Money and Magic in Early Modern Drama

ARDEN STUDIES IN EARLY MODERN DRAMA

Series editors:

Lisa Hopkins, Sheffield Hallam University, UK
Douglas Bruster, University of Texas at Austin, USA

Money and Magic in Early Modern Drama

Edited by David Hawkes

THE ARDEN SHAKESPEARE

LONDON • NEW YORK • OXFORD • NEW DELHI • SYDNEY

THE ARDEN SHAKESPEARE
Bloomsbury Publishing Plc
50 Bedford Square, London, WC1B 3DP, UK
1385 Broadway, New York, NY 10018, USA
29 Earlsfort Terrace, Dublin 2, Ireland

BLOOMSBURY, THE ARDEN SHAKESPEARE and the
Arden Shakespeare logo are trademarks of Bloomsbury Publishing Plc

First published in Great Britain 2023

Cover image: Albrecht Dürer, *Allegory of Avarice*, 1507,
Kunsthistorisches Museum Wien

A catalogue record for this book is available from the British Library.

A catalog record for this book is available from the Library of Congress.

ISBN: HB: 978-1-3502-4704-8
ePDF: 978-1-3502-4706-2
eBook: 978-1-3502-4705-5

Series: Arden Studies in Early Modern Drama

Typeset by Integra Software Services Pvt. Ltd.

To find out more about our authors and books visit www.bloomsbury.com
and sign up for our newsletters.

To Barbara Traister

CONTENTS

ACKNOWLEDGEMENTS

This collection originated in a seminar at the conference of the Shakespeare Association of America, which was held online in April 2020. The conversation was fascinating throughout, and all the participants deserve thanks. At the Arden Shakespeare, Lara Bateman has been a superb editor, combining patience and efficiency in exemplary fashion, Alice Moore has also been a tremendous help, and the two anonymous readers provided a detailed, sensitive analysis of each chapter. Most of my work on this project was completed during my sabbatical leave in 2020–21, and I'm grateful to Arizona State University (ASU) for providing that opportunity. Krista Radcliffe has been a wonderful Chair of ASU's English Department, and the intellectual conversation of friends like Julia Friedman, Joe Lockard, Richard Newhauser and Kathy Romack was especially important over the last two years, when regular contact with professional colleagues was suspended. My wife Simten and my son Ali were a joy, as always.

NOTES ON CONTRIBUTORS

William Casey Caldwell's work focuses on intersections between citizenship and economics in early modern drama. His manuscript in progress, tentatively titled *Economies of Citizenship in Early Modern Drama*, explores how playwrights use various financial concepts to reconceive notions of urban citizenship and its labour-based underpinnings, especially in relation to citizenship's others, including strangers, foreigners and denizens. Caldwell earned his PhD in English literature from Northwestern University, and he holds an MFA in Shakespeare and Performance from Mary Baldwin University in Partnership with the American Shakespeare Center, as well as an MA in Philosophy from the University of Auckland. Caldwell teaches at Carthage College in Kenosha, Wisconsin. He is also editor for *The Hare*, a journal which publishes untimely reviews of 'old' scholarship in early modern studies.

Kaitlyn Culliton is Assistant Professor of English in the Department of Humanities at Texas A&M International University in Laredo, Texas. She holds a PhD from Trinity College in Dublin, Ireland. From 2018 to 2019, she taught as a visiting assistant professor at Palacký University in Olomouc, Czechia. Her research interests include sixteenth-century British literature, particularly Shakespeare, folklore and children's literature. Her current project examines the connection between fairy lore and the development of chimneys in early modern houses. She is also the founder of the Border Literature Project, which seeks to support early childhood literacy in border communities by increasing access to diverse children's literature and educating and promoting multicultural authors.

Hugh Grady is Professor Emeritus at Arcadia University in Glenside, Pennsylvania, where he specialized in Shakespeare, early modern English literature and critical theory. He has authored numerous articles and several books on Shakespeare, including *The Modernist Shakespeare* (1991), *Shakespeare, Machiavelli and Montaigne* (2002), and *Shakespeare and Impure Aesthetics* (2009). He is co-editor (with Terence Hawkes) of *Presentist Shakespeares* (2007) and (with Cary DiPietro) of *Shakespeare and the Urgency of Now* (2013). His most recently published book is *John Donne and Baroque Allegory: The Aesthetics of Fragmentation* (2017). His next, *Shakespeare's Dialectic of Hope*, is forthcoming.

David Hawkes is Professor of English Literature at Arizona State University. He is the author of seven books, most recently *The Reign of Anti-Logos* (2020). He has edited four books, including John Milton's *Paradise Lost* (2004). His essays and reviews have appeared in the *Times Literary Supplement*, *The Nation*, *The New Criterion*, *Quillette*, *Modernist Cultures*, the *Journal of the History of Ideas*, the *Journal of Interdisciplinary Economics*, *Literature and Theology*, *Studies in English Literature*, *English Literary History*, *English Literary Renaissance*, *Renaissance Quarterly*, *Renaissance Studies*, *Shakespeare Quarterly*, *Shakespeare Studies*, *Milton Quarterly*, *Milton Studies* and many other popular and academic journals. His main current interest is the cultural influence of usury.

Ja Young Jeon is a PhD candidate at the Graduate Center, City University of New York. She is currently working on her dissertation project titled *Ventriloquizing and Ventriloquized Women on Shakespearean Stages: Speech, Agency, and Authorship*. She has written and presented widely on early modern drama, including a recent article on *The Spanish Tragedy*'s engagement with puppet theatre, which will appear in the spring 2022 issue of *The Journal of English Language and Literature*, and an essay on Echo's resonances with female kinship in *Twelfth Night*. She is also interested in Asian Shakespeare adaptations: her essay on a South Korean film's transcultural reworking of *Romeo and Juliet* will appear in a forthcoming issue of *Adaptation*.

Rebecca Steinberger is Professor of English and Program Director of Theatre at Misericordia University. In addition to Shakespeare and early modern cultural studies, her research interests include contemporary Irish drama, adaptation studies, the city of London, literary treatments of terrorism and disability studies. She is the author of *Shakespeare and Twentieth-Century Irish Drama: Conceptualizing Identity and Staging Boundaries* (2008) and contributing editor of *The Renaissance Literature Handbook* (2009), Adam Max Cohen's *Wonder in Shakespeare* (2012) and *Encountering Ephemera 1500–1800: Scholarship, Performance, Classroom* (2012).

Kemal Onur Toker hails from Istanbul, Turkey. He is currently a researcher at Brandeis University and a teaching fellow at Osher Lifelong Learning Institute. The focus of Toker's research and teaching is the heated conflict between two rival paradigms of social value – the paradigm of monetary capital versus the paradigm of infinitely shareable public goods – in the works of William Shakespeare, Thomas Hobbes, John Milton and John Locke. Toker's research project aims to uncover the now neglected history of a fundamental conceptual clash that not only played a decisive role in the ideological elaboration of modern liberalism, but which has also recently resurfaced as an urgent problem in the world of twenty-first-century digital information capitalism.

Melissa Vipperman-Cohen is Lecturer in the Eleanor Roosevelt College Writing Program at the University of California San Diego. She received her PhD in literature from the University of California San Diego. Her work focuses on the intersections between economic exchange, queer theory and early modern theatre to argue for the inherent and valuable queerness of English proto-capitalism. She is currently adapting this research for a book-length project titled *Queer Capitalism and Global Economies of Desire on the Early Modern English Stage.*

Daniel Vitkus holds the Rebeca Hickel Endowed Chair in Early Modern Literature at the University of California, San Diego. He is the author of *Turning Turk: English Theater and the Multicultural Mediterranean, 1570–1630* and of numerous articles and book chapters on the literature and cultural history of the sixteenth and seventeenth centuries. Vitkus has also edited *Three Turk Plays* *from Early Modern England* and *Piracy, Slavery and Redemption: Barbary Captivity Narratives from Early Modern England.* He currently serves as the editor of the *Journal for Early Modern Cultural Studies.* His interests include Shakespeare, early modern theatre, Renaissance literature, travel writing, literary and cultural theory, Islamic culture and its representation in the West, the origins of global capitalism and the cultural history of empire.

Introduction

David Hawkes

In *The Alchemy of Finance* (1983), George Soros argues that the modern world has witnessed the ultimate triumph of alchemy. Lead has not been transformed into gold, but a substance of no value has certainly been transformed into one of real value. The widespread use of paper money represents, according to Soros, the victory of the magical mindset. The idea that an intrinsically worthless piece of paper can contain real value is fundamentally fetishistic. The fact that this value exists only symbolically is no obstacle to its efficacy, for its efficacy rests on the assumption that the manipulation of symbols can achieve objective effects. The magician believes that sticking pins in an image of a person will harm the real person. Magic depends on the power of performative signs, and our society is dominated by the performative symbol known as 'money'. But Soros observes that financial value is usually conceived as a referential rather than a performative sign:

> Stocks are supposed to have a true or fundamental value as distinct from their current market price. The fundamental value of a stock may be defined either in relation to the earning power of the underlying assets or in relation to the fundamental value of other stocks. In either case, the market price of a stock is supposed to tend toward its fundamental value over a period of time, so that analysis of fundamental values provides a useful guide to investment decisions.[1]

Here Soros describes what he calls the 'fundamentalist' theory of stock prices. This well-established approach assumes a referential model of representation. It presupposes the existence of a 'true or fundamental value', which is determined either by a company's real-world performance or by relation to other true or fundamental stock values. The stock's nominal price is supposed to represent its real value. The price is the sign; the value is the referent. In Soros's opinion, however, this theory of prices is erroneous. Prices do not passively express a real, authentic value that somehow pre-exists them. On the contrary, they exert an active role in the determination of the value they are traditionally supposed to represent. As Soros explains:

> I take a totally opposite point of view. I do not accept the proposition that stock prices are a passive reflection of underlying values, nor do I accept the proposition that the reflection tends to correspond to the underlying value.... Stock prices are not merely passive reflections; they are active ingredients in a process in which both stock prices and the fortunes of the companies whose stocks are traded are determined. In other words, I regard changes in stock prices as part of a historical process.
>
> (52)

Thus, 'value' is incorporated into 'price', which the fundamentalist approach had regarded as merely its expression. The medium of representation asserts its agential, determining power and becomes part of the 'historical process', rather than a reflection of it. In short, Soros proclaims that financial value is not a referential but a performative sign. In the third decade of the twenty-first century, his claim has been resoundingly vindicated. Since he wrote, the forms taken by financial value have grown progressively more abstract, and the distance separating them from anchorage in the world of use-value has grown ever greater. Today most financial value takes the form of speculative 'derivatives' whose prices do not even refer to any underlying commodity in the imaginary world of finance, let alone in the real world of use-value.[2]

The shift of opinion recounted by Soros is only the latest stage of a long historical process whereby financial value has taken increasingly abstract, symbolic forms. That process began in sixteenth-century Europe, when massive, sudden fluctuations in the price of currency made it obvious that financial value was something separable from its material incarnation in gold bullion. Value was not identical with precious metal; it was an abstract quality, grafted onto gold by the human imagination. It became clear, in other words, that value was a sign. With this conceptual leap bank notes became generally acceptable, and over the next four centuries they were followed by ever more obviously symbolic forms of finance. By the twentieth century, the practical power of signs was acknowledged across a wide range of disciplines. In describing the latest stage of financial value's symbolic abstraction, Soros gives economic expression to developments that were initially noted in the field of linguistics. Ferdinand de Saussure incorporated the conceptual signified into the sign, just as Soros incorporates underlying value into nominal price. J. L. Austin argued that verbal statements can be performative as well as referential, just as Soros claims that price can determine value as well as express it. Just as post-structuralist philosophers deny that ideas exist prior to their expression in language, so twenty-first-century finance denies that value can be separated from its manifestation as price. In financial as in linguistic postmodernity, *il n'y a pas de hors-texte*.[3]

Today's triumph of the performative sign has its roots in early modernity. In pre-Enlightenment Europe, magicians aspired to influence the objective environment, and the subjective *psyche*, by means of signs: the occult symbols, runes and incantations of ritual magic. The Renaissance revived the intelligentsia's interest in ancient magical techniques. In the sixteenth and seventeenth centuries, alchemy attracted many of Britain's best minds, from John Dee to Isaac Newton. As Soros argues, the incorporation of 'real' value into 'nominal' price is alchemy continued by other means. Today's financial 'derivatives' conjure value out of pure representation, as if by magic. The ancient dream of the alchemists that a substance of no worth might magically acquire substantive value was realized with the invention of paper money and consolidated by the legalization of usury, which ratified the reproductive capacity of financial representation. Alchemy did not disappear from modern science because its efforts to create value ex nihilo were finally recognized as futile, but because they succeeded so completely as to render themselves imperceptible. Modern Westerners do not believe in magic, just as fish do not believe in water.

The efficacious sign grew to prominence simultaneously across the spheres of religious liturgy, ritual magic, aesthetics and economics. With the incremental legitimization of usury over the sixteenth and seventeenth centuries, financial value manifested itself as an efficacious symbol. As money acquires the capacity to reproduce, which is a definitive characteristic of life, it simultaneously acquires its own needs, interests and desires. Like any living creature, money desires above all to breed. Since physical metal cannot breed, while semiotic significance is infinitely fertile, the growing prevalence of usury confirmed that financial value did not reside in the physical body of precious metal but was instead an independent and auto-reproductive symbol: a sign possessed of practical power.

The chapters collected in this volume look back to an era when practical magic was a matter of urgent public controversy. In early modern London the performative power of signs was emergent, and often stigmatized or persecuted, rather than hegemonic as it is today. The witch-hunts of the sixteenth and seventeenth centuries were only one aspect of the reaction against the rise of efficacious representation. The adoration of religious icons, the attribution of independent agency to money, and the rise of the commercial public theatre were also conceived as manifestations of the tendency to treat signs as efficacious. By the mid-sixteenth century it was clear that the media of representation were acquiring an independent power that transcended the differences between their verbal, financial, aesthetic and liturgical forms. Under the Tudors and Stuarts, British people came to understand that the common element uniting ritual magic, liturgical idolatry, financial usury and theatrical aesthetics was the practical power of the performative sign.

Witch-hunting, iconoclasm, anti-theatricalism and popular opposition to usury were united in their hostility to efficacious representation. In the popular imagination they tended to coalesce around particular figures. In the Christian tradition, for instance, the paradigmatic magician is Simon Magus, whose basic heresy was to misconstrue miracles as magic. Magus assumed that the miraculous power of divinity, which he mistook for magic performed by the Disciples, was a commodity that might be purchased for money (Acts 9–24). He supposed that money and magic could be exchanged for each other because, as systems of performative signs, they were essentially similar in nature. This mode of thought led him to conceive of magical power as resident in the rituals and symbolic tools of the magician's trade. Thus, Irenaeus claims that the sect of Simon is notorious for its excessive concern with 'exorcisms and incantations. Love-potions, too, and charms'.[4] Hippolytus of Rome confirms: 'The disciples, then, of this (Magus), celebrate magical rites, and resort to incantations. And (they profess to) transmit both love-spells and charms.'[5] In sixteenth-century Europe, the composite magician known as 'Doctor Faustus' provided a similar nexus onto which various forms of performative efficacy were easily projected.[6]

The 'hedge magic' practised by 'cunning folk' had been integrated into British culture for centuries. Towards the middle of the sixteenth century, however, such practices were quite suddenly stigmatized. Any effort to achieve real effects by the manipulation of symbols began to seem evil. Many people began to identify such practices as 'black' magic or 'witchcraft'. It made no difference whether the witch's intention was to work *beneficia* or *maleficia*; it did not even matter whether the magic he or she practised was genuinely efficacious: the mere attempt to alter the condition of the world by using images was officially and popularly judged to constitute an agreement with the devil. The logic behind this judgement ran as follows. As Church Fathers from Augustine to Aquinas emphasized, signs do not naturally possess a capacity for autonomous action. Yet magicians claimed that they could achieve objective effects by means of what Christopher Marlowe's Faustus calls '[l]ines, circles, letters, and characters', and their claims were widely believed. Since signs are not truly efficacious, however, and since God does not deal in illusion, the agency behind magic's apparent effects could only be demonic. Furthermore, the Patriarchs reasoned, a sign is by definition addressed to a recipient, and there was only one possible candidate for the addressee of magical symbols. However innocent or inept their efforts may have been, the witch's attempts to put symbols to performative use ipso facto constituted a 'pact' with Satan.

Between 1550 and 1650, panic at the perceived power of Satanic witchcraft produced persecutions that tore through Europe in a concerted attack on traditional folk magic. Although the witch-hunts were sanctioned and generally directed by the state, the literature of the day suggests they enjoyed considerable popular support. The iconoclasm of the Reformation reflected a similarly visceral fear of fetishized icons, as mobs broke into churches to physically assault their enemies of wood and stone. At the same time, a popular reaction against the rise of usury started to find literary expression. The chronic shortage of ready cash meant that small-scale loans between acquaintances were commonplace, and resentment tended to focus on the character of the individual usurer or 'money-bawd'. Thomas Middleton's Pecunius Lucre, Ben Jonson's Moth Interest and Phillip Massinger's Giles Overreach are among the most egregious of the seventy-one archetypal usurers who stalked the London stage between 1553 and 1642.[7]

The idea that signs can do things had come to seem pernicious. The autonomous power of performative representation threatened to undermine the distinction between divinely created 'nature' and the human works of 'custom'; it obtruded artificial spectacles between the subjective observer and objective reality; it systematically collapsed essence into appearance. The rise of the independently efficacious sign seemed almost intended to deconstruct all mutually constitutive binary oppositions. Performative representation is the dialectical antithesis of logocentrism, which insists that meaning and value derive from a source prior to their symbolic expression. The Gospel of John identifies *logos* with the Second Person of the Trinity. In the early stages of its rise to power, performativity was recognized as an imminent threat to *logos*, and in this sense early modern moralists were correct when they identified as 'Satanic' such apparently diverse phenomena as the reproduction of exchange-value, the worship of religious icons, the conjurations of ritual magicians and the influence of the public theatre.

London's commercial stage provided a forum where the moral and practical impact of performative representation could be displayed, debated and turned into profit. The public theatre had been criticized for confusing essence with appearance since its earliest appearance in ancient Greece. Plutarch describes the proverbially wise Solon asking the actor Thespis:

> [I]f he was not ashamed to tell so many lies before such a number of people; and Thespis replying that it was no harm to say or do so in a play, Solon vehemently struck his staff against the ground: 'Ah,' he said, 'if we honor and commend such play as this, we shall find it some day in our business.'[8]

Solon understood that the theatre's systematic displacement of reality by representation cannot be confined to the stage. It manifested and inculcated a general tendency to attribute efficacy to symbols, which must inevitably find its way into practical affairs. The anti-theatrical campaigners of sixteenth-century London were equally quick to condemn the commercial theatre for its propagation of illusory 'spectacles' in pursuit of profit.[9] For the duration of the drama, the audience must take the actor for the character he represents. This deliberate replacement of essence by appearance, combined with the public theatre's commercialized aesthetics, convinced many observers that plays did not merely depict the displacement of reality by representation but actually caused it. As Helen Ostovich and Lisa Hopkins observe, '[p]lays which are about magical transformation may ... *do* some magical transformation of their own'.[10]

The idea that play-going might damage the individual *psyche*, or even disrupt the social order, was not marginal or eccentric. On the contrary, it was generally accepted by moralistic opponents and professional practitioners of the theatre alike. Playwrights like Anthony Munday and Stephen Gosson wrote anti-theatrical pamphlets in their spare time. Even serious dramatists like Ben Jonson endorsed much of the anti-theatrical case while others, including William Shakespeare, took it seriously enough to refute it at length. Shakespeare's diagnosis of the relation between money, magic and theatricality is especially acute in *Timon of Athens, The Comedy of Errors, Antony and Cleopatra* and *A Winter's Tale*, and several chapters in this book concentrate on these plays. Others consider a broader array of issues around which money, magic and theatricality coalesced, including the popular lore of fairy gold, the theatre's charging of admission fees, the practice of ventriloquism on stage, and the commodification of fake news in the 'dotages' of Ben Jonson.

The contributors approach these issues from a wide variety of theoretical and generational perspectives. They range in age from their seventies to their twenties and in rank from Professor Emeritus to graduate student. Some published their first monographs in the twentieth century, while others may conceivably still be publishing in the twenty-second. As might be expected of so diverse a cohort, the contributors utilize many different methods of analysis, including post-Marxist materialism, post-structuralist formalism, politicized feminism and a number of hybrid, intersectional positions too nuanced to name. Most of the chapters subordinate theoretical reflections to textual analysis, but the book opens with a rousing manifesto on the current state of theory in early modern studies: Daniel Vitkus's 'The Perverse Eco-Politics of Object-Oriented Criticism: Money, Magical Thinking, and the New Materialism'.

Vitkus provides a formidable critique of the 'new materialism' or 'object-oriented ontology' inspired by philosophers like Bruno Latour, Jane Bennett and Graham Harman. Although it is widely regarded as a radical, innovative approach, Vitkus identifies this methodology as a postmodern form of 'magical thinking'. Like the sorcerers of the past, 'object-oriented ontology' attributes a 'mystical' agency to matter, and Vitkus describes this bestowal of determining power on objects as 'reductionist'. He observes that, in practice, the 'new materialism' tends to produce 'a loose kind of thematic eco-criticism' that elides 'urgent questions about class and economics', and he concludes by calling for criticism to acknowledge the dialectical inter-penetration of subject and object. Such a criticism, Vitkus suggests, might address the urgent task of deconstructing the imaginary, supernatural agency that financialized capitalism attributes to symbolic exchange-value.

The volume's focus then shifts from theory to critical practice. William Casey Caldwell's '"Ye pay all alike:" The Vice of Collecting Money in *Mankind*' concentrates on what is arguably the earliest appearance of abstract exchange-value on the English stage. In the fifteenth-century morality play *Mankind*, the 'Vice' characters who represent modernity ('Nowadays' and 'New Guise') solicit real money directly from the audience. As Caldwell notes, this may be the first-ever example of a play dramatizing its own commodification. In exchange for their cash payment, the audience is rewarded by the appearance of Titivillus, an especially spectacular and villainous demon, often associated with Satan himself. This method of remuneration conspicuously departs from traditional compensation by patronage or *largesse* and, by making the appearance of Satan the immediate return for their payment, the play forces the audience to confront the ethical implications of exchanging entertainment for money.

Commodification uses financial signs to impose an apparent, artificial equivalence on objects that are essentially, naturally different. This power of transformation was treated as magical well into the modern era, and the effects of commodification were often represented as supernatural on stage. As Kaitlyn Culliton shows in 'Cozening Queens and Phony Fairies: Fairy Counterfeits in Early Modern Drama', English dramatists naturally turned to supernatural lore when they tried to conceptualize the commodity, and an entire genre of 'fairy stories' developed in response to the rise in exchange-value's independent power. These were often lightly fictionalized treatments of real-life events, and the number of 'counterfeit fairies' prosecuted in court suggests that the prospect of supernatural enrichment frequently drove avarice to the point of delusion. Culliton compares several real-life cases with the counterfeit fairies of Shakespeare's *The Merry Wives of Windsor*, Jonson's *The Alchemist* and *The Honest Lawyer* by 'S.S.' In both real and fictional cases of 'fairy couzening', she notes, ritual magic is employed as an instructive synecdoche for morally dubious financial reproduction.

My own contribution, 'The Sign of Abel Drugger: Fake News, Finance and Flattery in Ben Jonson's "Dotages,"' offers a reconsideration of Jonson's last complete plays: *The Staple of News*, *The New Inn* and *The Magnetic Lady*. Since John Dryden dismissed them as 'dotages', critics have assailed these plays as inaccessible and convoluted, largely because of their juxtaposition of apparently unrelated themes. Each play features a double plot involving financial trickery on the one hand and linguistic deception on the other, and the homology Jonson draws between the 'abuse' of money and the misuse of language was not always visible to eighteenth- or nineteenth-century critics. From today's perspective, however, we can see that Jonson is denouncing the simultaneous influence of the performative sign on financial and verbal systems of representation. He refers to the systematic use of verbal sophistry as 'canting' or 'jeering', which are his approximate equivalents of what English translators of Plato called 'flattery' (κολακεία). Several of Jonson's late works feature a 'Master-Cook' who embodies the power of representation, and this figure alludes to Plato's *Gorgias*, where Socrates uses 'cookery' as his paradigmatic example of 'flattery'. By 'cookery', Socrates means the use of flavourings and seasonings that are not nutritious but make the food taste pleasant. He explains that cookery stands in the same relation to nutrition as fashion to gymnastics, sophistry to reason, and drugs to the mind. In each case, 'flattery' deploys carnal appearances to alter or obscure ulterior reality.

Just as Jonson's last plays personify 'flattery' as a 'Master-Cook', so they represent exchange-value as a wealthy, attractive but capricious woman: Lady Pecunia in *The Staple of News*, Lady Frampul in *The New Inn* and Lady Loadstone in *The Magnetic Lady*. Personification or *prosopopeia* is an ancient trope for portraying money, but Jonson adapts it to include verbal as well as financial representation. Each of his last three plays depicts the Lady's attempted seduction by a motley pack of usurers and sophists. In *The Staple of News*, for instance, Penniboy Junior plots to spread sophistry throughout the land by founding a '*Canter's Colledge* ... I and my Pecunia'. Too often dismissed as a feeble-minded mélange of disparate obsessions, Jonson's last plays actually evince a prescient knowledge of the financial and verbal media that still dominate our society today.

At this point, the volume's focus shifts to Shakespeare. In 'Coins, Counterfeit, and Queer Threat in *The Comedy of Errors*', Melissa Vipperman-Cohen argues that Renaissance England's widespread fear of counterfeit coinage exerted a 'queer' influence on traditional notions of both economic and aesthetic value. She points out that in Shakespeare's Ephesus 'the culture of credit supersede(s) the affective bonds of the heterosexual family structure, by prioritizing the homosocial production of financial wealth'. *The Comedy of Errors* is 'concerned with the construction of selfhood in a commodified world created by credit, defined by money, and filled with false copies of both'. Antipholus of Syracuse believes that Ephesus is full of '[d]ark-working sorcerers' and '[s]oul-killing witches' (1.2.97–101), and this chapter confirms his worst suspicions. Not only does the conjunction of commerce and sorcery threaten to spread 'queer' conceptions of identity throughout society; it raises the even more disconcerting prospect of 'the individual as *its own counterfeit*'.

Financial value emerged from its material shell as the inflations and debasements of the sixteenth century revealed its independence from precious metals. Hugh Grady's 'The Magic of Bounty in *Timon of Athens*: Gold, Society, Nature' shows how Shakespeare and Middleton's collaborative play addresses the supernatural quality that money consequently acquired: an anonymous (and thus generic) poet dubs it the '[m]agic of bounty' (1.1.8). Grady envisages *Timon* as a 'thought experiment' which imagines a society completely dominated by usury – that is to say, one that closely resembles our own. In a series of influential speeches, Timon declares that usury's economic hegemony has induced a complete breakdown in traditional social roles and moral values, especially in the realm of sexuality. *Timon* has been recognized as prophetic of financialization since Friedrich Engels and Karl Marx's commentary in the *Economic and Philosophical Manuscripts of 1844*. In the twenty-first century, several well-received productions, together with a notable revival of critical interest, confirm the play's continued pertinence to the postmodern condition.

But *Timon* is hardly alone in this regard. Kemal Onur Toker's '"An Antony that Grew the More by Reaping": The Immeasurable Bounty of the Sharing Economy in Cleopatra's Egypt' discovers an incisive critique of the performative verbal sign in *Antony and Cleopatra*. As the titles of their chapters indicate, Grady and Toker are both concerned with Shakespeare's concept of 'bounty', but while Grady studies its economic implications, Toker applies it primarily to linguistics. His chapter concentrates on 'eponymy': the process whereby proper names are translated into common predicates so that, for example, it becomes possible to talk about 'an Antony' (*Antony and Cleopatra*, 1.3.91; 2.5.14; 4.2.18; 5.2.86; 5.2.98). This translation of the 'proper' into the 'common' is a matter of economics as well as of aesthetics: saying 'an Antony' transforms a proper name into a common noun that partakes of the shareable 'bounty' of reason and speech alike.

Toker explains how, like Timon of Athens, Antony's preferred mode of being in the world is to share his financial and verbal 'bounty'. Like Juliet, his capacity for sharing knows no bounds. Juliet's 'the more I give to thee, / The more I have' (2.1.176-177) finds its counterpart in Cleopatra's 'Antony ... / That grew the more by reaping' (5.2.86-87). Antony transposes Juliet's 'They are but beggars that that count their worth' (2.5.32) into his own 'There's beggary in the love that can be reckoned' (1.1.15). Cleopatra illustrates the moral peril of performativity when she kills the Messenger, misconstruing him as an efficacious agent of what he reports, rather than a mere representative. Shakespeare thus identifies performativity with arbitrary rule and, by falling in love with Cleopatra, Antony risks devolving into a tyrant. If he ends as a new Juliet instead, this is because Shakespeare had at his disposal cultural resources that enabled him to discern in 'an Antony that grows the more by reaping', a formula that reveals the foundations of human sociability and rationality.

Like Antony, Shakespeare's Margaret of Anjou makes the arduous journey from particular individual to generic abstraction, as Rebecca Steinberger shows in 'Woman, Warrior, or Witch? Fetishizing Margaret of Anjou on the Early Modern Stage'. The modes of fetishization to which Margaret is subjected evolve markedly over the four plays in which she appears, but the fact of her reification remains constant, and it dominates its various manifestations. The objectification imposed on the young Margaret is primarily erotic, but her substantial dowry adds an element of financial reification too. Over the four plays, Shakespeare progressively associates Margaret's money and sexual glamour with overtly supernatural forces of attraction. She is soon claiming that her enemies use magic against her, while she herself resorts to curses and imprecations. By her final appearance in *Richard III* Margaret's erotic and financial appeal has been transformed into the black magic of a 'foul, wrinkled witch' (1.3.168). The irony is that she thereby regains the same kind of independent agency that she once exerted through sexual and financial sorcery.

There were many forms of magical agency available in Renaissance England, as Ja Young Jeon reminds us in '"The Stone Is Mine": Theatre, Witchcraft, and Ventriloquism in *The Winter's Tale*'. Jeon traces the history of ventriloquism from the Delphic *Pythia* to early modern witches, defining it as 'a form of autonomously powerful verbal performance, in which linguistic signs operate in the absence of a speaking subject' and thus as 'the paradigmatic form of an autonomous speech-act'. Ventriloquism's central role in *The Winter's Tale* reflects the period's preoccupation with the occult effects of performative signs – including spells, money and the theatre – and it thus offers a convenient way of examining the ethical status of efficacious representation in general.

Departing from the traditional conception of ventriloquism as divine or demonic possession, Shakespeare's Paulina secularizes it as a thespian stage skill. The idea of ventriloquism as a technical craft resonates with the professional actor's habitual adoption of a fictional identity. Just as Paulina imitates and summons Hermione through her vocal performance, the actor manipulates his voice to bring a character to life. This was one reason the anti-theatricalists claimed that theatrical illusions were just as dangerous as magical effects. The figurative language of drama, like the incantations of ritual magic, can distort the senses and prompt people to credit illusions. This model of theatrical fraudulence implicitly identifies the playwright with the witch.[11] Yet Jeon argues that 'Paulina's embrace of the witch's role challenges the pejorative associations of magic'. By deploying Paulina's redemptive ventriloquism as a figure for the performative power of the playwright, Shakespeare offers an implicit but nonetheless passionate defence of the theatre as 'an art/ Lawful as eating' (5.3.137-38).

The default position today is to agree with Shakespeare. We no longer believe that Paulina is 'assisted / By wicked powers' (5.3.111-12). Few twenty-first-century commentators perceive an ethical problem in the proliferation of performative signs. Most agree with the 'object-oriented' philosopher Graham Harman when he demands that 'essences must be replaced by events and performances'.[12] Those who still insist on the distinction between appearance and essence, or who claim that signs designate a reality logically prior to representation, are often convicted of political conservativism. The power of financial signs is now so great that it seems almost perverse to deny a similar power to other media of representation. The notion that meaning derives from *logos* is generally considered oppressive. The idea that the human essence consists in a non-material core of subjectivity is widely regarded as superstitious. The young generation apparently experience their own identity, even their own gender, as performative rather than essential. The data of sense-perception are simply equated with reality. The triumph of reification appears complete. As the chapters collected in this volume remind us, however, one of the theatre's most salutary functions is to demonstrate that appearances are necessarily deceptive.

Notes

1   George Soros, *The Alchemy of Finance* (Hoboken, NJ: John Wiley & Sons, 1983), 21.

2   David Hawkes, 'Against Financial Derivatives: Towards an Ethics of Representation', *Journal of Interdisciplinary Economics* 31, no. 2 (Spring 2019): 119.

3   Jacques Derrida, *Of Grammatology*, trans. Gayatri Chakravorty Spivak (Johns Hopkins University Press, 1976), 159.
4   Irenaeus, *Against Heresies* 1.23.4. Retrieved from https://www.newadvent.org/fathers/0103123.htm 04/02/22
5   Hippolytus of Rome, *Philosophumena*, chapter XV. Retrieved from https://www.ewtn.com/catholicism/library/refutation-of-all-heresies-books-vix-philosophumena-11417 04/02/22.
6   David Hawkes, *The Faust Myth: Religion and the Rise of Representation* (Palgrave Macmillan, 2007).
7   Arthur Bivins Stonex, 'The Usurer in Elizabethan Theater', *PMLA* 31, no. 2 (1916): 190–210, 191.
8   Plutarch, 'Life of Solon', in *Plutarch's Lives*, trans. John Dryden (New York: Cosimo Classics, 2008), 182.
9   David Hawkes, 'Idolatry and Commodity Fetishism in the Antitheatrical Controversy', *Studies in English Literature* 39, no. 2 (Spring 1999): 255–73.
10   Helen Ostovich and Lisa Hopkins, 'Introduction: Transformations and the Ideology of Witchcraft Staged', in *Magical Transformations on the Early Modern English Stage* (London: Routledge, 2016), 4.
11   Stephen Greenblatt, 'Shakespeare Bewitched', in *Shakespeare and Cultural Traditions*, ed. Tetsuo Kishi, Roger Pringle and Stanley Wells (University of Delaware Press, 1991), 136.
12   Graham Harman, 'The Well-Wrought Broken Hammer: Object-Oriented Literary Criticism', *New Literary History* 43, no. 2 (2012): 183–203, 188.

Works cited

Derrida, Jacques. *Of Grammatology*, trans. Gayatri Chakravorty Spivak. Johns Hopkins University Press, 1976.
Greenblatt, Stephen. 'Shakespeare Bewitched', in *Shakespeare and Cultural Traditions*, ed. Tetsuo Kishi, Roger Pringle and Stanley Wells. University of Delaware Press, 1991.
Harman, Graham. 'The Well-Wrought Broken Hammer: Object-Oriented Literary Criticism', *New Literary History* 43:2 (2012), 183–203.
Hawkes, David. 'Idolatry and Commodity Fetishism in the Antitheatrical Controversy', *Studies in English Literature* 39:2. Spring, 1999, 255–73.
Hawkes, David. *The Faust Myth: Religion and the Rise of Representation*. Palgrave Macmillan, 2007.
Hawkes, David. 'Against Financial Derivatives: Towards an Ethics of Representation', *Journal of Interdisciplinary Economics* 31:2. Spring, 2019, 1–19.

Hippolytus of Rome. *Philosophumena*. Retrieved 04/ 02/22 from: https://
    www.ewtn.com/catholicism/library/refutation-of-all-heresiesbooks-vix-
    philosophumena-11417

Hopkins, Lisa and Helen Ostovich. 'Introduction: Transformations and
    the Ideology of Witchcraft Staged', in *Magical Transformations on the
    Early Modern English Stage*. London: Routledge, 2016.

Irenaeus, *Against Heresies*. Retrieved 04/ 02/22 from: https://www.
    newadvent.org/fathers/0103123.htm

Plutarch, *Lives*, trans. John Dryden. New York: Cosimo Classics, 2008.

Soros, George. *The Alchemy of Finance*. Hoboken, NJ: John Wiley &
    Sons, 1983.

Stonex, Arthur Bivins. 'The Usurer in Elizabethan Theater.' *PMLA* 31:2
    (1916): 190–210.

1

The perverse eco-politics of object-oriented criticism: Money, magical thinking and the new materialism

Daniel Vitkus

[A]ctor-network theory ... posits a specious ontological flattening: it insists that there is no difference in the ability of 'actors' – whether they be human or non-human – to act. There is a distribution of agency to everything and hence an agential privileging of nothing, since nothing can exert more power than anything else. It ignores the disparities in agency and hierarchies of power that actually exist.

ALEXANDRE LESKANICH[1]

As early modernists and scholars working in the humanities, we are called on to pursue research, writing and teaching that looks to the

I would like to express my profound gratitude to the editor of this volume, David Hawkes, for his many substantial suggestions during the revision process – his help has greatly improved this chapter. I would also like to thank Celine Khoury, currently a doctoral candidate at UC San Diego, for her contributions to this project as a graduate student research assistant.

past, responds to the present and helps us to prepare for the future. And today, climate change presents a global crisis that has motivated certain presentist modes of literary and cultural study. With good reason, many scholars in the humanities are turning green, jumping on an eco-bandwagon that has been picking up momentum and passengers for decades now. As they do so, they are seeking ways to theorize, authorize and inform their ecocritical interpretations of particular texts. Our present predicament calls on us, as scholars focusing on early modern culture and history, to assume an ecocritical stance as we undertake our interventions. How then can we theorize and empower our approach so that it will answer that call?

We desperately need to raise awareness about the history of ecocide, to discuss humankind's coexistence with and dependence on a non-human 'nature' and to point out the destructive consequences of anthropocentrism – these are key lessons to impart to our fellow world-citizens. But given the difficult political obstacles faced by the green movement, and the powerful inertia of our unsustainable global economy, consciousness-raising about speciesism is not enough. Rather, the role of human thought and action must be recentred, or restored, to its position as the collective subject that has forgotten how to live sustainably in the material world. We must confront the deep socio-structural, cultural and historical causes of ecocide so that we can enact effective political solutions. What must be taught and learned, first and foremost, is the fact that *human* institutions and economies, enabled by linguistic and technological abilities that set our species apart from all others, have brought us to this pass. At this moment of planetary crisis, scholars in the humanities and literary studies must do their part to address the fundamental source of the problem, its origins and perpetuation in the cultural formation of capitalism: that is to say, in a form of political economy that emerged during the time of Shakespeare. In a famous article published in 2015, Simon Lewis and Mark Maslin pointed to the year 1610 as a crucial turning point in the onset of the Anthropocene.[2] In as much as the early modern period gave rise to the global systems that would bring on the Anthropocene, it behoves us to link the early modern past with the post-human present – to trace the origins of extractive imperialism and global capitalism back to the sixteenth century.

There is, however, a deep pitfall to be avoided here – a misdirected ecocriticism that fails to foreground and target the powerful socio-economic forces (operating in the form of a class system, dominated by the capitalist class) that, for centuries, have been driving the destruction of habitat and the increase in atmospheric levels of carbon dioxide and other greenhouse gases. Inclined to avoid questions of political economy, and swayed by the current tendency to fixate on questions of identity instead, many scholars have resorted to a post-human, undialectical 'new materialism'. But this approach is politically ineffective insofar as it leads us away from deep causes – away from human agencies, responsibilities and solutions – and into an uncanny, 'weird'[3] world where all is connected and dispersed through magical-material agentic flows of 'thing power'. The latter term is derived from one of the movement's foundational texts, Jane Bennett's *Vibrant Matter*, where it is used to describe 'the curious ability of inanimate things to animate, to act'.[4] In that work, she draws on Bruno Latour's Actor Network Theory, which owes something, in turn, to the rhizomes of Deleuze and Guattari. Through terms such as 'thing power', Bennett refers to nothing less than the re-enchantment of the world. She dismisses any autonomous agency of the individual human subject as illusory. In reality, she argues, our actions and perceptions are determined by innumerable non-human 'actants', often invisible, that constantly hover around us, exerting occult influences of which we are largely unaware. The effect is to challenge the very idea of 'humanity':

> [I]f human culture is inextricably enmeshed with vibrant, nonhuman agencies, and if human intentionality can be agentic only if accompanied by a vast entourage of nonhumans, then it seems that the appropriate unit of analysis for democratic theory is neither the individual human nor an exclusively human collective but the (ontologically heterogeneous) 'public' coalescing around a problem.
>
> (108)

The new materialism as a literary and cultural critical practice finds its origins in sensible premises and in an admirable desire to do eco-friendly work. After all, it is true that we humans-as-objects all exist in an entangling network of objects that includes carbon dioxide molecules, rocks, trees, insects, oysters, cows, gloves, communion wafers, early printed books, keyholes, lecture halls, oil rigs and our own bodies. But which material beings possess the agency, the consciousness, the technology and the social organization to 'cause'

climate change? And who might be able to slow its 'progress'? Who
created, shaped, maintained and celebrated the capitalist system
that has driven our petrochemical technologies and brought on
what Jason W. Moore calls 'the capitalocene'?[5] Neither animals,
nor plants, nor rocks. Furthermore, the idea that 'Nature' and
'Society' are separate, alien entities is itself a consequence of the
human imposition of symbolic exchange-value on the non-human.
As Moore argues, 'the view of Nature as external is a fundamental
condition of capital accumulation' (5). In short, human beings
alone bear the responsibility for the climate emergency. But we also
possess the ability, if we act together against neoliberal power, to
reduce the damage. Whether or not we are able to unite as a species
and take collective action to alleviate the coming crisis is an open
question, perhaps the greatest question of all time. The fate
of our species rests on the answer.

My general thesis in this chapter is that our intellectual efforts, if
moved by a sufficiently urgent sense of ethical responsibility, should
avoid the kind of ecocriticism that neglects human power and
responsibility, that endows material objects with a kind of magical-
theological animism, or that merely thematizes our entanglement
with nature, matter and objects. In spite of Bill Brown's confident
declaration that 'our relation to things cannot be explained by the
cultural logic of capitalism',[6] and his equally confident denial that
the metamorphosis of people into things 'can be fully explained by
the so-called reifying effects of a society permeated by the commodity
form' (13), we cannot afford to indulge in micro-materialist fiddling
while neoliberalism marches on and the planet burns. Ecocriticism
that does not engage sufficiently with our all-too-human political
economy is the equivalent of the liberal 'environmentalism' that
celebrates the beauty and complexity of nature, and even advocates
its 'preservation', but fails to address the deep structural source of
our planetary crisis in capitalism.[7] Friedrich Engels's declaration in
the *Anti-Dühring* (1877) is more pertinent now than ever: 'If the
whole of modern society is not to perish, a revolution in the mode
of production and distribution must take place.'[8] Rosa Luxemburg's
later slogan, coined in the face of a senseless world war, must be
rephrased for our own postmodern condition: 'Ecosocialism or
barbarism!'

The more perceptive theorists of the 'new materialism' sometimes
acknowledge the connection between the agency they attribute to

objects and the reversal of subject and object entailed in commodity fetishism. For example, Bennett alludes to 'the capacity of things – edibles, commodities, storms, metals ... to act as quasi agents or forces with trajectories, propensities, or tendencies of their own'. She fails, however, to acknowledge the vital difference between commodities and the other objects for which she claims agency. Commodities *appear* to act independently of human beings only because they have been falsely fetishized. Their action is illusory. That is why Karl Marx describes capitalism as 'an enchanted, perverted, topsy-turvy world, in which Monsieur le Capital and Madame la Terre do their ghost-walking as social characters'.[9] Marx condemns what he calls 'the magic and necromancy' of commodity fetishism as an ontological and ethical error. For him it is obviously absurd, and obviously evil, to suppose that objects can act independently of human beings. In direct contrast, Bennett and the 'new materialists' appear to rationalize, or even to celebrate, the quasi-magical agency of objects.

Given its political and philosophical limitations, how far should we go in pursuing a micro-materialism – with its emphasis on vibrant matter, agentic things, material objects and so on – as a guide to reading literary texts? What are the advantages and shortcomings of ecocritical readings motivated by 'the ethics of human enmeshment within an agentic material world'?[10] The various theoretical sub-genres that make up 'new materialism' (or what I will call 'micro-materialism') include Bill Brown's 'thing theory', the 'object-oriented ontology' and 'speculative realism' associated with Graham Harman, Levi Bryant, Timothy Morton and Ian Bogost, Jane Bennett's 'vital materialism', Bruno Latour's 'actor-network theory', and some versions of Deleuzian 'assemblage' or 'rhizomic theory'. Despite their many differences, these theories share a hostility to anthropocentric ontologies or causalities that would centre and prioritize human being, subjectivity, identity, consciousness or agency. They reject the Marxist 'old materialism', which is historical, dialectical and cultural.[11] They replace the Hegelian subject-object dialectic with an eliminative materialism that reduces human thought and consciousness to matter. Morton rejects the 'correlationist dyad' that conceives of subject and object as a mutually constitutive binary opposition, happily reducing the former to the latter: 'We've become so used to hearing "object" in relation to "subject" that it takes some time to acclimatize to a view in which there are only objects, one of which is ourselves.'[12] The practitioners of object-oriented ontology insist on the radical inaccessibility of the objective world to the human mind, which they call the 'withdrawal of things'. Left entirely to themselves, things take on a supernatural agency. In *Realist Magic*, Morton reflects on the implications of his work:

> To think this way is to begin to work out an object-oriented view of causality. If things are intrinsically withdrawn, irreducible to their perception or relations or uses, they can only affect each other in a strange region out in front of them, a region of traces and footprints: the aesthetic dimension.[13]

Morton presents aesthetics as a realm in which the fantastic agency acquired by things can be brought to fruition, and his claim has recently provided the basis for a plethora of 'object-oriented' literary-critical projects. He suggests that this is 'why philosophers have often found [the aesthetic dimension] to be a realm of evil', and he describes the aesthetic dimension as 'a place of illusions, yet they are real illusions' (18). Aesthetics, in this view, is a sphere of Baudrillardian hyper-reality and simulacra, a proto-postmodern realm in which images come to life, throwing the 'correlationist' binaries between subject and object, image and reality, human and non-human into radical doubt. Walter Benjamin once lamented the 'aestheticization of politics', which he equated with fascism, but Morton appears to applaud the aestheticization of reality itself when he claims that '*the aesthetic dimension is the causal dimension*' (20, emphasis in original). If causation is aesthetic, Morton notes, then '[a]ction at a distance happens all the time', and 'in Plato's time they used to call action at a distance demonic' (20). In short, *Realist Magic* describes postmodernity as a 'demonic' and 'weird' environment in which 'objects and their sensual effects crowd together like leering figures in a masquerade', and 'nothing is going to tell us categorically what counts as real and what counts as unreal' (19).

I am not suggesting here that epistemology, ontology and phenomenology as philosophical fields have not benefitted from or been energized by the micro-materialists' insights: in the context of specific philosophical discourses they have considerable pertinence and power. But how do they translate into the practice of textual interpretation, or assist in the reconstruction of cultural history, or contribute to our understanding of early modern drama? What is their politics? And above all, how might the new materialism help us to carry out the kind of scholarship and teaching that will directly address, and even help to dismantle, the forms of neoliberal capitalism that continue to destroy our 'natural' environment and push our planet towards ecological disaster?

Recently, many literary critics who focus on the vibrant life of things, or pursue the post-human, have begun to draw on the authority of micro-materialist theory. Like other influential theories that begin in the discipline of philosophy and then emigrate to a variety of other humanistic disciplines, object-oriented ontology and speculative realism first gained attention as philosophy, then as 'theory', before being imported, adapted and applied to the interpretive practice of rank-and-file literary and cultural critics. As Harman notes, his ideas have 'rapidly gained influence in fields outside academic philosophy' (183). This popularity suggests that the new materialism strikes a resonant chord with the postmodern *Zeitgeist*. These originally philosophical developments have lent a new authority, and a new intellectual impetus, to three already existing tendencies in literary-historical studies.

First, they have been utilized to advance the admirably anti-anthropocentric intentions of ecocriticism and animal studies, which have rightly questioned the concept of the 'human', deconstructed the human-natural binary, and presented us instead with a single, interdependent environment. A rich and compelling body of recent ecocritical work in early modern studies has drawn our attention to species boundaries and the entanglement of human with non-human being. Second, and perhaps less admirably, they have been alleged to support the undialectical, reductionist materialism of 'material culture studies' to provide a framework for studying the 'materiality' of gloves, writing tablets and keyholes, for pursuing cultural analyses of horses, herrings, tulips, stones, guns, germs, steel and so on. Third, they have informed recent scholarship in the 'history of the book', especially those developments that fetishize the 'materiality' of the text, and in doing so often ignore or de-emphasize larger political questions. According to David Hawkes, the danger here is that 'this attention to things, objects, or matter can degenerate into what has been called "tchotchke criticism" ..., an interest in objects for their own sake which, ironically enough, frequently eschews the cultural contexts in which objects acquire meaning'.[14] When objects are endowed with vibrant lives, thrilling with actor-network connectivity and distributive agency, human subjects are correspondingly decentred and ontologically downgraded. We have been kicking objects around for far too long, the micro-materialists argue, and so it is high time that we acknowledge more fully our interwovenness with non-human matter. In my view, however, micro-materialist ontologies seek to reorient reality in ways that have troubling limitations for the practice of both politics and cultural analysis.[15]

Micro-materialist theorists like Bogost and Bennett ask such questions as, '[w]hat's it like to be a computer?' (Bogost 9). They may stumble upon a clump of garbage in the gutter and find it redolent with vibrant, relational being and 'thing-power' (Bennett 4–6). Brown reminds us that 'one way Marx tries to give us a sense of commodity fetishism is by showing us ideas in things' (8), but he seems to find the notion implausible when he recalls 'trying to notice whether this thing or that – a crushed Styrofoam cup, a stone bench, a horse chestnut – might have an idea in it' (6). Bennett glimpses non-human agency through close encounters with a glove, a bottle cap and a stick that give off what are probably best conceived as 'weird vibes':

> I caught a glimpse of an energetic vitality inside each of these things, things that I generally conceived as inert. In this assemblage, objects appeared as things, that is as vivid entities not entirely reducible to the contexts in which (human) subjects met them, never entirely exhausted by their semiotics.
>
> (5)

Presumably the inference is that the non-human is implicated in the human and vice versa. But according to object-oriented ontology, and to micro-materialism in general, material objects form the very definition and model of being. The new materialists grudgingly acknowledge that human beings can be included in the world of things, but not as autonomous perceivers of, or central participants in, that world. And never as subjects. The usual ecocritical or post-human critique of anthropocentrism does not go far enough in decentring humankind for the radical micro-materialists. Their emphasis on a complex and all-inclusive 'materiality' that refuses to separate 'nature' from technology, social structures or culture is a welcome philosophical position, insofar as it breaks down the classical humanist alienation of the autonomous subject from animals, plants, inanimate objects and their networks. But when micro-materialism is imported into the cultural politics of literary interpretation, it threatens to distract attention from wider social and subjective agencies, ideologies and political economies. There is no doubt that non-human objects are continually interacting with us, but they lack consciousness and the will to political action. For such capacities, we must take full responsibility. Human work, human thought and human action are the forces that have given us a political economy, and they are also the only forces capable of changing capitalism before it is too late.

In part, the limitations of micro-materialism arise from a problem of disciplinary positionality. Its insights afford a more effective purchase in the context of a specialized philosophical inquiry into matter and objects. But once micro-materialist principles are brought to bear on human cultures and meanings, once they are directed towards the composition and consumption of literary texts, they rapidly become a hindrance to incisive cultural analysis and effective political action. For micro-materialism is haunted by a problem of deep structure. Its networks or assemblages, its occult, enchanted correspondences between objects, form a shifting matrix of the local and the specific that can serve to conceal overarching, persistent human-made structures like social class. Its focus on the instantiation of objects disarms us by distracting from the shaping power of human ideas, actions and economies to affect materiality – including terrestrial, even planetary, materiality. At the level of a philosophical description of the fundamental principles of ontology, we may surmise that there are heterogeneous networks that include both human and non-human actants, distributed in intricate rhizomic assemblages, and not manifested in clearly defined hierarchies. But in terms of political and critical practice, we need to prioritize human thought, the human class system and the large-scale economic structures that human beings produce.

We should not, in short, become fixated on the occult being of the non-human objects that interact with human being. We should not fetishize matter. As Slavoj Zizek has remarked of David Chalmers's reduction of consciousness to matter: 'The temptation to "see" thought as an additional component of natural/material reality itself is the ultimate vulgarity.'[16] Indeed, one urgent justification for a continued focus on *human* thinking and action is our need to understand (and possibly even control) the large-scale effects of human activity on the non-human world, with which we coexist and on which we are dependent for our survival. As we face the current crisis of global capitalism, we must not lose sight of the causal connection between the history of capitalism (from its emergence in the early modern period to its current ascendency as a global neoliberal order) and the onset of the Anthropocene. The mode of human activity determined by the capitalist economy is the formal cause of climate change.

In *Vibrant Matter*, Bennett describes politics as 'not … a formed thing or fixed entity, but … an unruly activity or indeterminate wave of energy' (106). This does not seem a promising basis for effective political action. Bogost only grudgingly concedes that humanity might 'possess a seemingly unique ability to agitate the world, or at least our corner of it (although this too is a particularly grandiose assumption, given that humans interact with only a tiny sliver of the universe)' (9). I am not advocating an anti-intellectual, blanket dismissal of micro-materialist thinking: there is certainly a place for rarified speculation of this kind, especially when philosophers debate philosophers. Nonetheless, it hardly seems the theoretical paradigm to keep literary studies ethically and politically viable or to advance the struggle against socio-economic injustice and neoliberal ideology. Nor will it assist our efforts to slow a climate crisis whose roots lie in the nature of capitalism itself. If scholars in the humanities are to engage with the most urgent ethical and political issues of our time, then we will need a more robustly dialectical theory, one that fully acknowledges the profound effects of human economic and cultural organization on the material health of our planet.

Claiming the status of a new and rigorous methodology, new materialist theory has been applied to a variety of historical contexts, and to diverse literary texts, from the medieval mystics, through the poetry of Lord Byron, and onto postmodern media ecologies.[17] Anti-anthropocentrism is its central ethical position, but often the Latourian zeal to identify a kind of sympathetic magic as the key to all events and agencies becomes an animistic faith in matter itself. The idea that humans have lorded it over the rest of creation for centuries, and that we have failed to acknowledge how human being is indebted to the power of non-human objects, must be joined with an acknowledgement of the structuring influence of the class system, supported by ideology – as it is for example in the work of Jason W. Moore. Historical, contextual considerations that link our readings of literary texts to an understanding of the long process of capitalism's emergence and its destructive deformation of 'human nature' should form the basis for an ethical, political reading today. While our approach to textual terrestriality is grounded (or mired) in local, dead, inanimate objects, without paying adequate attention to large-scale political phenomena, and to *human* agencies, it will remain incapable of understanding the intertwined histories of ecocide and capitalism that connect the early modern emergence of political economy with the economic crises of today.

*   *   *

Shakespeare and Middleton's *Timon of Athens* undoubtedly invites us to examine the question of materiality. But that does not necessarily mean regarding the text itself as an object, in the micro-materialist sense.[18] *Timon*'s movement from the human to the non-human is not represented through the materiality of the text, but through the plot, characters and language of the play. By such means Shakespeare and Middleton tell a cautionary tale of the social and economic problems raised by early capitalism.[19] The play also warns that withdrawal from society, or abstinence from consumption, does not provide solutions to those problems. It shows how usury destroys anyone who does not play by the social rules of thrift or who fails to fulfil the obligations of a monetized marketplace, but also it reveals how retreat from the human leads only to deadly isolation and political disaster. His self-exile beyond the city walls does not bring Timon to a 'natural' refuge in asceticism or solitude. His misanthropic turn towards the non-human is a model for self-destruction, not an effectual protest against usury or a prototypical form of eco-activism.

From the misanthropic perspectives of Timon, Apemantus and Alcibiades, Athens is a city run by greedy lords and corrupt senators, which has degenerated into a subhuman condition devoid of charity, hospitality or gratitude. Apemantus claims '[t]he commonwealth of Athens is become a forest of beasts' (4.3.346-47) while, according to Alcibiades, Athens there is 'no meat' like 'a breakfast of enemies' (1.2.75-8).[20] The old codes of male friendship and patronage are barely residual, persisting as mere rhetoric. Yet the radical turn away from humankindness and commonwealth towards the non-human terrestrial is politically and personally counter-productive for Timon. Nor is Timon a lone, tragic protagonist; his hostility to humankind affects Athens as a whole. The rise of an economic structure based on monetary value rather than on blood, and the replacement of the relationship between aristocrats and commons by relations between creditors and debtors, threatens to release a populist spirit of murderous vengeance. The defection of Alcibiades seems likely to bring a blood-letting that will purge the sick, unjust society of all that ails it. The frightening pronouncement that concludes the play is radically indeterminate: Alcibiades will '[m]ake war breed peace, make peace stint war, make each/Prescribe to other, as each other's leech' (5.5.81-82). It is not clear whether this is a violent but necessary prescription that will heal the body politic of its moral and economic corruption, or a recipe for the permanent war of all against all, provoked by an incurable disease: 'the malice of mankind' (4.3.446).

Timon ends with Athens under occupation by a mercenary army (the most costly form of unproductive labour, then as now). This concludes the events set in motion by the collapse of the traditional economy based on hospitality, gifts and feudal, household patronage. Timon's personal debts function as a synecdoche for the replacement of feudal relations by the 'unnatural', usurious logic of debt that mercilessly squeezes any individual defaulter, no matter how noble in birth or character. As Timon falls from wealth to poverty, and from generous giving to bitter misanthropy, Shakespeare and Middleton focus closely on the process of his alienation. Timon attempts to detach himself from a community that can no longer conceive of gift-giving as reciprocal charity but perceives it as a credit-based payment with strings attached. Timon's furious rejection of the human specifically means turning his back on a particular society structured and bound by abstract relations of financial credit and debt.[21] In this play, ancient Athens is plagued by the same forces of emergent capitalism, the same species of usury and debt bondage, that were starting to affect Shakespeare and Middleton's own society.[22]

The play's opening acts exhibit the reification of human beings into objects of 'use'. Shakespeare and Middleton portray objectification as a degrading process of dehumanization, rather than as the harmless levelling of the human-object playing field advocated by the micro-materialists. The people of early modern England still had moralistic objections to the conversion of beings with consciousness and spirit into lifeless commodity-things. One of Timon's creditors describes the complex network of credit that mercilessly abstracts and compels the human will:

> I must serve my turn
> Out of mine own. [Timon's] days and times are past,
> And my reliance on his fracted dates
> Have smit my credit. I love and honor him,
> But must not break my back to heal his finger.
> Immediate are my needs.
>
> (2.1.20-25)

Here time itself is commodified by the customs and laws of a community in which Timon and his creditors are bound by the rules of usury, which are diametrically opposed to traditions of hospitality and gratitude. The immediate need for ready cash trumps the obligation to repay past gifts. The later discovery of gold, which Timon finds accidentally while digging for roots to eat, provides the 'agentic materiality' that drives the play's final two acts. An object-oriented critic might well find in this an example of how inanimate objects can exhibit a kind of vitalism that coexists with and determines human behaviour. But such a reading would ignore the underlying logic of money, which is often *perceived* as an autonomously efficacious, magical fetish, but which is not enchanted in reality. Insofar as it is regarded as financial value, gold is merely a congealed representation of human labour-power. This idea is articulated in Timon's paean to gold in act 4, which is glossed in Karl Marx's famous interpretation. According to Marx, the efficacy of gold 'lies in its *character* as men's estranged, alienating and self disposing *species-nature*. Money is the alienated *ability of mankind*'.[23] In this form of alienation, humans translate their own subjective activity, their very lives, into the money-form. In other words, they reify themselves. In doing so, however, they also trick themselves into making a superstitious mistake: they come to believe in the magical efficacy of their own fetish.

This belief in the efficacy of exchange-value is an ideological self-delusion, and not (as some might have it) a blast of essential, material thing-power emanated by money as vibrant matter. Commodity fetishism, after all, is the superstitious folly, the barbaric image-worship of the capitalist who mistakes the unjust economic mechanisms of exchange-value for a magical creation of value from nothing. As Marx declares in *Capital*, 'social power becomes a private power in the hands of a private person.... Modern society which, when still in its infancy, pulled Pluto by the hair of his head out of the bowels of the earth, acclaims gold, its Holy Grail, as the glittering incarnation of its inmost vital principle'.[24] Timon's turn from the human to the terrestrial, his attempt to take refuge in solitude, to return to human rootedness in natural, non-human processes, forces him to labour – literally to dig in the dirt for food. Indeed, he prays for food to the Earth, the 'common mother – thou / Whose womb unmeasurable and infinite breast / Teems and feeds all' (4.3.176-77). Yet the same Nature that rewards his labour with a root to eat also provides the golden metal for which human beings steal and kill. Timon declares that Nature has enough for all human needs, but this is contradicted by his characterization of humanity as a species that is monstrous, and even worthy of annihilation, because its nature is the antithesis and the enemy of Nature. Through Timon, Shakespeare and Middleton suggest that human beings naturally want, and naturally take, more than they naturally need.

Any political ecology worth the name must be based on human, social and political economies. The market currently defines relations between human and non-human: all nature is a storehouse of potential commodities, and so nothing is purely 'natural'. This is also the implication of Shakespeare and Middleton's tragedy. Timon learns, and then loudly proclaims, that human relations with nature have been distorted by the fetishization of gold. He tells the thieves who come to steal his gold that even their murderous labour partakes of the general social pattern: 'take wealth and lives together, / Do villainy, do, since you protest to do't like workman' (4.3.428-30). Their theft is patterned after nature itself:

> the earth's a thief
> That feeds and breeds by a composture stol'n
> From general excrement. Each thing's a thief.
> The laws, your curb and whip, in their rough power
> Has unchecked theft.

>   (4.3.435-39)

Thus, humanity projects its own vision of reality onto nature. Timon's personal back-to-nature programme and his choice of a cave as dwelling and of roots as food are efforts to break free from society. Ironically, however, his hatred of humankind continues to bind him firmly to his fellow human beings through the gold that he discovers and they desire. Timon's withdrawal from the city does not bring solitude or separation – that would hardly make for good drama. His misanthropic vituperations continue to connect him to the community he once loved but now hates. His cave-life is not rooted in natural, terrestrial processes any more than his life in the city had been. Even at the periphery of the city and the edge of the sea, humanity pursues Timon with all its acquisitive intent. Nature itself is commodified in the form of the gold, which provides the source of Timon's second wave of giving – but this time his gift is a curse and a 'planetary plague', not a charitable response to the needs of friends and clients.

The only real way out of social species-being, and thus the sole true escape from humankind, is not exile but death. Timon even tries to protect his inanimate body-object in the grave from any lingering social ties in the form of visitors or mourners. His epitaph warns: 'Here lie I, Timon, who alive all living men did hate, / Pass by and curse thy fill, but pass and stay not here thy gait' (5.5.70-71). Alcibiades rather generously declares Timon's lines a 'rich conceit' that '[t]aught thee to make vast Neptune weep for aye/On thy low grave, on faults forgiven' (5.5.75-77). But this pseudo-Christian consolation is offered by a notably unforgiving, vengeful soldier about to enter Athens and slaughter all his enemies. The audience is offered little consolation from the play's conclusion. Social and personal faults, like financial loans, will be forgiven only as part of an endless cycle of blood-letting. Such dark ironies constitute the satirical force of Shakespeare and Middleton's play, juxtaposing human values and agency with an implacable nature, in which human beings are certainly imbedded, but which they systematically commodify and consume through the violent extraction of exchange-value. Alcibiades's closing reference to 'faults forgiven' does not apply to the faults of proto-capitalist Athens, with its epidemic avarice and usury. It refers to Timon's personal faults, both his overly generous giving and his overly bitter cursing. The play's discordant and puzzling conclusion, ending with the harsh drumbeat of war and the certainty of impending massacre, seems designed to force the original London audiences to consider the unnatural structure of their own socio-economic system. Such historical considerations link *Timon of Athens* to capitalism's deformation of 'human nature', and they can still enable politically transformative readings of the play.

We must abjure the rough magic that would re-enchant matter so that we can focus our collective power against the class-based economy that is driving us towards global disaster. We must do this while refusing to neglect either the climate emergency itself or its causes in human agency. This is a time of urgency, indeed of emergency. The esoteric animism and magical tendencies of the 'new materialism' will not save humanity from itself. Human agency, human responsibility, and collective, eco-socialist political action offer our only human hope. To the extent that it is adopted by literary critics, the 'new materialism' seems likely to lure us away from crucial questions about, and effective resistances to, the deep, ecocidal structures of class, power and political economy. While acknowledging that anthropocentrism and a delusional sense of human separation from nature have helped bring us to the present emergency, we must not be drawn away from the primary cause of the crisis – capitalism – or become entangled in a rarified, micro-materialist web of distributed agencies. Only human action can slow the acceleration of harm. And only an acknowledgement of human action as the original source of the problem can lead to such restorative action being taken.

With admirable anti-anthropocentric urgency, post-humanism takes the species boundary as the final frontier of identity politics. Like other forms of identity politics, however, it will fall short of its liberatory goals unless informed by economics and the politics of class struggle. In economic terms, the reduction of human beings to objects is known as 'reification'. The reification of human labour-power into agential, financial form is the ultimate cause of ecological crisis because, unlike actual human beings, the reified, symbolic form of human labour-power owes no allegiance to nature. The idea that money can breed money, as it does so prolifically today, was in Shakespeare and Middleton's day regarded as Nature's very worst enemy. In *Timon of Athens* and a host of other early modern plays, the agency of money is treated as destructive and unnatural, precisely because it represents human subjective activity in objective form. The concomitant dangers of reification and commodification, which alarmed early modern writers like Shakespeare and Middleton, have been sustained and reinforced over the centuries through the proliferation of capitalist ideology, something that exists only through and in human culture and subjectivity. As it developed and spread over the centuries, that ideology, with its insistence on increased profits and unsustainable growth, supported tremendous material suffering in our class-based human society and produced staggering levels of ecological destruction. It continues to do so. The micro-materialists of today would do well to consider the possibility that, far from evoking a beneficent sympathy with the non-human environment, their reduction of human beings to pure matter is the main ideological effect of ecocidal capital run amok.

Notes

1   From a 'Review of Latour's *Facing Gaia*' by Alexandre Leskanich in the *Los Angeles Review of Books*, http://blogs.lse.ac.uk/lsereviewofbooks/2017/08/24/book-review-facing-gaia-eight-lectures-on-the-new-climatic-regime-by-bruno-latour/

2   Simon L. Lewis and Mark A. Maslin, 'Defining the Anthropocene', *Nature* 519 (2015): 171–80.

3   'Weird' is Graham Harman's term. See his *Weird Realism* (Winchester: Zero Books, 2012), which unsurprisingly announces that all the leading exponents of 'object-oriented ontology (OOO)' are inspired by the fiction of H. P. Lovecraft.

4   Jane Bennett, *Vibrant Matter: A Political Ecology of Things* (Durham: Duke University Press, 2012), 6.

5   See Jason W. Moore, *Capitalism in the Web of Life: Ecology and the Accumulation of Capital* (London: Verso, 2015), and the essays in Jason W. Moore, ed., *Anthropocene or Capitalocene? Nature, History, and the Crisis of Capitalism* (Oakland: PM Press, 2016).

6   Bill Brown, *A Sense of Things: The Object Matter of American Literature* (University of Chicago Press, 2003), 5–6.

7   The literature linking capitalism (as cause) with ecocide and the climate emergency (as effects) is of course vast, but good places to start include Ian Angus, *Facing the Anthropocene: Fossil Capitalism and the Crisis of the Earth System* (New York: Monthly Review Books, 2016); Kate Aronoff, *Overheated: How Capitalism Broke the Planet and How We Fight Back* (New York: Bold Type Books, 2021); John Bellamy Foster, Brett Clark and Richard York, *The Ecological*

Rift: Capitalism's War on the Earth (New York: Monthly Review
Press, 2010); Naomi Klein, *This Changes Everything: Capitalism vs.
The Climate* (New York: Simon & Schuster, 2015); Fred Magdoff
and John Bellamy Foster, *What Every Environmentalist Needs to
Know about Capitalism* (New York: Monthly Review Press, 2011);
and Andreas Malm, *Fossil Capital: The Rise of Steam Power and the
Roots of Global Warming* (London: Verso, 2016).

8   Friedrich Engels, *Anti- Dühring*, 'Part II: Political Economy', https://
www.marxists.org/archive/marx/works/1877/anti-duhring/ch13.htm

9   Karl Marx, *Capital*, vol. 3, cit. M. C. Howard and J. C. King, *The
Political Economy of Marx* (New York University Press, 1975), 107.

10 'Introduction' to *Object Oriented Environs*, ed. Julian Yates and
Jeffrey Jerome Cohen (Punctum, 2016): vi–xxv.

11 As Graham Harman puts it: 'The Marxist idea that there is
economics and all the rest is ideology was once a fresh approach
to the human sciences, but eventually became petulant, robotic and
blind'. 'The Well-Wrought Broken Hammer: Object-Oriented Literary
Criticism', *New Literary History* 43, no. 2 (2012): 183–203, 200.

12 Timothy Morton. 'Here Comes Everything: The Promise of Object-
Oriented Ontology', *Qui Parle* 19, no. 2 (2011): 163–90, 165.

13 Timothy Morton, *Realist Magic: Objects, Ontology, Causality*
(Ann Arbor: Open Humanities Press, 2013), 17–18.

14 David Hawkes, 'Against Materialism in Literary Theory' in *The
Return of Theory in Early Modern English Studies: Tarrying with
the Subjunctive*, ed. Paul Cefalu and Bryan Reynolds (New York:
Palgrave Macmillan, 2011).

15 For recent critiques of the new materialism, including Latour's ANT,
see R. H. Lossin, 'Neoliberalism for Polite Company: Bruno Latour's
Pseudo-Materialist Coup' in *Salvage* (1 June 2020), https://salvage.
zone/articles/neoliberalism-for-polite-company-bruno-latours-
pseudo-materialist-coup/; Andreas Malm, 'On What Matter Does:
Against New Materialism', chap. 3 of *The Progress of This Storm*
(London: Verso, 2018): 78–118; Slavoj Žižek, 'Marx Reads Object-
Oriented-Ontology', in *Reading Marx* (Cambridge: Polity, 2018);
and Hylton White, 'Materiality, Form, and Context: Marx contra
Latour', *Victorian Studies* 55, no. 4, Special Issue: The Ends of
History (Summer 2013): 667–82.

16 Slavoj Zizek, 'Interview with Ben Woodard', in *The Speculative Turn:
Continental Materialism and Realism*, ed. Levi Bryan, Nick Srnicek
and Graham Harman (Melbourne: re.press, 2001), 406–15, 407.

17 For examples, see *Animal, Vegetable, Mineral: Ethics and Objects*,
ed. Jeffrey Cohen (Washington, DC: Oliphaunt/punctum books,
2012); Paolo Bartoloni, *Objects in Italian Life and Culture: Fiction,*

Migration, and Artificiality (New York: Palgrave Macmillan, 2016); and Susan Signe Morrison, *The Literature of Waste: Material Ecopoetics and Ethical Matter* (New York: Palgrave Macmillan, 2015).

18   Following Jason W. Moore's definition of the capitalocene, but emphasizing the object-oriented critique of 'human exceptionalism', Katherine Gillen offers a new materialist reading of *Timon* in her article, 'Shakespeare in the Capitalocene: *Titus Andronicus, Timon of Athens*, and Early Modern Eco-Theater', *Exemplaria* 30, no. 4 (2018): 275–92. Typical of the apolitical, thematic school of new materialist criticism is Joanna Grossman's article, 'Timon of Ashes', *The Journal of Ecocriticism* 6, no. 2 (2014): 1–20.

19   Useful economic readings of *Timon* include the following: Michael Chorost, 'Biological Finance in Shakespeare's *Timon of Athens*', *English Literary Renaissance* 21, no. 3 (1991): 349–70; David Hershinow, 'Cash Is King: Timon, Diogenes, and the Search for Sovereign Freedom', *Modern Philology: Critical and Historical Studies in Literature, Medieval Through Contemporary* 115, no. 1 (August 2017): 53–79; Eike Kronshage, 'Conspicuous Consumption, Croyance, and the Problem of the Two Timons: Shakespeare and Middleton's *Timon of Athens*', *Critical Horizons: Journal of Social & Critical Theory* 18, no. 3 (2017): 262–74; Sandra K. Fischer, '"Cut My Heart in Sums": Shakespeare's Economics and *Timon of Athens*', in *Money: Lure, Lore, and Literature*, ed. John Louis DiGaetani (Westport, CT: Greenwood Press, 1994): 187–95; John Jowett, 'Middleton and Debt in *Timon of Athens*', in *Money and the Age of Shakespeare: Essays in New Economic Criticism*, ed. Linda Woodbridge (New York: Palgrave Macmillan, 2003), 219–35; Derek Cohen, 'The Politics of Wealth: *Timon of Athens*', *Neophilologus* 77, no. 1 (January 1993): 149–60; Hugh Grady, '*Timon of Athens*: The Dialectic of Usury, Nihilism, and Art', in *A Companion to Shakespeare's Works, Volume I: The Tragedies*, ed. Richard Dutton and Jean E. Howard (Oxford: Wiley-Blackwell, 2006): 431–51; Katherine A. Gillen, '"What He Speaks Is All in Debt": Credit, Representation and Theatrical Critique in *Timon of Athens*', *Shakespeare Jahrbuch* 150 (2014): 79–109.

20   All quotations from the play are taken from the Arden edition: Thomas Middleton and William Shakespeare, *Timon of Athens*, ed. Anthony B. Dawson and Gretchen E. Minton (London: Bloomsbury, 2008).

21   On the fictionality of credit relations in early modern England and in *Timon*, see Laura Kolb, *Fictions of Credit in the Age of Shakespeare* (Oxford University Press, 2021), especially Chapter 3,

which includes her reading of *Timon*. Kolb understands credit as both dangerous and empowering for early modern people, but she neglects to discuss credit and debt as 'usury' or to interpret *Timon* in critical terms with reference to emergent capitalism.

22 See Amanda Bailey's chapter on 'Timon of Athens, Payback, and the Genre of Debt', in *Of Bondage: Debt, Property, and Personhood in Early Modern England* (Philadelphia: University of Pennsylvania Press, 2013) and David Hawkes, *The Culture of Usury in Renaissance England* (New York: Palgrave Macmillan, 2010).

23 Karl Marx, *Economic and Philosophical Manuscripts of 1844, Collected Works*, vol. 3 (1976), 323–5.

24 Cited in John Jowett's introduction to the Oxford Shakespeare edition of the play, William Shakespeare and Thomas Middleton, *The Life of Timon of Athens* (Oxford: Oxford University Press, 2004), 54.

2

The vice of collecting money in *Mankind*

William Casey Caldwell

Midway through the late-medieval morality play *Mankind*, three 'Vice' characters named New-Guise, Nowadays and Nought suddenly demand cash payment from the audience: if they want the play to continue, the Vices warn, real money must change hands. Written around 1465–70 for performance in East Anglia, *Mankind* belongs to a medieval performance tradition that predates the emergence of the London professional theatre. Douglas Bruster and Eric Rasmussen argue that 'the evidence suggests *Mankind* was probably written for and performed by highly talented, highly organized actors who happened to be monks at the abbey of St Edmund of Bury', at that time the 'virtual heart of theatrical activity in England'.[1] The abbey at Bury was not a secluded and detached location, but rather a 'massive, rich, powerful and sometimes aggressive corporation that dominated life in its part of East Anglia', and this religious building could have served as one of the sites for *Mankind*'s staging.[2]

Scholars have generally regarded this play's collection scene as prefiguring the rise of the professional theatre. David Bevington claims that this 'taking up of a collection during the performance is the first recorded instance in England of openly commercial acting'.[3] Most readings of the monetary collection note its innovation: the Arden edition claims that this is 'the first reference we have to money being paid by those attending a play in England'; Walter K. Smart remarks that, so far as he knows, 'in no other extant medieval play [...] is the collection made a part of the play as it is here'; William Tydeman suggests that this is 'the earliest English text to integrate the need for a collection into its dramatic structure'.[4] While *Mankind*'s collection scene undoubtedly represents an important moment in theatre history, however, the critical focus on originality or precedent can be limiting. We can interpret the collection scene within a varied continuum of performative contexts and dramatic forms, which often recall such theatrical precedents for collecting money, mummers' plays, traditional and emergent funding structures for theatre troupes, and morality play character types.

If the collection does anticipate the rise of openly commercial acting, it does so in a peculiar way: rather than paying an intermediary to keep the gate or door, as would become the norm in London's professional playhouses, this drama involves the audience members handing money directly to a fictive character. Furthermore, this moment of contact between audience and player pointedly raises the question of what happens when money as payment becomes a condition of possibility for dramatic production. How is the dialectic between spectator and performer altered by monetary exchange?

Mankind is full of financial imagery. Mercy refers to Mankind as 'dear bought' (10) and to Christ as 'him that bought me dear' (255), before urging Mankind: 'Lose not through folly that is bought so dear'. Mischief and New Guise also swear 'by him that me bought' (415). Mischief's first lines anticipate the collection: 'unshut your gates and take an ha'penny' (52).[5] Nought urges Mercy to leave the Vices alone with Mankind: 'I have seen a man lost twenty nobles in as little time' (270). The Vices' bawdy, scatological humour is woven into a monetary lexicon, in a manner that presages Freud's link between money and defecation. For instance, New-Guise's reference to his 'great purse' refers to his testicles, which Mankind has just kicked, an act that New-Guise calls the '*recumbentibus* of my jewels'. He also refers to a 'pardon belly-met' (likely a reference to the sale of indulgences) granted by 'Pope Pockett'. Having been beaten by Mankind, Nought complains, 'I have such a pain in my arm / I may not change a man a farthing' (390–91) and later claims that his purse is 'as clean as a bird's arse' (479). All of the Vices repeatedly pun on farthings/fartings (496; 489).[6]

The collection scene brings real money into play, involving the audience directly in the drama. As Tison Pugh has recently observed, throughout the morality play tradition, the audience is 'called to interpolate themselves into the dramatic plot by envisioning the moral choices of the protagonists' actions as directly relevant to their own lives'.[7] Here they are asked to conjure the devil, using money. Late in the play, Mercy makes explicit what has been suggested all along: 'properly Titivillus signifieth the fiend of Hell' (886). Sarah Beckwith suggests that 'the audience is implicated in [Titivillus's] appearance and indeed financially underwrites that appearance', while Pamela King notes that 'the motive for calling up a spectacular devil slips from the fictional one of destroying Mankind to the factive one of entertaining a paying audience', so that the audience contributes to something resembling a black mass by conjuring the devil onto the stage.[8]

Mankind uses money to implicate the audience in the devil's appearance but also to stage an ethical conflict inherent in paid acting. The play extends this conflict to the audience and the actor/vices' relationship with the host, or the 'goodman of the house', who is 'entertaining' everyone under his roof. The fact that the play can be staged with a few simple props and only six actors has led scholars to suggest that it was intended either for a small itinerant troupe or a local group of actors.[9] Scholars also cite *Mankind*'s 'base' humour to suggest that it was meant for a popular audience, perhaps in an outdoor venue like an innyard or a temporary staging area like a local field. In direct contrast, others suggest that the play's frequent use of Latin indicates that it was intended for a more educated, elite audience in a private, indoor venue. King, Bruster and Rasmussen agree, however, that *Mankind* is written to be highly adaptable not just in terms of playing space but also of audience demographic and that the play could have been performed in many potential sites including private halls, inns and monasteries.[10]

While we cannot know for certain the identities of *Mankind*'s actors or the breadth of its performance locations, we can make inferences about its staging conditions from basic theatrical technologies of the time and also from evidence internal to the play. Some of *Mankind*'s playing conditions, particularly the audience/actor dynamics, would have closely resembled those of the early London commercial playhouses. Whether an innyard, a private hall or a religious building, the playing space would have involved constant, shared lighting over the actors and the audience. This lighting would have facilitated moments of direct address between the audience and a fully visible character, where each would often (if not always) be performatively aware of the other.[11] It is often suggested that the playing space would have been mostly in the round, with the audience surrounding the stage on most sides.[12] In the opening monologue addressed to the audience, Mercy refers to 'ye sovereigns that sit and ye brethren that stand right up', indicating that the social division implied by 'sovereigns' as opposed to 'brethren' would have mapped onto the division between seating and standing areas in the same manner as early modern commercial playhouses.[13] The Vices may have also entered and exited through the audience, rendering the space between actor/character and audience even more permeable than would be possible in Shakespeare's day.

Mankind's genre also critically shapes its approach to the monetary conditions of dramatic production. It is typically grouped with plays like *Everyman* and *The Castle of Perseverance* as a morality play.[14] Whereas the Chester and York cycles dramatize biblical history from the Fall of Lucifer to the Last Judgement, the morality plays instead feature an everyman figure whose spiritual crisis is dramatized as a fight between 'personified abstractions' such as vices and virtues.[15] The play's central protagonist, Mankind, shares the stage not with biblical figures like Abraham, Herod or Mary but with embodied character traits like Mercy or Mischief, New-Guise, Nowadays and Nought. The names of these last four characters invoke the vices with which the play is centrally concerned: 'New-guise' and 'Nowadays' both reveal an interest in fashion and keeping up with the moment, whereas 'Mischief' and 'Nought' refer to bad behaviour. The central spiritual crisis that the Vices precipitate is depicted through a single teachable moment. As William Tydeman puts it, morality plays generally tend to focus 'not on the whole span of a man's life, but one allegorical incident'.[16]

In *Mankind,* the 'allegorical incident' involves the titular character becoming distracted from good, honest labour on his plot of land. After being warned about the Vices by Mercy – to 'convert your conditions all their means shall be sought' – Mankind for a time manages to fend off New-Guise, Nowadays and Nought while he struggles to farm his land (296). He is eventually conquered, however, when Titivillus magically induces him to dream that Mercy has died. Losing hope, Mankind falls in with the Vices and for a time follows their bad example, nearly driving himself to suicide, before Mercy returns and Mankind repents. This relatively straightforward allegorical arc is developed with a richly idiosyncratic language that swings between scatological abuse and Latinate rhetoric, as well as through deeply entertaining moments of audience interaction, prominent among which is the collection of money.

The collection occurs midway through the play, immediately after Mankind has beaten the Vices off the stage with his shovel and left to get more grain to plant. Returning to the stage after their trouncing, New-Guise, Nowadays and Nought meet with Mischief and decide to have an 'interlection', or consultation, because 'it were good to have an end' to their struggle with Mankind (449–50). In order to complete their 'interlection', they signal for Titivillus to enter the stage. Titivillus is a common character, generally associated with idle words and loose talk in the medieval period, though in this play he is specifically associated with the Devil.[17] The Vices then turn to the audience, requiring them to pay up if they want to see this new attraction. New-Guise declares:

> We shall gather money unto,
> Else there shall no man him see.
> Now, ghostly to our purpose, worshipful sovereigns,
> We intend to gather money, if it please your negligence,
> For a man with a head that is of great omnipotence.
>
> (457–61)

The phrase 'worshipful sovereigns' is applied to the audience with sarcasm, and this speech evidences the kind of malapropic wordplay that the Vices often engage in (e.g. 'negligence' for 'reverence'). There does not seem to be an additional pun on 'sovereign' in the monetary sense, as one would expect in later plays, as this was not yet the name of a coin.[18] Apart from the angel, however, *Mankind* names every domestic coin in circulation during Edward IV's reign.[19] The Vices use the tantalizing prospect of seeing Titivillus to induce the audience to pay as much as possible: 'He loveth no groats, nor pence of two pence./ Give us red royals if ye will see his abominable presence' (464–5). New-Guise declares they will start their collection with 'the goodman of this house', mockingly blessing him while also protesting: 'Ye say us ill, yet ye will not say nay' (466–8). It is at this point that the *New Mermaids* edition inserts the stage direction '*They take a collection*', during which New-Guise instructs the audience, 'Ye pay all alike' – that is, everyone must pay and they must pay equally (470).[20] Resorting to playful Latin, the Vices confirm that they must receive sufficient money before they will consent to summon Titivillus. Eventually Nought asks: '*Estis vos pecuniatus?* [are you full of money?] / I have cried a fair while' to which Nowadays responds, '*Ita vere, magister* [yes indeed master]'. Titivillus enters on being called to 'come forth your *patus* [gates]', and his first request is 'Sir New Guise, lend me a penny!' (472). He immediately begins demanding money from the Vices, asking Nowadays, 'What is in thy purse?' and exclaiming to Nought: 'Hark now! I say thou hast many a penny' (482; 486). Eventually Titivillus 'discovers the collected monies', whereupon he sends the Vices out to scour the country to see 'if ye may catch ought'. As they depart, Titivillus reminds them, 'Come again, I warn, as soon as I you call, / And bring your advantage into this place' (523–4), anticipating the sense of 'advantage' as 'illegitimate or usurious profit', as Shylock uses the term in *The Merchant of Venice* (1.3.395). The audience may begin to suspect that it has purchased the means of its own destruction, especially when Titivillus threatens to fine them if they speak: 'Not a word, I charge you, pain of forty pence' (590).

While many scholars have stressed the unprecedented nature of the collection scene, it is actually an appropriation of an older performance ritual from folk drama. This was known as the *quête* – the collection of money by characters at the end of a mummers' play.[21] E. K Chambers describes a typical mummers' play as consisting of three parts: the presentation, the drama and the *quête*. In the presentation, a prologue-figure requests welcome from the audience and introduces the main characters; the drama usually features a fight and resurrection, as a doctor cures dead characters, sometimes even beheaded ones.[22] The *quête* was often taken at the end of the performance by a devil/Beelzebub character, played by an actor wearing a large mask or fake head and carrying a club, ladle or frying pan (Smart 23). W. K. Smart has pointed out that the action surrounding the collection of money in *Mankind* incorporates these three elements of the earlier mummers' plays.

Immediately before the collection, *Mankind* features a parodic fight and resurrection that also recalls the mummers' play and its magic-show elements, as well as anticipating later Renaissance plays that involve magic or conjuring. The Vices return to the stage complaining of their various bodily injuries after Mankind's beating. After New-Guise's bawdy complaint about the pain in his 'privity' and his seeming offer to expose himself and show the wound to Mischief, Nowadays bemoans an injury to his head, prompting

Mischief to declare he will cure the pain by 'smit[ing] off thy head and set[ting] it on again' (429; 435). There is probably some stage device at work here, involving the actor playing Nowadays ducking his head beneath his shirt to make it appear that his head is cut off, then popping it back out to declare, 'And my head is all safe and whole again' (447). One can draw a line directly from the mummers' play ritual fight and resurrection, through *Mankind*'s parodic Vices, to a less allegorical play like Marlowe's *Doctor Faustus*, in which the magician fools a horse-courser into believing he has pulled off Faustus's leg. The stage business presumably involved a removable prop leg and the actor simply pushing his real leg back out for the audience to see, much like Nowadays with his head. The effect is to stress the theatricality of undermining bodily integrity in a manner reminiscent of the modern-day magic shows in which a magician saws an audience member in half.

Another element *Mankind* shares with later London commercial plays is an investment in the magic of conjuring. In addition to the black-mass-style conjuring that the Vices ask the audience to pay for, Mercy inadvertently conjures the Vices onto stage near the start of the play.[23] Similar conjuring moments occur when Faustus summons Mephistopheles; in Shakespeare's *2 Henry VI*, when Gloucester's wife calls upon devils to aid her husband's ambitions; when Macbeth 'conjures' the weird sisters to show him his future; and even when Lady Macbeth invokes the 'spirits / That tend on mortal thoughts' (1.4.38-39). Ben Jonson parodies such conjuring in *The Alchemist*, when Subtle disguises himself as a Priest of Fairy, who conjures up the Fairy Queen in order to con Dapper of his money. Jonson's puncturing of theatrical illusion (the Fairy Queen is the con artist, Doll Common, in disguise) is close kin to *Mankind*'s playful appropriation of the mummers' *quête*.

Mummers' plays also invoked the host of the performance, often during the collection of money. E. K. Chambers notes that the *quête* typically featured an 'obeisance to the master of the house', much as New-Guise calls upon 'the goodman' at the start of the collection.[24] This obeisance may have involved a single person or the whole cast, and it would have preceded the collection. Chambers also notes that a character named 'Little Devil Dout' would frequently enter and threaten to sweep the audience into graves if they do not hand over money, thus mirroring the role of the three Vices in preparing Titivillus's entrance.[25]

The Vice's reference to the 'goodman of the house' explicitly alludes to the traditional funding relation between the master of a household and a playing troupe. Due to draconian anti-vagabond laws, acting troupes often sought livery status within a household under the patronage of a master.[26] Initially, local troupes were funded primarily in the form of a *largesse* or honorarium, understood as a monetary gift from the benevolent head of a household, rather than as wages paid for services rendered. Glynne Wickham describes the gradual mutation in the role of the *largesse* over the fifteenth century, such that the actors 'continued to receive *largesse* from the master of the house whether that house was [their] own or belonged to someone else: it was the multiplication factor that translated individual *largesse* into regular income' (188). Throughout the fifteenth century, troupes were compensated for their performances in the form of monetary gifts, either from their own patrons or from the 'goodmen' of the households they visited. It was the ability to multiply *largesse* through touring that led to a sustainable way of life for actors. Paul Whitefield White has suggested that these sponsored acting troupes were central to the 'feudal practice of gift-giving and hospitality' on the part of their host, both as an extension of the master's hospitality to the homes of the peers they visited and as an enactment of the master's beneficence towards the local community, for example through Christmas performances open to all levels of society (6).

Money given to acting troupes was framed, therefore, as a gift, rather than as a payment, and this was supposed to convey the hospitality of the host. The various ways in which money was funnelled to local and travelling acting troupes in return for their performances included ecclesiastical and civic sources as well as aristocrats, but the *largesse* system was prominent and definitive among them. As Wickham suggests, ecclesiastical and civic funds were best understood 'in the nature of gifts or honorariums, that is to say as "largesse" or bonuses voluntarily bestowed, rather than as an obligatory payment exacted for a service professionally rendered'.[27] Money collected from audiences during or after mummers' plays should also be seen as 'optional gifts' and not as obligatory fees or wages.[28] Everyone in late medieval England, from patron to audience, seems to have associated the actors' income with gratuities or honoraria rather than payment for their labour.

There was a history of reluctance to commodify the labour of entertainment, and *Mankind*'s collection scene is one of the earliest attempts to subvert this reluctance – in part, by making an explicit spectacle of that subversion.

Yet *Mankind* is also part of a long tradition in which fictional characters solicit money directly from audience members. The play's main innovation was to appropriate the structure of the mummers' performance and relocate it in the middle of the play. This makes the payment of money into a spectacle and integrates it into the action. Rather than marking the end of the play (as in the mummers' tradition) or the beginning (as with the early modern London playhouses), the collection is part of the performance. This relocation of the *quête* makes the continuation of the show contingent on payment so that the performance is held hostage – the actors may even have threatened to halt the show altogether if the transaction does not occur. There is hardly any distinction between the plot and the extra-mimetic frame at this point. As Mankind successfully fends off the Vices, forcing them to summon Titivillus to do their job for them, this in turn forces them to collect the money that will induce him to appear. The audience's payment is not only the precondition of the play's continuing; it materially advances the action, and it is accounted for as an element within the plot.

Whether *Mankind* was performed before a host in charge of an abbey, inn or private hall, the Vices comically violate the familiar *largesse* or honorarium framework when they demand payment from him.[29] In the process they invert and monetize the traditional blessing offered to the host and household in the mummers' play tradition. They mock-bless the host, demanding money while preemptively accusing him of protesting ('ye say us ill, yet will not say nay'). The line 'God bless you, master' repeats the mummers' blessing, but since it is uttered while demanding money from the host, its sincerity is less clear than in the traditional form. The guest-host relationship has been monetized: the host ought to be blessed for providing the space for the performance, but he is instead asked to give money to the Vices. This dramatic violation of the gift form is repeated when the Vices turn to the audience, asking them to pay as well.[30]

Mankind also appropriates the demonic role from the *quête*, and Titivillus provides a nexus for the convergence of money and theatricality. Vice-figures traditionally addressed the audience directly, thus calling attention to their theatrical status and connecting it with their own immoral behaviour. In Nicholas Udall's *Respublica* (1553), the idea of disguise is specifically connected to Avarice:

> My very true, unchristian name is Avarice ...
> To work my feat, I will my name disguise
> And call my name Policy instead of Covetise ...
> So that, under the name and cloak of Policy,
> Avarice may work many facts, and scape all jealousie.

Scholars have linked Titivillus's large head to his predecessor in the mummers' plays, and editors suggest that he enters carrying a net – a prop characteristic of the devil, and reminiscent of the ladles or frying pans used by the mummers to gather up the audience's cash.[31] Although Titivillus does not necessarily take the collection himself in *Mankind*, Smart notes that he is 'closely associated with it' and that he attempts to collect the money from the other Vices, although each denies having any.[32] In his edition, Lester has Titivillus eventually take the money, as indicated by the stage direction inserted after his final request to the Vices: 'Titivillus *discovers and confiscates the collected money from behind Nought's back*' (489).[33] Titivillus thus fulfils the role played by his character type in the mummers' play *quête*.[34] Whether or not Titivillus actually collects the money from the Vices, the audience is made to believe that they are paying to see him and that he will ultimately receive the money. *Mankind* thus seems to mock the traditional *quête*, invoking the mechanics of its collection and the character who would normally receive it, only to audaciously deny the Devil his due. Even if the Vices do finally hand over the money, their refusal to transfer the collected funds effectively simulates the audience's response. Anyone who may have felt like refusing to pay is confronted with visible Vices hypocritically exhibiting the same attitude and thus presumably encouraged to eschew their reprobate example.

Once he has been safely paid, however, Titivillus undermines the stable reality of money itself in a direct address to the audience. After playing several magical pranks on Mankind while invisible, including making his corn and spade seem to disappear and inducing

him to urinate, Titivillus offers the audience practical advice on
how to counterfeit money:

> If ye have any silver, in hap pure brass,
> Take a little powder of Paris and cast over his face,
> And even in the owl-flight let him pass.
> Titivillus can learn you many pretty things.
>
> (569–72)

Powder of Paris is a white powder much used in magic and alchemy.[35]
Titivillus is suggesting that one can sprinkle this powder on a brass
coin to make it pass as silver in the poor light of dusk ('the owl-
flight'). He will undermine anything that putatively confers value,
and he does so by undermining the value of value itself: money.
Titivillus's alchemical advice can be turned against him, though, as
the audience will presumably now know how to counterfeit money
the next time they are asked to pay him.

Mankind's violation of traditional *largesse* forces the audience's
attention onto the figures who solicit their money. The play
dramatizes a metatheatrical exchange, whereby a real audience
gives real money to individuals who remain within the mimetic
frame of the performance. The actors do not formally mark a hiatus
in the play while they take up the money, or explicitly announce
that they are actors who need to get paid for their show; nor do
they relate the purchase's value to the quality of their performance
or to the star quality of some fifteenth-century Richard Burbage.
Mankind nevertheless shares certain traits with the prologues of
early modern plays, especially those of Ben Jonson, that overtly
grapple with the commercial nature of the London theatre.

Although the public London theatres did not, so far as we know,
require audiences to pay fictional characters at the door in order
to see a show, early modern playwrights did frequently deploy
meta-prologues that made a point of foregrounding the audience's
relationship with the play and the actors. Plays like Francis
Beaumont's *The Knight of the Burning Pestle*, John Day's *The
Isle of Gulls*, Ben Jonson's *Cynthia's Revels*, John Marston's *The
Malcontent* and the anonymous *Wily Beguiled* feature prologues
that are interrupted by actors pretending to be audience members,
by fights between actors over who will play the prologue, even by
an actor who changes the play that will be performed. *The Isle of*

Gulls begins with three 'Gentleman, as to see a play' who demand of the prologue that his play feature their preferred themes and content.[36] John Webster's induction to Marston's *The Malcontent* features the actors Richard Burbage and Henry Condell speaking in their own voices, as they seek to vindicate their production to a fictional audience member sitting on stage.

While many of these metatheatrical prologues allude to the audience's having paid to see the show, Jonson's *Bartholmew Fair* explicitly discusses the contractual nature of the producer/consumer relationship which *Mankind* treats in such a novel way. After a 'stage-keeper' enters to attack the play the audience is about to see, a 'book-holder' and a 'scrivener' enter to draw up an official contract, or 'Articles of Agreement', between 'the *Spectators* or *Hearers*, at the *Hope* on Bankside, in the County of *Surrey* on the one party; And the Author of *Bartholmew Fayre* in the said place, and County on the other party' (Induction 58–61).[37] The scrivener enumerates a series of articles to be ratified by the audience, including an agreement that each spectator will 'remain in the places' that 'their money and friends' have put them in for the duration of the show; a right to judge the play according to how much they have paid; and a concluding request that 'as you have preposterously put to your Seales already (which is your money) [, if] you will now adde the other part of suffrage, your hands, The Play shall presently begin' (66–71; 77–87; 137–9). To be 'preposterous' is literally to put the first last: here the preposterousness consists in the audience's payment of money before they have received their commodity.

The humour in Jonson's claim that this seal is formed preposterously, or backwards, springs from the fact that this was actually the norm at the playhouse. The payment seals the tacit contract before the audience enters. In contrast, Jonson insists on applause as prologue to the performance and thus on an *a priori*, non-commercial sealing of the pact. Jonson desires an uncommodified exchange between audience and playwright that would preface, supplant or even nullify commercial exchange. Unlike the Vices in *Mankind*, who will not let a popular character enter the stage until they have been paid, Jonson suggests that the play will not even start until the audience (who have already paid) provide their applause.

By contrast, *Mankind* is well underway before it issues its metadramatic demand for the audience's money. The collection scene activates various layers of association between the actors and the Vices – associations that have been at work throughout, but which coalesce here around the notion of payment for performance. The idea of the collection is introduced by Mischief, who reminds New-Guise and Nowadays that during their 'interlection' he 'spake of *si dedero*' (456).[38] The phrase *si dedero* means 'if I give'. Here it appears to be shorthand for asking for money, as New-Guise's response confirms: 'Yea, go thy way! We shall gather money unto, / Else there shall no man him see' (457–8).[39] The collection is suggested by Mischief to two Vices that he names, rather than by an actor dropping out of character to address two other actors. New-Guise also announces that the collection is a prerequisite for seeing an unspecified 'him'. Turning to address the audience directly and referring to them as 'worshipful sovereigns', he explains that the Vices are gathering money 'for a man with a head that is of great omnipotence'. Nowadays adds that if the audience refuses to pay they will not 'see his abominable presence' (459–65). After the collection Nowadays simply declares: 'He is a goodly man, sirs; make space and beware!' (474). He teasingly builds audience anticipation by delaying the full announcement of exactly who is on the way.

By coyly refusing to name Titivillus during the collection, the players are able to maintain a wide range of possible associations related to him and to the characters who demand payment in return for seeing him. The audience is kept in suspense concerning the precise nature of the commodity it has just purchased. In fact, *Mankind* suggests that the audience is paying for a multivalent presence that is described as simultaneously omnipotent, abominable and 'goodly'. The irreligious invocation of godly qualities (along with a hint of omnipotence there is perhaps a pun on 'godly' in 'goodly') amplifies the allure of the figure about to enter the stage, while also increasing the audience's awareness of the money they have already paid. Declining to narrow its focus to a particular character, the play connects the audience's payment to a more abstract, theatrically and morally charged stage presence, thus expanding the metadramatic significance of the collection.

The alleged monetary value of this metatheatrical presence is raised further when Nowadays informs the spectators that 'he' (i.e. Titivillus) does not love small change but only high-value coins. This is quickly amended by New-Guise's remark: 'Yet that may not pay the tone, pay the tother', which reveals a comically profit-driven attitude that demands to get paid, regardless of the amount (466). New-Guise's subsequent declaration that 'Ye pay all alike' introduces a democratic quality to the cash nexus between the audience and the theatrical presences demanding payment: everyone must pay, and everyone must pay the same amount. This demand levels class distinctions, forging an egalitarian, inclusive (and universally obliging) relationship between the spectators even as the Vices simultaneously evince an immorally commercial attitude that effectively holds the performance hostage.

Constantly referred to as being just offstage, Titivillus is titillatingly presented as a paid-for attraction within an explicitly metatheatrical context. His entrance takes place in front of the host and an onstage audience, rather than on Mankind's plot of land or some other fictional scene. It is made clear that the audience's payment is the precondition for a new stage presence that promises to be even more entertaining than the Vices they have already seen. Instead of dropping character to reveal the real actor beneath, the collection scene is introduced by actors, speaking as Vices who are aware of their conditions of performance. The play refuses to fully cancel either actor or character, suggesting that the two are fundamentally linked. This fusion of real and fictional presences is then mobilized to seek payment for a further, more dramatically charged theatrical-theological presence on stage. The play fuses an ensemble of entertaining, yet immoral, stage presences fully cognizant of their host, their audience and their theatrical environment into a metatheatrically aware theatrical troupe providing an entertainment for which they are charging money.

By staging the audience's payment as a direct interaction with the morally dubious theatrical figure of Titivillus, the play raises the question of whether the conversion of the *largesse* into a wage-payment is itself a 'vice'. If the actors had stopped the show and asked for money out of character, the moral interrogation of that manoeuvre would not have applied, at least not to the same degree. By framing the players as an evil, albeit ludic, group of entertainers not fully identified as either actors or Vices, the collection scene allows *Mankind* to hold up to moral scrutiny the transition from honorarium to payment for services rendered.

Mankind further expands its ethical analysis of remuneration for acting through the likely doubling of the actor playing Mercy and Titivillus.[40] When the actor who played the sole embodiment of virtue early in the play reappears as the Devil, the audience's experience will be metatheatrical, especially since this is presumably the only such doubling in the play. This immoral, yet entertaining, character that the audience has explicitly paid to see is played by the same actor who impersonated the relatively dull avatar of conventional morality. The monetary value of Titivillus's stage presence is putatively higher than that of Mercy, which forces the audience to wonder whether commercialized entertainment can be subjected to ethical evaluation at all.

After working through this complicated, moral metatheatre of payment, *Mankind* extends its implications beyond the collection scene to complicate broader elements of the play. The immorality of the collection is intensified when the star Vice, for whose presence the audience has just paid handsomely, is propelled into a confrontation with the representative of ethical labour. The core morality at the heart of *Mankind* is based on gainful work: at the centre of the play is a stand-in for the audience, Mankind, whose good honest toil as an agrarian labourer represents the primary strategy for fending off evil. Mercy's final exhortation to Mankind before the first entrance of the Vices is 'do truly your labour and be never idle' (308). Left alone on stage, Mankind turns to digging with his spade to help him ignore the taunts of the Vices, and in response to their first major onslaught, he yells:

> Hie you hence, fellows, with braiding!
> Leave your derision and your japing!
> I must needs labour, it is my living.
>
> (348–50)

Mankind then literally weaponizes his labour, using his shovel to beat the Vices off stage. Later Titivillus explains that his attack on Mankind is aimed at stopping his work: 'To irk him of his labour I shall make a frame' (532). The Vices mock Mankind's labour as financially unprofitable, and Nowadays asks: 'Shall all this corn grow here / That ye shall have next year? / If it be so, corn had need be dear, / Else ye shall have a poor life' (352–5).[41]

The play's central crisis does not focus on the ethical temptations faced by the audience's avatar, as for example in *Everyman*, but rather on the moral fortitude involved in earning a basic living. The threat to morality issues from a group of Vices who have revealed themselves as paid actors. After the Vices have comically violated the honorarium model, the star actor playing Titivillus successfully, if temporarily, puts a stop to Mankind's morally fortifying labour. In staging this tension, *Mankind* suggests that the historical shift towards paid acting – compensation for services rendered, rather than the *largesse* system – is morally problematic and fraught with contradictions. Paying the Vices as actors undermines the ethical and financial value of proper work.

While *Mankind* still playfully alludes to the familiar critique of the theatre as a pastime that distracts its audience from higher pursuits, the dynamic of the collection scene also suggests that paid actors and ethical labour cannot coexist on the same stage. The anti-theatricalists of early modern London levied similar complaints against the theatre, ranging from charges that it corrupted the spectator's soul and drew them away from their honest daily work, to complaints that actors prostituted themselves on stage, or that the playwrights commodified drama. Stephen Gosson compares the theatre to the famous Royal Exchange when he writes that theatres are 'the very markets of bawdry, where choice w[i]out shame hath been as free as it is for your money in the Royal Exchang[e], to take a short stock, or a long, a falling band, or a French Ruff'.[42] Gosson's anxiety is that the role of money in the theatre opens the door to bawdy, illicit desires pursued without shame, precisely because money is the condition of possibility of this form of freedom. It is tempting to see a play such as *Mankind* as anticipating the moralizing of an anti-theatricalist like Gosson – and this is precisely the historical trajectory that many scholars have plotted between the two.[43]

Although Mankind resolves his personal crisis by returning to Mercy and repenting, however, the play does not offer a resolution to the moral crisis it reveals at the heart of commercial performance. Claire Sponsler detects a similar dynamic when she notes that the Vices' effects linger well past the putative moral resolution. Just as the weddings at the end of Shakespeare's romantic comedies can be anticlimactic and reductive compared to the complex possibilities for social and erotic experiment explored earlier in the plots, so in *Mankind* the Vices' dramatic charisma and subversive potential are not cancelled by their ultimate defeat. They are 'models of misbehavior', writes Sponsler, who 'provide a way of exploring the relationship between the violation of the norms of bodily propriety and the transgression of social and economic norms'.[44] In addition to embodying values related to corporeal integrity, the Vices raise questions about the relationship between violations of theatrical and economic norms. While Mankind's conflict is resolved, the metadramatic misbehaviour exemplified by the Vices is not meant to be washed away, but rather to persist in the minds of the audience beyond the bounds of the play.

In addition to portraying the historical movement from a patron dispensing *largesse* to an audience paying for acting troupes, *Mankind* suggests that this shift introduces an irresolvable moral problem to the nascent commercial theatre. Irresolvable moral conflict is always dramatically interesting, especially when the conflict occurs not at the level of plot, but at the level of the mechanisms that permit dramatic representation. *Mankind* gets to have it both ways: the character of Mankind finds Mercy, but the fate of the souls of the professional Vice-actors is left an open question. This problem is bequeathed to early modern London commercial theatre.

Finally, the audience's own moral status is brought into question by the fact that money has become a condition of possibility for dramatic production. By drawing buyers into direct contact with the commodified spectacle staged by a troupe of entertaining yet amoral payees, *Mankind* forces the audience to confront the ethical implications of this new monetary relationship. The audience's status as guests of the goodman of the house is altered at the moment that they pay. As Jonson's prefaces reveal, the shift from an optional *largesse* or gift of money to a compulsory payment imbues the audience with a different set of presumed rights. The transition moves the audience closer to a relationship with their host that resembles the exchange between publican and customer at a 'public house' or inn, rather than that between host and guest in a private household.

Like customers at an inn, audiences paying for a show are presumed to have certain rights that come along with purchasing the opportunity to be in that space. The Vices have already drawn the audience into an adversarial relationship with their host, insofar as the traditional model of beneficence from the 'goodman' to his guests has been replaced by the need to make a profit from paying customers. The audience is therefore empowered and undermined at the same time. It attains the rights belonging to customers, while simultaneously being forced into becoming purchasers rather than patrons and receiving a palpably commodified product in return for their money. *Mankind* stages its own audience ironically, as paying to undergo a metadramatic conflict that queries, subverts and ultimately recoups their relationship to the commercialized performance in which their own experience is represented back to them.

Notes

1   Douglas Bruster and Eric Rasmussen, eds., *Everyman and Mankind* (A&C Black, 2011), Introduction 25, 8.
2   Bruster and Rasmussen, eds., *Everyman and Mankind*, Introduction 23.
3   David Bevington, *Medieval Drama* (Hackett Publishing, 2012), 901.
4   Bruster and Rasmussen fn.456; Walter K. Smart, 'Mankind and the Mumming Plays', *Modern Language Notes* 32, no. 1 (1917): 22; William Tydeman, *English Medieval Theatre, 1400–1500* (Routledge & K. Paul, 1986), 32.
5   Bruster and Rasmussen suggest that 'take' can mean here either 'take' or 'give'; the former would refer to a priest taking alms, whereas the latter would allude to a festival door-knocking ritual. See Bruster and Rasmussen fn.52.
6   Sigmund Freud's paper, 'Character and Anal Eroticism', in *The Freud Reader* (W. W. Norton & Company, 1995) associates the desire to retain faeces with miserliness and discusses connections between the underworld, money and faeces in Western mythology. See Freud, 'Character and Anal Eroticism', 293–301.
7   Tison Pugh, 'Excremental Desire, Queer Allegory, and the Disidentified Audience of *Mankind*', *JEGP, Journal of English and Germanic Philology* 119, no. 4 (2020): 457–83.
8   Sarah Beckwith, 'Language Goes on Holiday: English Allegorical Drama and the Virtue Tradition', *Journal of Medieval and Early Modern Studies* 42, no. 1 (1 January 2012): 118; Pamela K. King, 'Morality Plays', in *The Cambridge Companion to Medieval English Theatre*, ed. Richard Beadle and Alan J. Fletcher (Cambridge University Press, 2008), 247.
9   Scholars often suggest that the characters of Mercy and Titivillus were doubled. See David Bevington, *From Mankind to Marlowe: Growth of Structure in the Popular Drama of Tudor England* (Harvard University Press, 1962), 69–71; Susan E. Phillips,

Transforming Talk: The Problem with Gossip in Late Medieval England, 1 et edition (University Park, PA: Penn State University Press, 2007), 204; Katie Normington, *Medieval English Drama* (John Wiley & Sons, 2013), 119.

10   See King, 'Morality Plays', 245; Bruster and Rasmussen, Introduction 8. For the debate about *Mankind*'s venue see Lawrence M. Clopper, '"Mankind" and Its Audience', *Comparative Drama* 8, no. 4 (1974): 347–55; Neville Denny, 'Aspects of the Staging of "Mankind,"' *Medium Ævum* 43, no. 3 (1974): 252–63; King. Generally, aside from Beckwith and King, scholarship on the money collection in *Mankind* has focused on establishing the original venue.

11   By 'performatively aware', I mean that an audience member or character's awareness of the presence of the other is itself often available for performative value in itself – a mere wink from a Vice to an audience member is sufficient to elicit a laugh.

12   On the spatial conditions of medieval theatrical performance in relation to morality plays, see Richard Southern, *The Medieval Theatre in the Round. A Study of the Staging of the Castle of Perseverance and Related Matters* (Faber & Faber, 1957); Denny, 'Aspects of the Staging of "Mankind"'; Jessica Brantley, 'Middle English Drama beyond the Cycle Plays', *Literature Compass* 10, no. 4 (2013): 331–42.

13   Cf. line 29. Unless noted otherwise, all citations are from Bruster and Rasmussen, eds., *Everyman and Mankind*. I follow editorial tradition in not imposing act and scene breaks upon *Mankind*; thus all citations are to line numbers only.

14   The manuscript for this play is untitled, so scholars have adopted the title from the name of the central protagonist, 'Mankind'. Like *Everyman* and *The Castle of Perseverance*, *Mankind*'s author is unknown; though scholars have speculated about his possible identity. See Bevington, *From Mankind to Marlowe*; Bruster and Rasmussen, *Everyman and Mankind*; Lester, G. A., ed., *Three Late Medieval Morality Plays* (Bloomsbury Academic, 2008); King, 'Morality Plays'.

15   Bevington, *Medieval Drama*, 792.

16   Tydeman, *English Medieval Theatre, 1400–1500*, 9.

17   For Titivillus's modified role in this play, compared to his usual stock role in performances of the period, see Phillips, *Transforming Talk*, 203–5.

18   The *OED* suggests that 'sovereign' first came to refer to an English coin in 1503. See n.4a.

19   See Sarah L. Peverly, 'Political Consciousness and the Literary Mind in Late Medieval England: Men "Brought Up of Nought" in Vale,

Hardyng, Mankind, and Malory', *Studies in Philology* 105, no. 1
(10 January 2008): 18.

20 Both Lester's and Bruster and Rasmussen's editions insert the stage
direction for the collection immediately before the invocation of the
goodman of the house, after line 466.

21 Smart was the first to argue for the role of the *quête* in Mankind.
I discuss his argument below.

22 Edmund Kerchever Chambers, *The Mediaeval Stage* (Oxford:
Clarendon Press, 1903), 211.

23 Editors note that it is in a section of the manuscript that is now
lost that the Vices make their first entrance on stage. Based on lines
that come later (e.g. 110–14), it appears that Mercy inadvertently
conjures the Vices onto stage while talking with Mischief. See
Bruster and Rassmusen fn.71.

24 Chambers, *The Mediaeval Stage*, 208.

25 Ibid., 217.

26 Glynne Wickham, *The Medieval Theatre* (Cambridge University
Press, 1987), 188.

27 Ibid., 181.

28 Ibid., 181–2. Wickham suggests that the often close-knit communal
ties between actors and audience involved in mummers' plays made
the gift exchange context for the audience's money more aggressive:
if one did not give money, the actors knew where one lived.

29 Lester notes that the Vice's invocation of the 'goodman of the house'
could refer either to 'the master of this household' or to 'the host of
this inn', depending on the performance space; Bruster and Rasmussen
add that, along with a private hall or inn, this could refer to the master
of a 'religious house' (Lester fn.467; Bruster and Rasmussen fn.467).
While my argument does not require that we know which particular
'goodman' *Mankind* was written for, my opinion persists that the play
should be read as touring all three kinds of sites.

30 For scholarship on early modern hospitality and its possible
decline since the medieval period, see Katherine Blankenau,
'From Plays-Within to Players Without: Theatrical Hospitality *in
Hamlet and* Sir Thomas More', *English Literary Renaissance* 52,
no. 2 (*forthcoming*); Julia Reinhard Lupton and David Goldstein,
Shakespeare and Hospitality: Ethics, Politics, and Exchange
(Routledge, 2016); Julia Reinhard Lupton, 'Hospitality', in *Early
Modern Theatricality*, ed. Henry Turner (Oxford University Press,
2013); Daryl W. Palmer, *Hospitable Performances: Dramatic Genre
and Cultural Practices in Early Modern England* (Purdue University
Press, 1992); Felicity Heal, *Hospitality in Early Modern England*
(Clarendon Press, 1990).

31 See Smart, *Mankind and the Mumming Plays*.

32 Smart 23. Smart also notes how this section of *Mankind* replicates, in comic form, Chamber's middle 'drama' section of mummers' plays, with its fight-resurrection structure. He detects 'four, perhaps five' elements from mummers' plays, which, 'it is particularly to be noted, all occur in one passage of less than fifty lines' (24).

33 G. A. Lester, ed., *Three Late Medieval Morality Plays* (London: Bloomsbury Academic, 2008).

34 For further elaboration on Smart's argument about the mummers' influence, see Denny. On the impact that a writer of mummers' plays like John Lydgate may have had on morality plays in the East Anglia regions, see John Lydgate, *Mummings and Entertainments*, ed. Claire Sponsler (Medieval Institute Publications, Western Michigan University, 2010), 1–2; 5fn.18. Lydgate was a monk at Bury St Edmonds, the same abbey where *Mankind* may have originally been performed.

35 See Bruster and Rasmussen fn.570.

36 See John Day, *The Ile of Gulls as It Hath Been Often Playd in the Blacke Fryars, by the Children of the Reuels* (London, 1606).

37 All quotes from *Bartholmew Faire* were taken from Ben Jonson, *Bartholmew Fair*, ed. G. R. Hibbard (A & C Black Publishers Ltd, 2014).

38 Lester suggests that there is an implied stage direction for the Vices to whisper together after the call for an interlection. Bruster and Rasmussen insert '*They whisper with their heads together*', after line 450.

39 Bruster and Rasmussen cite a similar usage in John Lydgate's *Isopes Fabules*, claiming it invokes the 'corrupting power of money' (fn.456). The passage reads as follows: 'Si dedero ys now so mery a song, Hath founde a practyk by lawe to make a preef To hang a trew man & saue an errant theef' (*Minor Poems*, ll. 327–9).

40 See fn.9.

41 Note that 'corn' in this period referred to various cereal plants or their seeds, especially in an agricultural context. C.f. *OED*, 'corn', n.1.III.3.

42 Stephen Gosson, 'Plays Confuted in Five Actions', in *The English Drama and Stage under the Tudor and Stuart Princes, 1543–1664*, ed. W. C. Hazlitt (London, 1869), 157–218, 214–15.

43 These are the same scholars that emphasize the first-ness of the collection in *Mankind*. See fn.1 above. See also David Kathman, 'The Rise of Commercial Playing in 1540s London', *Early Theatre* 12, no. 1 (2009): 15–38.

44 Claire Sponsler, *Drama and Resistance: Bodies, Goods, and Theatricality in Late Medieval England* (University of Minnesota Press, 1997), 81.

3

Cozening queens and phony fairies: Fairy counterfeits in early modern drama

Kaitlyn Culliton

At the climax of Ben Jonson's *The Alchemist*, a trio of tricksters convinces a gullible clerk named Dapper that he is favoured by the fairy queen. Believing that the fairies' influence will help him gamble and 'win up all the money in the town', Dapper undergoes a series of humiliating ritual 'trials' which rob him of his worldly possessions. The tricksters' performance, punctuated by the appearance of the prostitute Dol Common as the fairy queen, is one of several instances wherein the play ruminates on the monetary potential of dramatic performance. With each new client, their witty improvisations generate real profit. The play's central motif of alchemy functions as a metaphor for the con artists' 'magical' ability to create monetary reward out of seemingly nothing. While the play never suggests the reality of preternatural occurrences, their fairy impersonation effectively results in financial gain because of the con artists' ability to conceive and express the rapidly changing economic landscape using the conceptual vocabulary of magic.

Of all their various victims, Dapper alone remains convinced of the plausibility of his experience. After meeting Dol Common disguised as the fairy queen, Dapper departs grateful and credulous. Dol's impersonation of the fairy queen is just one of many 'counterfeit fairies' in Renaissance drama.[1] This character type typically appears when a con artist of lower social status dupes someone who possesses (frequently undeserved) wealth. Such plots are well suited to the social satire of the city comedies, so it is not particularly surprising that fake fairies similar to Jonson's appear in plays like *The Honest Lawyer* by 'S. S.' (1616) and Shakespeare's *Merry Wives of Windsor* (1597). It is, perhaps, more surprising that Dapper's experience with the counterfeit fairy queen had numerous real-life analogues in early modern England.[2]

Like Jonson's tricksters, real-life scammers such as Alice West and Judith Philips convinced their victims that they were favoured by the fairy queen and that, if furnished with money and specific household goods, they could perform a ritual to summon her. After much costly delay, the con artist would appear disguised as a fairy, rob their victim and disappear. At the core of these encounters, both victim and perpetrator shared an implicit understanding that fairy mythology offers the possibility of reward. Of course, this reward only manifests for the con artist, but several accounts recorded between 1602 and 1615 reveal that at least a portion of the early modern English population was re-evaluating fairy mythology with a newly pecuniary consciousness.

I want to suggest that the relatively sudden appearance of counterfeit fairies in plays, and also in the historical record, was connected to the development of a money economy in seventeenth-century England. Amid rapid economic changes, counterfeit fairies presented a logic that their victims might easily accept: rapid upward social mobility often seemed to be indiscriminate, and the consequent, sudden acquisition of capital and commodities certainly looked similar to gifts from the fairies.[3] Urban migration not only brought fairy lore from the countryside to the capital but also offered unprecedented opportunities for the kind of 'magic' that could transform country transplants into middle-class tradespeople and merchants.[4] As the tales indicate, involvement with fairies, as with investments or trade ventures, was extraordinarily risky but could generate outlandish profit, seemingly out of thin air. Fairies had the ability to see, and to test, someone's true character, regardless of external appearances, and to reward or punish accordingly. Those who spoke about the origins of their fairy gifts or displeased the fairies, like those who invested poorly, revealed trade secrets, or spoke openly about the value and whereabouts of their possessions, were likely to see their 'fairy gold' disappear, as if by magic.[5]

Many scholars have focused on the common elements shared between plays and historical accounts.[6] Despite a recent resurgence of critical interest in the supernatural, however, little attention has been paid to the construction of the counterfeit fairy as a cultural and literary phenomenon. The false fairies who feature in the cons played by Judith Philips and Alice West, like those who appear in *The Merry Wives of Windsor*, *The Alchemist* and *The Honest Lawyer* demonstrate how rural fairy lore was adapted to urban contexts, as a means of interpreting (and exploiting) the social transformations and moral implications of rapid economic change. Each manifestation of the fairies is highly theatrical: the historical accounts describe fraudsters using fairy magic as a medium through which dramatic performance could be turned into financial gain, and the plays are metatheatrically aware of their own complicity in profiting from dramatic depictions of such fraud on the stage. This theatricality suggests that counterfeit fairies represent a performance by those whose voices were least represented in earlier economic systems – women, servants, rural transplants – that expresses a widespread aspiration for advancement within an emerging middling class and urban proletariat.

Fairies and counterfeits

At the turn of the sixteenth century, fairy mythology was hugely popular in England. As Elizabeth I's reign progressed more or less peaceably, her courtiers sought to 'devise a means of presentation of the queen which would equate her iconographic position [as an unmarried woman] with her actual position as head of church and state'.[7] In masques and entertainments, Elizabeth was frequently compared to the 'fairy queen', a figure of supernatural beauty, whose favour could bestow riches and social elevation on her adoring knights.[8] The fairies in these early entertainments often gave elaborate gifts as a part of these performance, as in the Entertainment at Woodstock wherein the fairy queen gave Queen Elizabeth a costly gown.[9] These gift-giving rituals may have partly operated as socially countenanced vies for royal favour. With the publication of Edmund Spenser's *The Faerie Queene* in the 1590s, the epithet of 'the fairy queen' for Elizabeth was widely popularized.[10] In the romance tradition that inspired Elizabeth's courtiers, the vacillating moral and physical characteristics of fairy figures 'foreground the testing of chivalric values as an integral part of the hero's journey toward self-realization'.[11]

In popular folklore, by contrast, the liminal moral position of fairies was problematic, and their potential status as physical or spiritual threats was the subject of much debate.[12] Fairies had a reputation for pinching people who displeased them, abducting adults and stealing children.[13] In theory, mortals were needed to strengthen fairy bloodlines, and abductions or pinches might have erotic or vampiric undertones.[14] One description of fairies by Reginald Scot even suggests that 'pinches' might be euphemisms for brutal rapes, kidnappings and mutilations:

> Many such have been taken away by the sayd Spirits, for a fortnight, or month together, being carryed … over Hills, and Dales, Rocks and Precipices, till at last they have been found lying in some Meddow or Mountain bereaved of their sences, and commonly of one of their Members [limbs] to boot.[15]

It is unclear if Scot, a fairy sceptic, attributed this dismembering to accidental causes or to deliberate attacks, but his account confirms that fairies were widely regarded as capable of inflicting serious bodily harm on human beings. While the plays I examine remain within the genre of comedy, and none of the victims are seriously injured, it is worth considering what real-life con artists might have been willing to do under the apparently plausible guise of fairies.

The risks of a close encounter with the fairies might well have seemed worth taking; fairies were known to reward those they favoured with erotic experiences, supernatural abilities and above all gold. John Aubrey describes one recipient of fairy money:

> There was a labouring-man, who for many dayes together found a nine pence in the way that he went [to work]. His wife wondering how he came by so much money, was afraid he gott it not honestly: at last he told her; and afterwards he never found any more.[16]

As Aubrey's example shows, 'fairy gold' was a notoriously capricious gift, and it was common to lose favour with the fairies by speaking about them.[17] This idea is frequently referenced in Jacobean drama,

as in Beaumont and Fletcher's *The Honest Man's Fortune*, where
the French nobleman Montague explains to the lady Lamira: 'For
when they talk once, 'tis like fairy money, They get no more.'[18] As
Maureen Duffy explains, the whole fairy realm is 'without real
substance and may vanish at any moment'.[19] Its illusory quality
makes it intrinsically untrustworthy – it is always likely to disappear
and may never yield any of the substance it promises.[20] 'Fairy gold'
was thus an apt metaphor for ineffable, and frequently unstable,
forms of wealth, such as financial value, speculative investment or
even royal favour, that were nevertheless inextricably linked with
socio-economic privilege.

Fairy gold also evoked unremunerated labour since fairies were
known to carry out or reward tedious domestic tasks, particularly
those traditionally ascribed to women.[21] Fairies are 'inconsistently
represented', sometimes completing household tasks in exchange
for a bowl of cream or piece of bread, but just as often rewarding
housewives and servants for housework (and its associated moral
virtue). Eberly suggests that leaving food out for the fairies may have
been a way of referring to a social contract between householders
and 'rough men' or other social outcasts who might perform difficult
household tasks in exchange for a meal.[22] Richard Corbert's poem,
written in 1647, reflects, perhaps with some degree of sarcasm, on
the prevalence of earlier fairy beliefs:[23]

> Farewell rewards and Fairies
> Good housewives now may say,
> For now fowle sluts in Dairies
> Do fare as well as they;
> And though they sweepe their hearths no lesse
> Then maides were wont to doe,
> Yet who of late for cleanlinesse,
> Findes Six pence in her shooe?[24]

The poem makes clear the connection between household
cleanliness, chaste behaviour and fairy reward. As the poem suggests,
fairies were apt to leave money hidden around the household,
particularly in shoes. Likewise, the anonymous play, *The Wisdome
of Doctor Dodypoll* (1600), opens with a servant named Haunce
describing the fairy money left in his shoe. Haunce details how
a young gentleman staying in the house 'goes to see the Fayries'

nightly and concludes, 'I am glad we are so haunted by Fairies: For I cannot set a cleane pump down, but I find a dollar in it in the morning.'[25] Haunce presumably understands that the 'fairy money' left in his shoe is a means of buying Haunce's silence in regard to the gentleman's nightly visits to his mistress, rather than an actual fairy reward for good housekeeping. However, the reference evokes a multitude of understandings about fairy money as a currency for otherwise unremunerated tasks – from household labour to illicit bribes – and why it was liable to disappear if openly spoken about. This multiplicity of associations leads Mary Ellen Lamb to suggest that references to fairies do not imply belief in their literal existence but rather constitute performative speech-acts deployed within particular discursive communities 'to provide remedies outside established institutions'.[26] To Lamb, for example, the 'fairy gold' in Aubrey's narrative signifies the husband's refusal to reveal the actual source of his money, presumably a mistress or illegal activity.

As disparate discursive communities converged on London from all over England, various forms of fairy lore would have mingled and been interpreted in many different ways. As Marjorie Swann's examination of Stuart fairy poetry suggests:

> English fairylore was traditionally bound up with normative concepts of a precapitalist social formation; thus, as England shifted from a rural household-based mode of production to an urban, commercial and increasingly mercantile economy, fairylore became a particularly apt vehicle for mystifying the profound socioeconomic changes of the early modern period.[27]

Swann suggests that poets drew on Shakespearean references to the diminutive nature of the fairy world in order to imagine a kingdom lavishly, even excessively, filled with miniature commodities. In widely circulated popular verse, fairy largesse offered a commentary on the conspicuous consumption of the upper classes. In plays, fairy lore was likewise employed as a means of interpreting economic changes, but the interpretation operated differently for the members of London's public theatre audience, for whom the conspicuous consumption of the upper classes was no more accessible than a fairy story. Given the plethora of depictions of fairy money in vernacular expression and on the commercial stage, all of which were consumed by the numerous discursive communities newly arriving in London, it is hardly surprising that tricksters such as the Wests profited from their ability to adjust the language of fairy lore to numerous social groups. As Gary Butler describes, when a 'reference is shared between speaker and hearer and when the speaker's presuppositions accurately conform to their interlocutors' knowledge, the result is successful communication'.[28] The con artists who impersonated supernatural beings rely on a calculated *mis*communication: the term 'fairy' has a different meaning for the con artist than for the victim. From the latter's perspective, fairies were real, ontological beings who offered a potential source of financial or erotic reward. For the con artists, fairies may or may not have been understood as the ontological beings of folklore, but they undoubtedly provided a very real means of 'magically' making very real money.

Fake fairies

A 1595 pamphlet titled *The Brideling, Sadling and Ryding of a rich Churle in Hampshire* describes Judith Philips's cozenage of the eponymous unfortunate. The author explains that Judith left her husband, a man named Pope, for a life of crime because of his 'poor state of living'. The titular churl was at first dubious when Judith claimed to see the fairies' favour written on his forehead, but 'to confirm her words for a truth, she took an oath upon the Bible that she came from the Pope: which was true for her husband's name was Pope'.[29] From the outset, Judith's fairy narrative relies on her witty ability to adapt language to her purposes.

The churl, 'in hope to attaine to great wealth', followed Judith's instructions to 'get a saddle and a bridle with two new girths' and to 'have the largest chamber of your house be hung with the finest linen you can get, so that nothing about your chamber but white linen cloth be seen'.[30] At the appointed hour, Judith saddled the churl in the yard and 'sat upon his backe in the saddle, and rid him three times betwixt the chamber and the holly tree'.[31] Then she made him lie down outside while she entered the house, supposedly to summon the queen of fairies.

Predictably, Judith stole everything she could carry. The items that most interest her – the linen, candlesticks and gold coins – had all been conveniently arranged in a single chamber to make a 'holy and unspotted place' fit to welcome the fairy queen.[32] Judith's request for clean linen was a reliable standard in accounts of counterfeit fairies. Domestic cleanliness (and its association with moral purity) was a prerequisite for fairy reward, and good cloth represented an expensive, portable commodity that could be quickly sold in secondary markets. Under the guise of ritual purity, Judith 'took down all the linen clothes from the walls of the chamber and wrapped them up close in a bundle, and all the gold from under the candlesticks and put them in her purse'.[33] Instead of immediately leaving, however, Judith gave the churl and his wife the fairy encounter they have been hoping for:

> [P]utting herself in a fair white smock, somewhat disguised, with a thing on her head all in white, and a stick in her hand, she appeared onto him and his wife, using some dalliance, as old wives say spirits with night spells do, she vanished away, and again entered the chamber where her pack lay ready, and so roundly went away, leaving the churl and his wife in their cold lodging.[34]

Judith's appearance as the fairy queen can certainly be interpreted as a way to win some get-away time – the churl and his wife might be slower to enter the house if they perceived some evidence of fairy activity. Yet her actions seem less economic than 'personal and even aesthetic, because they are such spectacular exhibitions of her complete mastery of the situation and of her victims' complete gullibility'.[35] The overtly theatrical nature of the encounter recalls the various roles and disguises that the con artists in *The Alchemist* must deftly adopt and discard as they cozen their victims. With the right words and a bit of household linen, Judith is able to deliver on her promise: she indeed 'finds' a significant sum of money by performing rituals to summon fairies, although the gain turns out to be her own rather than the churl's.

A similar pamphlet titled *The Several Notorious and Lewd Cozenages of John West and Alice West* describes a pair of married tricksters who impersonate fairies in order to cozen one Thomas Moore of Hammersmith. The couple requested clean linen and money 'to performe the due rites of sacrifice to his great patron, the king of fayries'. The ceremony took months of preparation, and the Wests repeatedly requested more resources, pretending 'that something or other was eyther neglected'.[36] Moore eventually began to lose patience, so the Wests staged a meeting with the fairies:

> They brought [Moore] into a vault, where they shewed him two attired like the king and queene of fayries, and by them little elves and goblings, and in the same place an infinite company of bags, and upon them written, 'This is for Thomas Moore,' 'This is for his wife,' but would not let him touch any thing, which gave him some incouragement to his almost despairing hope; but still he received no profit.[37]

Such performances instilled complacency in the dupes, using the avarice of their victims to perpetuate a cycle of temptation and delayed gratification. Moore eventually sought advice from a friend but inexplicitly became lame shortly thereafter. The pamphlet suggests that Alice's 'sorceries' have caused his sudden affliction, thus indicating that, while the pamphlet maintains that Alice's fairies are counterfeit, the author believes her quite capable of committing preternatural *maleficia* by other means. Alice told Moore that 'his purpose to blab the secrets of the fairies was come to the ears of Oberon, for which he enraged, had inflicted this punishment upon him'.[38] After paying additional money for a healing ritual, Moore was resolutely silent and continued to pay the Wests, even borrowing money in order to do so.

The outlandish theatrics of these historical accounts resemble nothing so much as an especially implausible Renaissance comedy. However, Orgel reminds us that, as in *The Alchemist*, 'the risk works not because [the victim] is preposterously gullible, but because the charlatans are excellent actors who ... have produced an entirely credible scam'.[39] But there is another practical element to the tricksters' evocation of fairies, which explains their willingness to risk such brazenly theatrical performances. Describing the West's plot, the pamphlet explains that 'because they knew common cousonages had for the most part common discovery, and so consequently a common and ordinary punishment denounced against offenders in that kinde, they therefore devised a new forme'.[40] Con artists were often punished less severely than other

criminals because 'unlike many other crimes of fraud, where the
unsuspecting victim did nothing to deserve the loss, cozenage of
people who believed in fairies often shows greed all around: greed
on the part of people hoping to earn the fairies' favor as well as
those who preyed on them'.[41] New and creative forms of cozenage
were not only unexpected by the victims but also likely to have less
severe consequences for the perpetrators.[42]

Of course the accounts of counterfeit fairies were published,
and doubtless diligently edited, by printers whose main motive
was profit. Booksellers were presumably aware of the popularity
of *The Merry Wives* and *The Alchemist*, which may account for
some of the similarities between events on stage and details of the
real-life fairy cons.[43] Many writers were keen to cash in on the
craze for 'cony catching' pamphlets like Robert Greene's accounts
of London's criminal underworld, which became popular during
the 1590s. Greene claimed to highlight cozenages in order to make
'honest, simple, and ignorant men' aware of criminal activity,[44]
but the virtue of his intentions was mingled with commercial
considerations. The entertaining stories told and sold about con
artists were widely enjoyed, and this growing fascination with
the *demimonde* may even have given the criminals a degree of
protection – victims were perhaps less likely to come forward
when their credulity was the subject of public derision. Although
the cover image and title of *The Brideling, Sadling and Ryding
of a Rich Churle in Hampshire* clearly advertise the cozenage of
the titular churle, Judith was neither tried nor convicted for this
offence. The salacious details of the churl's stories came to light
at Judith's trial for the cozenage of the Trype widow, which is also
detailed in the account.

The cover image of the Wests' pamphlet depicts them in the
stocks outside the prison awaiting trial for the titular cozenage of
Thomas Moore of Hammersmith. The courts probably suspected
that, like Judith Philips, the Wests were repeat offenders, and this
punishment allowed other victims to come forward and testify –
by the time the pamphlet was published, eleven more cases had
come to light. The fairy queen features in several of their other
cons; the Wests also cozen a maid out of 'seven years wages of her
good housekeeping', convincing her to sit naked in a garden with
a pot of dirt in her lap 'promising that ere morning the queen of

fairies should turn it into gold'.[45] Another con resembling Dapper's
experience in *The Alchemist* is the far more violent trick on a
prentice goldsmith whom Alice convinced that the queen of fairies
'did most ardently dote on'. She told the prentice to bring several
gilt plates to a close outside of the shop to meet the queen of fairies,
where her waiting conspirators beat the young man until 'his corage
was cold for meeting the Q. of fayries'.[46] This outright beating
resembles the appearance of a counterfeit fairy in Robert Armin's
The Valient Welshman (1612). In the play, a foolish knight named
Morion decides he is in love with the queen of fairies and is lured
into a ditch by a con artist disguised as the queen of fairies, where
he is beaten and robbed.[47]

In addition to being an opportunity for others to come forward,
the pillory's public nature also helped spread new lore about
the power and exploits of fairies, both real and counterfeit.[48] As
Willard suggests, 'there is no doubt that the pamphlet's author and
publisher knew their market' and their readership probably 'took at
least as much pleasure in the descriptions of the crime as in those of
the punishment'.[49] Several pamphlets circulated about the exploits
of the Wests and one pamphlet detailing Judith's cons claims the
story of the churl was circulating 'abroad in every corner'.[50] In this
way, the pamphlets suggest that the counterfeit fairy phenomenon
was connected to the larger economy, in which fairy narratives and
occult knowledge operated as commodities to be exchanged and
consumed in print, on stage and in real life.

The Alchemist

Like many of Jonson's other comedies, *The Alchemist* is metatheatrically concerned with its own participation in profiting from
performance. The play opens on a cautionary note: 'If thou art
an understander, and then I trust thee. If thou art one that takest
up, and but a pretender, beware of what hands thou receivest thy
commodity; for thou wert never more fair in the way to be cozened,
than in this age, in poetry, especially in plays.'[51] The commodity
the text offers its readers is likened to the various occult services
in which the play's tricksters trade – alchemy, cozenage, the theatre
(and arguably even prostitution) each entails a process in which

personal gain is achieved through a seemingly magical but actually illusory performance. As Face's closing lines put it:

> And though I am clean
>   Got off from Subtle, Surly, Mammon, Dol,
>   Hot Ananias, Dapper, Drugger, all
>   With whom I traded: yet I put my self
>   On you, that are my country: and this pelf
>   Which I have got, if you do quit me, rests
>   To feast you often, and invite new guests.[52]

By this point in the play, Face has surrendered his ill-gotten wealth to Lovewit so that 'this pelf / Which I have got' refers to the profit made by the playhouse rather than to the commodities purloined within the play.

As in the historical accounts, the 'magic' practised by Jonson's fraudsters depends on a miscommunication by which ordinary processes are misconstrued as supernatural occurrences. Face explicitly tells Kastrill the nature of Subtle's business, recalling that he 'made me a Captain. I was a stark pimp Just o' your standing, 'fore I met with him'.[53] Face himself is a counterfeit – a servant posing as a 'suburb captain' in his master's absence. While Kastrill takes Face's sudden social elevation literally, Subtle has only made Face a 'captain' by costuming him appropriately and teaching him some of the soldier's vocabulary. When Kastrill questions the ethics of such ventures, Face explains:

> You shall have a cast commander, (but can get
> Credit with a glover, or a spurrier
> For some two pair, of either's ware, aforehand)
> Will, by most swift posts, dealing with him,
> Arrive at competent means to keep himself,
> His punk, and naked boy, in excellent fashion.[54]

In outlining his alchemical methods, Face recounts the process of the 'commodity swindle' as described in Greene's cony catching pamphlets. This 'was the practice by which a money-lender would take advantage of a client in order to force him to accept part of the loan in unwanted commodities'.[55] Describing such tricks in the language of alchemy makes them seem, at least to Kastrill, more magical than criminal – although as the play demonstrates, the distinction between magical transactions and dubiously legal forms of exchange was often very narrow in practice.

When Dapper asks Subtle, Face and Dol for a familiar spirit to help him win at gambling, 'Captain' Face and Subtle, disguised as the priest of fairy, convince him that he is 'of the best complexion the fairy queen loves' and that he will win huge sums of money if he can only contact her. Dapper reveals that with his winnings, he 'shall leave the law'. His desire to leave his job motivates his lust for fairy gold just as it motivates his gambling ventures, and fairy money, like gambling winnings or other income not earned by the labour of its recipient is frequently lost quickly. The con artists begin their fairy performance by blindfolding Dapper and pinching him. While Dapper is blindfolded, Doll and Face speak in their own made-up fairy language, which Subtle pretends to translate, further emphasizing the linguistic character of their 'magical' skills. When the scene is interrupted, they lock Dapper in a privy to be 'fumigated'. Not until act 4 does he finally enjoy his long-awaited fairy encounter, when Dol Common disguises herself as the fairy queen. Dapper crawls to kiss the edge of her gown, as she prophesizes: 'Much, nephew, shalt thou win, much shalt thou spend,/Much shalt thou give away, much shalt thou lend.'[56] Dapper is elated that the prophesy focuses so directly on financial gain and loss. As so often in this play, the dupes are unable to distinguish between the language of alchemy and the language of political economy, and Face's aside – 'much indeed!' – suggests that the trio have already planned a way of exploiting the 'give away' portion of the 'prophesy' for their own benefit.

Like the fairies they impersonate, the scammers expose those whose wealth can be attributed to personal vice, and they delight in redistributing the money of the undeserving. A person's willingness to deal with fairies in the first place marked them as 'somewhat fantastical', as Judith's wealthy churl is described and often as exaggeratedly avaricious.[57] Dapper is careful to assert the moral integrity of his request, promising to give half his winnings to Subtle and Face, ironically immoral characters themselves. Their fairy ritual embodies just this sort of moral contradiction, when they inform Dapper that 'the elves are come. To pinch you, if you tell not truth'.[58] Subtle, Face and Dol play on the common assumption that lying incurs the displeasure of the fairies, but by telling the truth about a silver bracelet around his wrist, Dapper reveals the location of his personal wealth, thus making him easier to rob.

The Merry Wives of Windsor

The victims of fairy cons were often seen as morally 'unclean', and this characteristic was likewise reflected in their physically dirty state. In *The Merry Wives of Windsor*, Mistress Quickly, disguised as the fairy queen, orders her attendants to punish lazy housemaids: 'Where fires thou find'st unraked and hearths unswept, / There pinch the maids as blue as bilberry: / Our radiant queen hates sluts and sluttery.'[59] Falstaff is described as a 'greasy knight', guilty of the same indecorum and uncleanliness. The tricks that the wives play on him, culminating in his encounter with the counterfeit fairies, begin with Falstaff being pressured into a laundry basket. Forced to remain quiet for fear of discovery, Falstaff is physically dumped into Dachet Mead along with 'foul shirts' and 'greasy napkins'. As with Subtle's suggestion that Dapper put on a clean shirt – 'who knows what grace her grace may do you in clean linen' – or Judith Philips's call to hang a chamber in pristine linen, concealing Falstaff in a basket of soiled clothing identifies him as the sort of domestic pollution with which fairies might be called to help.

Falstaff's lechery is certainly uncouth, but his real affront to Windsor society is his transgression of class boundaries. Penniless, Falstaff tries to position himself as a con artist: 'I must cony catch. I must shift.' He therefore schemes to seduce the wives, claiming that when he becomes 'cheater to them both ... they shall be exchequers to me; they shall be my East and West Indies'.[60] The wives' first revenge for his exploitative plotting is fitted to Falstaff's personal and domestic transgression: they declare the cleanliness of their virtue by washing him along with soiled underclothes. In the second trick, they emasculate him by dressing him as the Witch of Brentford. On the third occasion, however, it is not just transgressions against individual households that are revenged. As a knight, Falstaff is a living remnant of medieval feudalism. In medieval romance, fairies function as a test of chivalric values, but Falstaff's immorality is a gross mockery of such values, and his poverty, juxtaposed with the burghers' obvious wealth, marks his obsolescence. The townspeople invoke fairy mythology to answer Falstaff's attempted usurpation of middle-class wealth and also to restore economic and social equilibrium.

The final fairy trick depicted in *The Merry Wives* highlights the theatrical nature of encounters with false fairies and also the suspension of disbelief required of their victims. At the end of the play, the wives lead the townspeople in a masque-like procession of fairies to pinch Falstaff. As the ruse comes to an end and the townspeople reveal themselves, Falstaff begins 'to perceive that I am made an ass'.[61] Struggling to reconcile two contradictory versions of reality, he wonders:

> And these are not fairies?
> ...
> the guiltiness of my mind, the sudden surprise of my
> powers, drove the grossness of the foppery into a
> received belief, in despite of the teeth of all
> rhyme and reason, that they were fairies.[62]

Immersed in the theatrical spectacle, Falstaff dismissed 'rhyme and reason' and embraced a belief 'received' partly from the unfolding spectacle before him and partly from his own cultural knowledge of folk tales. It would seem that real-life con artists relied on a similar willingness to suspend disbelief.

The Honest Lawyer

The use of 'fairy gold' to restore social justice is exemplified by *The Honest Lawyer*, attributed to 'S. S.' In the play, a landowner named Vaster has mortgaged his land to the usurer Gripe. On realizing that he cannot pay his debt, Vaster accuses his faithful wife of cuckolding him and leaves his family to pursue a life of crime. Meanwhile, Gripe is unable to collect on his mortgage because illness renders him unable to take possession of the land. To relieve his ailments, Gripe hires another con artist named Valentine, who is posing as a physician. As is typical of usurers in early modern comedy, Gripe's diseases are shown to be the result of his ill-gotten wealth and miserly habits. Valentine prescribes two 'cures' to rob the usurer of money: a nail through the toe and gunpowder in his bladder. During their initial encounter Valentine tells Gripe that, to cure his gout, 'this naile I must driue through your great toe'.[63] He duly nails Gripe's toe to the floor and steals his purse, but when Gripe is able to walk again, his son observes, 'Strange! that same Quack-saluer has done him good, against his will.'[64] Valentine's phony and violent remedies actually do cure Gripe's illnesses because they separate him from at least some of his ill-gotten wealth, thus alleviating some of the physical symptoms of his usury.

The counterfeit fairies provide another such 'cure'. After Valentine robs Gripe for the first time, he decides to 'spend these crownes, as I got them, in cony-catching'.[65] He teams up with Vaster and a fake abbot named Curfew, explaining: 'I haue often heard the gripulous Dotard talke of Fairies: and how rich the house proues that they haunt. I haue ripened the blister of his imagination to the full. Shall we launce it?'[66] The trio begin to leave the stolen coins throughout Gripe's house to convince him that fairies are rewarding him. Gripe describes his 'fairy' haunting:

> These three or foure nights I ha'bene haunted with Fairies: they dance about my bed-side, poppe in a peece of gold betweene the sheetes, scatter here and there fragments of siluer, in euery corner. I keepe my chamber swept, cleane linnen, fire to warme them euery night. I was at first afraide, they had beene spirits; now I see, they are good harmelesse Fairies. If I can please them, I shall grow rich, rich.[67]

Of course, the fairies are not truly offering him financial reward for his cleanliness. Like Falstaff, Gripe is a grotesque figure, ignorant of his own adverse impact on the communities he is harassing. On their final appearance, the con artists bind, gag and rob the usurer, making clear that the displeasure of the fairies is another illness that Gripe has brought upon himself:

VASTER
> Man-eater. Thou fetting Canker
> ...
> Whose belly has iust cause to sue an action of trespasse, gainst thy couetous lusts exaction: For detinie of many hundred meales, which it from others, and thy selfe too; steales. The Gowt.

VALENTINE
> The Dropsie.

CURFEW
> Collicke, Lunacie, Like Sprites and Fairies haunt thy
> company.[68]

The fraudsters' call for the usurer to repent may seem incongruous,
given their own moral transgressions throughout the play, but
it positions Gripe's usury at the heart of the sickness in society.
Although they have far worse intentions than the honest-but-merry
wives of Windsor, the counterfeit fairies in *The Honest Lawyer*
actually do restore Gripe to social grace. At the end of the play,
Gripe's son Benjamin, the titular honest lawyer, pressures each
character into a series of confessions in court. Gripe agrees to return
Vaster's lands: 'I haue drunke powerfull physicke, and the Dropsie
Of my (till now) nere quenched auarice, Dries vp like dew at the
ascending Sunne.' When Vaster realizes his wife has been mistaken
for one of the fairies and may be hanged, he confesses his part in
the fairy plot and is thus cured of his jealousy. Vaster also agrees
to return the 'lost three hundred pound. The fairie money, which
was iust the price Of my redeemed lands'.[69] The money in question
was both the sum of the mortgage that Vaster was unable to pay at
the beginning of the play and the amount he has stolen from Gripe
while disguised as a fairy. This means that, while money changes
hands frequently throughout the play, Vaster ultimately pays Gripe
with his own coin. His claim that the 'fairy money' is a 'just price'
for the redemption of his lands thus suggests that the tricksters are
morally justified in robbing a usurer, regardless of the law.

The correlation between fairy gold and usurer's profits in *The
Honest Lawyer* makes explicit some of the moral anxieties expressed
implicitly in tales of fairy gold. In early modern England money 'was
understood to be a facilitator of exchange rather than a commodity
in itself. Because it was fungible – consumed in use – ownership of
it could not be transferred, nor – like land or livestock – could it
reproduce itself; money therefore was sterile'.[70] However, fairy gold,
like compound interest, is not sterile in empirical terms; it can indeed
reproduce itself as if by magic, and this reproduction is steeped in an
erotic aura that defies – or perhaps necessitates – the sort of domestic
cleaning and sterilizing with which the fairies are so obsessed. The
fairies dance around Gripe's bed and 'poppe a piece of gold between
the sheets', an oddly eroticized means of becoming 'rich rich'.

As the one to name the contentious sum 'fairy money', Vaster can dictate his own terms to the court. His final speech of contrition allows him to end the play absolved of cozenage. It is reminiscent of the moment at the end of *The Alchemist*, when Face appeals to the audience to forgive him for his ill-gotten pelf. In Jonson's play a cautionary note to the reader frames Face's final address, warning about 'understanders' and the dangers of transacting as a 'pretender'. Face's last speech positions him as the ultimate 'understander', who is able to discern the true value of a commodity and explain its value to others, even if his explanations frequently serve to fool his victims. Like Face, who 'has clean got off', avoiding punishment for his dubious transactions, Vaster is ultimately left unpunished, and indeed better off than at the opening of the play.[71] The tricksters' use of folklore proves them apt 'understanders' of how to commodify the language and performance of fairy magic.

The language of counterfeits

In folklore, those who spoke of the fairies were often punished, and savvy tricksters took advantage of this convention to silence their victims. The deceivers generally claimed that the silence imposed on their dupes was part of a process of ritual purification, which aligned with the victims' expectations about fairy folklore. Subtle and Face force Dapper into silence by a parody of such methods. When their fairy ritual is interrupted by a knock on the door, Subtle warns his co-conspirators that Dapper 'must not see, nor speak To anybody'. Incorporating this interruption into their makeshift ritual, they lock Dapper in a privy to be 'fumigated', gagging him with a piece of gingerbread: 'gape, sir, and let [Subtle] fit you'.[72]

A similar scene is played out in *The Honest Lawyer* when the criminal trio break into Gripe's house to rob him. Binding and pinching the usurer while disguised as fairies, they taunt him: 'Now thou gap'st for a morgage?'[73] The trio take advantage of Gripe's inability to form words by stuffing cheese into his mouth: 'Here is a morsel for an Vsurer. / Gagge him … / A peece of Cheese of the Low-country Dairies. This is the vsuall diet of the Fairies.'[74] Whereas Dapper is gagged with gingerbread, Gripe's cheese gag alludes to the common association between fairies and dairy products: they were known to frequent dairies, enchant cattle and spoil milk.[75] In *The Merry Wives of Windsor*, Falstaff fears that the 'welsh Fairy' Sir Hugh Evans will '[t]urn me into a piece of cheese'.[76]

The victims of fairy tricks are usually grotesque figures, whose moral impurity is marked by their desire to consume. In the cases of Gripe and Falstaff, this consumption is as much an excess of gluttony as of avarice. Gagging them with food is not only a practical means of quenching their appetites, but it also symbolizes the seizure of discursive power by the con-artists. In both scenes, Dapper and Gripe willingly open their mouths to be silenced, 'gaping' for food as hungrily as they do for money.

In folkloric precedent, encounters with fairies are frequently ineffable, and the fraudsters rely on the victims being unable to articulate what has happened to them. They encourage secrecy, even enforced silence. Moreover, the victims' complacency and willingness to be silenced is itself a synecdoche for changing systems of exchange. The kind of people whose wealth might have given them voice in the past are now portrayed as gluttonous, greedy and easily silenced by upwardly mobile 'understanders'. The appearance of counterfeit fairies in comedies like *The Alchemist*, *The Merry Wives of Windsor* and *The Honest Lawyer* indicates that audiences would have found the victims' confusion humorous. Audiences were presumed to understand that fairies are not real ontological beings and that money does not magically materialize. However, the real-life success of several fairy impersonations (despite whatever warnings might have been gleaned from the theatre) suggests that the dupes truly believed it possible that fairies might grant them real money, even if they could not fully describe how it would happen.

After all, there is a sense in which the tricksters do deliver what they promise. As each of their victims gapes open-mouthed at the magical spectacle, the tricksters generate profit by making the fairies manifest to their victim. They evaluate moral character, and they issue or deny reward accordingly. Victims like Falstaff or Thomas Moore spring from the landed gentry, who trace their wealth to medieval land rights instead of to market exchange or wage labour. Their claim to ancestral fortunes is circumvented by those who possess the seemingly magical ability to make a profit by adapting folklore to an urban setting, in a way that the 'gaping heirs' of the aristocracy cannot grasp or describe. Particularly for those with a penchant for words and a flair for performance, early modern London offered unprecedented opportunities for financial advancement. The ability to 'translate' the language of fairy lore into the emerging vocabulary of political economy shows that the likes of Subtle and Face are indeed effective alchemists. They can generate value from nothing, just as they claim.

Notes

1   The term was coined by Katharine Briggs, *The Anatomy of Puck: An Examination of Fairy Beliefs among Shakespeare's Contemporaries and Successors* (London: Routledge and Kegan Paul, 1959), 50.

2   C. J. Sisson suggests *The Alchemist* is based on the swindle of Thomas Rogers of Dorset chronicled in the Chancery Records. 'A Topical Reference in *The Alchemist*', in *Joseph Quincy Adams Memorial Studies*, ed. James McManaway et al. (Washington, DC, 1948), 739–41. Richard Levin suggests not enough information exists to assume such a correlation. 'Another "Source" for "The Alchemist" and Another Look at Source Studies', *English Literary Renaissance* 28, no. 2 (Spring 1998).

3   Essex cleric William Harrison observed 'three things to be marvellously altered in England' in the last generation, including the replacement of straw mattresses with feather beds and wood tableware with pewter. *The Description of England*, ed. George Edelen (Ithaca: Folger Shakespeare Library, 1968), 200–1.

4   Regina Buccola, *Fairies, Fractious Women, and the Old Faith: Fairy Lore in Early Modern British Drama and Culture* (Selinsgrove, PA: Susquehanna University Press, 2006).

5   The association between fairies and their vanishing gold was common enough to be proverbial, as in *Woman Is a Weathercock*: 'I see you labor in some serious thing, / And think (like fairies' treasure) to reveal it, / Will cause it to vanish'. Nathan Field, *Woman Is a Weathercock* (London: William Jaggard for Iohn Budge, 1612), B2r. Early English Books Online.

6   Piotr Spyra, 'Ben Jonson's *The Alchemist*: The Essential Guide to Early Modern Fairy Belief', *Folklore* 128, no. 3 (2017): 292–313. See also Richard Levin, 'Another "Source" for "The Alchemist" and Another Look at Source Studies', *English Literary Renaissance* 28, no. 2 (Spring 1998): 210–30; Sisson, 'A Topical Reference'.

7   Jean Wilson, *Entertainments for Elizabeth I* (Totowa, NJ: D. S. Brewer, 1980), 21. For the iconography of Elizabeth see Roy Strong, *Gloriana: The Portraits of Queen Elizabeth I*

(London: Randomhouse, 2003); Susan Frye, *The Competition for Representation* (Oxford: Oxford University Press, 1993); Carole Levin, Jo Eldridge Carney and Debra Barrett-Graves, *Elizabeth I Always Her Own Free Woman* (London: Routledge, 2003); Julia Walker, ed., *Dissing Elizabeth: Negative Representations of Gloriana* (Durham, NC: Duke University Press, 1998).

8   Diane Purkiss, 'Old Wives' Tales Retold: The Mutations of the Fairy Queen', in *This Doubled Voice: Gendered Writing in Early Modern England*, ed. Danielle Clarke and Elizabeth Clarke (Basingstoke, Hampshire: Macmillan, 2000), 103–22.

9   Gabriel Heaton, ed., *Entertainment for Elizabeth at Woodstock*, in *John Nichols's The Progresses and Public Processions of Queen Elizabeth I: A New Edition of the Early Modern Sources, Vol. 2: 1572–1578*, ed. Elizabeth Goldring, Faith Eales, Elizabeth Clarke and Jayne Elizabeth Archer, 5 vols. (Oxford: Oxford University Press, 2014), 361–475.

10   Mathew Woodcock, *Fairy in the Faerie Queene: Renaissance Elf-Fashioning and Elizabethan Myth Making* (Aldershot, England: Ashgate, 2004).

11   Steve Bull, '*The Alchemist* and Medieval Faerie Romance', *Ben Jonson Journal* 6, no. 2 (2019): 210. https://doi.org/10.3366/bjj.2019.0255.

12   Daren Oldridge, 'Fairies and the Devil in Early Modern England', *The Seventeenth Century* 31, no. 1 (2016): 1–15. https://doi.org/10.1080/0268117X.2016.1147977.

13   The term 'changeling' was used throughout early modern Europe to refer to a child that has been swapped at birth for a fairy's baby. See Peter Narváez, ed., *The Good People: New Fairylore Essays* (Lexington: University Press of Kentucky, 1997). Especially Joyce Underwood Munro, 'The Invisible Made Visible', 250–83 and Susan Schoon Eberly, 'Fairies and the Folklore of Disability', 227–50.

14   See Maureen Duffy, *The Erotic World of Fairy* (Hachette, UK: Hodder and Stoughton, 1972); Jason Gleckman, '"I know a Bank …" *A Midsummer Night's Dream*, fairies, and the Erotic History of England', *Shakespeare* 10, no. 1 (2014): 23–45. https://doi.org/10.1080/17450918.2013.766237.

15   Reginald Scot, *The Discovery of Witchcraft* (London, 1584. Reprint 1665), Eee3r. *Early English Books Online*.

16   John Aubrey, 'Remaines of Gentilisme and Judaisme', in *Three Prose Works*, ed. John Buchanan-Brown (Fontwell, Sussex: Centaur, 1972), 203.

17   The origin of the term 'fairy gold' might date to the ancient Greek proverb 'our treasure turned out to be charcoal'. W. H. D. Rouse,

'Fairy Gold', *Folklore* 8, no. 4 (December 1897): 379. https://doi.org
/10.1080/0015587X.1897.9720431

18 Francis Beaumont and John Fletcher, 'The Honest Man's Fortune',
    in *The Dramatic Works in the Beaumont and Fletcher Canon*, ed.
    Fredson Bowers (Cambridge: Cambridge University Press, 1996), 3–
    144, 5.1.56–7. There is substantial evidence that dramatist Nathan
    Field may have contributed to this play, and Field seems to have
    been partial referencing fairy money proverbially in his own plays.
    Cf. n 5 above. Another reference suggests, 'Tis like fairies treasure;
    which but reueal'd, brings on the blabbers, ruine.' Philip Massinger
    and Nathaniel Field, *The Fatal Dowry* (London: Printed by John
    Norton, 1632). *Early English Books Online*.

19 Duffy, *Erotic World*, 75–6. Duffy also notes that 'fairies may steal
    the substance from things, leaving them superficially the same, but
    with all the goodness gone'.

20 John Brunner discusses how 'fairy gold' might have geological
    origins – ammonites are gold, coin-sized fossils that rapidly
    deteriorate when exposed to air. 'Ammonites and "Fairy Gold,"'
    Folklore 90, no. 2 (1979): 241.

21 Wendy Wall, 'Why Does Puck Sweep? Fairylore, Merry Wives, and
    Social Struggle', *Shakespeare Quarterly* 52, no. 1 (2001): 67–106
    Buccola, *Fairies*, 41.

22 Susan Schoon Eberly, 'Fairies and the Folklore of Disability', in *The
    Good People: New Fairylore Essays*, ed. Peter Narváez (Lexington:
    University Press of Kentucky, 1997), 227–50.

23 As Wall suggests, 'fairy discourse spanning many centuries
    designates belief in these spirits as both domestic and fading; that
    is, it constitutes a belief system held reverently until just *recently*'.
    'Why Does Puck', 68.

24 Richard Corbet, 'The Fairies Farewell', *Certain Elegant Poems*
    (London, 1647).

25 Anonymous. *The Wisdome of Doctor Dodypoll* (London, 1600),
    sig. A4r.

26 Mary Ellen Lamb, 'Taken by the Fairies: Fairy Practices and
    the Production of Popular Culture in *A Midsummer Night's
    Dream*', *Shakespeare Quarterly* 51, no. 3 (Autumn 2000): 279.
    Stephen Orgel takes an intermediary stance suggesting that while
    belief in fairies was real, most magic was 'about getting through
    ordinary life'. 'Secret Arts and Public Spectacles: The Parameters
    of Elizabethan Magic', *Shakespeare Quarterly* 68, no. 1 (Spring
    2017): 90.

27 Marjorie Swann, 'The Politics of Fairylore in Early Modern English
    Literature', *Renaissance Quarterly* 52, no. 2 (2000): 450.

28 Gary R. Butler, 'The Lutin Tradition in French-Newfoundland Culture: Discourse and Belief', in *The Good People: New Fairylore Essays*, ed. Peter Narváez (Lexington: University Press of Kentucky, 1997), 8.

29 *The Brideling, Sadling and Ryding of a Rich Churle in Hampshire* (London: 1595), 7. *Early English Books Online.*

30 Ibid.

31 Ibid., 7–8.

32 *The Brideling*, 8.

33 Ibid.

34 Ibid.

35 Levin, 'Another Source', 219.

36 *The Several Notorious and Lewd Cozenages of John West and Alice West, Falsely Called the King and Queen of Fairies* (London, 1613), B1r.

37 Ibid.

38 Ibid.

39 Orgel, 'Secret Arts', 91.

40 *The Several Notorious*, A4v.

41 Willard, 'Pimping', 492.

42 There is also some evidence to suggest that fairy queens (even ontologically real ones) were associated with the sort of trickery that is occurring in these plays, as in the ballad *A Monstrous shape. OR A shapelesse Monster*:

> Of Robin Goodfellow also,
> Which was a seruant long agoe,
> The Quéen of Fairies doth it know,
> and hindered him in fashion:
> She knew not what she did her selfe,
> She chang'd him like a Fairie elfe,
> For all his money, goods, and pelfe,
> she gull'd him.

(London: Printed by M. F[lesher] 1639). *Early English Books Online.* The printing of this ballad after the circulation of the pamphlets and dramatic works discussed in this paper suggests that these accounts coloured future ideas about fairies. Even in a ballad that seems to be describing ontologically real fairies, the fairy queen figure is depicted as something of a con artist.

43 Levin, 'Another Source'.

44 Robert Greene, 'A Notable Discovery of Coznage', in *Rogues, Vagabonds, & Sturdy Beggars: A New Gallery of Tudor and Early Stuart Rogue Literature Exposing the Lives, Times, and Cozening Tricks of the Elizabethan Underworld*, ed. Arthur Kinney (Amherst, MA: University of Massachusetts Press, 1990), 163–86.

45 *The Several Notorious and Lewd,* B3r.
46 Ibid., C4v.
47 Robert Armin, *The Valiant Welshman* (London, 1663), D4v.
48 As Alec Ryrie suggests, 'these accounts are taken from sensational pamphlets whose authors did not place any great value on accurate reporting. Many of the ancillary tales of Alice West and Judith Philips read as if they have grown in the telling; some are likely to be the work of other fraudsters, others are probably mere urban myths.' Ryrie is particularly sceptical of the tale of Judith riding the churl. *The Sorcerer's Tale: Faith and Fraud in Tudor England* (Oxford University Press, 2010).
49 Willard, 'Pimping', 493; 494.
50 Anonymous, *A Quest of Enquirie, / by Women to Know; / Whether the Tripe-Wife Were Trimmed / by Doll or No* (London, 1595), qtd. in Levin, 'Another Source', 214. For the many versions of this story in circulation, see Kirsten Uszkalo, 'Cunning, Cozening and Queens in *The Merry Wives of Windsor*', *Shakespeare* 6, no. 1 (2010): 20–33, https://doi.10.1080/17450911003643084.
51 *Alchemist*, 25.
52 Ibid., 5.5.159-65.
53 Ben Jonson, *The Alchemist*, ed. Elizabeth Cook, New Mermaids 2nd edition, (London: A & C Black, 2004), 3.4.44-5.
54 Ibid., 3.4.75-81.
55 Jonson, *Alchemist,* 56, n. 10-14.
56 Ibid., 5.4.30-1.
57 Many held the idea that Catholics were particularly inclined to fairy belief as a form of anti-Catholic propaganda. See Buccola, *Fairies,* 174.
58 *Alchemist*, 3.5.30-1.
59 Shakespeare, 'The Norton Shakespeare', in *The Merry Wives of Windsor*, ed. Stephen Greenblatt (New York: Norton, 2008), 5.5.41–7.
60 *Merry Wives*, 1.3.31; 67-9.
61 *Merry Wives*, 5.5.105; 119.
62 Ibid., 5.5.120-6.
63 S. S. *Honest Lawyer* (London: Printed by George Purslowe for Richard Woodroffe [etc.], 1616), B3v.
64 Ibid., C2r.
65 C3r.
66 C4r.
67 F1v.
68 E3r.
69 Ibid.

70   Judith M. Spicksley, 'Women, "Usury" and Credit in Early Modern England: The Case of the Maiden Investor', *Gender & History* 27, no. 2 (August 2015): 267.
71   *Alchemist*, 25.
72   Ibid., 4.1.74-7.
73   *The Honest Lawyer*, G3r.
74   *The Honest Lawyer*, G3r.
75   Buccola, *Fairies*, 99; cf. 'The Four Leafed Clover' in Briggs, *Anatomy*, 213.
76   *Merry Wives*, 5.5.82. Cheese was also stereotypically associated with the Welsh.

Works cited

Armin, Robert, *The Valiant Welshman, or, The True Chronicle History of the Life and Valiant Deeds of Caradoc the Great* ... (London, 1663). *Early English Books Online.*

Aubrey, John, 'Remaines of Gentilisme and Judaisme', in *Three Prose Works*, ed. John Buchanan Brown (Fontwell, Sussex: Centaur Press, 1972).

Beaumont, Francis and John Fletcher, 'The Honest Man's Fortune', in *The Dramatic Works in the Beaumont and Fletcher Canon*, ed. Fredson Bowers (Cambridge: Cambridge University Press, 1996), 3–144.

The Brideling, Sadling and Ryding of a rich Churle in Hampshire by the subtill practice of one Iudeth Philips, a professed cunningwoman, or fortune teller VVith a true Discourse of her vnwomanly vsing of a trype wife, a widow, lately dwelling on the Back Side of S. Nicholas Shambles in London, Whom She with Her Conferates, Likewise Cosoned: For Which Fact, Shee Was at the Sessions House without New Gate Arraigned, Where She Confessed the Same, and Had Iudgement for Her Offence, to Be Whipped through the Citie, the 14. Of February, 1594, (London, 1595). *Early English Books Online.*

Briggs, Katharine, *The Anatomy of Puck: An Examination of Fairy Beliefs among Shakespeare's Contemporaries and Successors* (London: Routledge and Kegan Paul, 1959).

Brunner, John, 'Ammonites and "Fairy Gold"', *Folklore* 90, no. 2 (1979): 241.

Buccola, Regina, *Fairies, Fractious Women, and the Old Faith: Fairy Lore in Early Modern British Drama and Culture* (Selinsgrove, PA: Susquehanna University Press, 2006). *ProQuest Ebook Central*, http://ebookcentral.proquest.com/lib/tamiu-ebooks/detail.action?docID=3116136.

Bull, Steve, 'The Alchemist and Medieval Faerie Romance', *Ben Jonson Journal* 26, no. 2 (2019): 206–26. https://doi.org/10.3366/bjj.2019.0255.

Butler, Gary R., 'The Lutin Tradition in French-Newfoundland Culture: Discourse and Belief', in *The Good People: New Fairylore Essays*, ed. Peter Narváez (Lexington: University Press of Kentucky, 1997), 5–21.

Corbet, Richard, 'The Fairies Farewell', in *Certain Elegant Poems* (London, 1647).

Duffy, Maureen, *The Erotic World of Fairy* (Hachette, UK: Hodder and Stoughton, 1972).

Eberly, Susan Schoon, 'Fairies and the Folklore of Disability', in *The Good People: New Fairylore Essays*, ed. Peter Narváez (Lexington: University Press of Kentucky, 1997), 227–50.

Erasmus, Desiderius, *Literary and Educational Writings. Volume 4: De Pueris Instituendis/De Recta Pronuntiatione*, ed. J. Kelley Sowards (Toronto, ON: University of Toronto Press, 1985).

Field, Nathan, *Woman Is a Weathercock* (London: William Jaggard for Iohn Budge, 1612). *Early English Books Online*.

Frye, Susan, *The Competition for Representation* (Oxford: Oxford University Press, 1993).

Gleckman, Jason, '"I Know a Bank …": *A Midsummer Night's Dream*, Fairies, and the Erotic History of England', *Shakespeare* 10, no. 1 (2014): 23–45. https://doi.org/10.1080/17450918.2013.766237.

Greene, Robert, 'A Notable Discovery of Coznage', in *Rogues, Vagabonds, & Sturdy Beggars: A New Gallery of Tudor and Early Stuart Rogue Literature Exposing the Lives, Times, and Cozening Tricks of the Elizabethan Underworld*, ed. Arthur Kinney (Amherst: University of Massachusetts Press, 1990), 163–86.

Harrison, William, *The Description of England*, ed. George Edelen (Ithaca: Folger Shakespeare Library, 1968).

Heaton, Gabriel, ed., *Entertainment for Elizabeth at Woodstock. In John Nichols's The Progresses and Public Processions of Queen Elizabeth I: A New Edition of the Early Modern Sources, Vol. 2: 1572–1578*, ed. Elizabeth Goldring, Faith Eales, Elizabeth Clarke and Jayne Elizabeth Archer (Oxford: Oxford University Press, 2014), 361–475.

Helgerson, Richard, 'The Buck Basket, the Witch, and the Queen of Fairies', in *Renaissance Culture and the Everyday*, ed. Patricia Fumerton and Simon Hunt (Philadelphia: University of Pennsylvania Press, 2014), 162–82.

Jonson, Ben, *The Alchemist*, ed. Elizabeth Cook, New Mermaids 2nd edition (London: A & C Black, 2004).

Klaassen, Frank and Sharon Hubbs Wright, *The Magic of Rogues: Necromancers in Early Tudor England* (University Park, PA: Pennsylvania State University Press, 2021).

Kolkovich, Elizabeth Zeman, 'Pageantry, Queens, and Housewives in the Two Texts of the Merry Wives of Windsor', *Shakespeare Quarterly* 63, no. 3 (2012): 328–54. https://doi.org/10.1353/shq.2012.0051.

Lamb, Mary Ellen, 'Taken by the Fairies: Fairy Practices and the Production of Popular Culture in *A Midsummer Night's Dream*', *Shakespeare Quarterly* 52, no. 3 (Autumn 2000): 277–312.

Latham, Minor White, *The Elizabethan Fairies: The Fairies of Folklore and the Fairies of Shakespeare* (New York: Columbia University Press, 1930).

Levin, Carole, Jo Eldridge Carney and Debra Barrett-Graves, *Elizabeth I Always Her Own Free Woman* (London: Routledge, 2003).

Levin, Richard, 'Another "Source" for "The Alchemist" and Another Look at Source Studies', *English Literary Renaissance* 28, no. 2 (Spring 1998): 210–30.

Massinger, Philip and Nathaniel Field, *The Fatal Dowry* (London: Printed by Iohn Norton, 1632). *Early English Books Online.*

A Monstrous shape. OR A shapelesse Monster, London: Printed by M. F[lesher], 1639. *Early English Books Online.*

Narváez, Peter, ed., *The Good People: New Fairylore Essays* (Lexington: University Press of Kentucky, 1997).

Oldridge, Daren, 'Fairies and the Devil in Early Modern England', *The Seventeenth Century* 31, no. 1 (2016): 1–15. https://doi.org/10.1080/0 268117X.2016.1147977.

Orgel, Stephen, 'Secret Arts and Public Spectacles: The Parameters of Elizabethan Magic', *Shakespeare Quarterly* 68, no. 1 (Spring, 2017): 80–91. https://doi.org/10.1353/shq.2017.0004.

Purkiss, Diane, 'Old Wives' Tales Retold: The Mutations of the Fairy Queen', in *This Doubled Voice: Gendered Writing in Early Modern England*, ed. Danielle Clarke and Elizabeth Clarke (Basingstoke, Hampshire: Macmillan, 2000), 103–22.

Purkiss, Diane, *Troublesome Things: A History of Fairies and Fairy Stories* (London: Allen Lane, 2000).

A Quest of Enquirie,/by Women to Know;/Whether the Tripe-Wife Were Trimmed/by Doll or No (London, 1595).

Rouse, W. H. D., 'Fairy Gold', *Folklore* 8, no. 4 (December 1897): 379. https://doi.org/10.1080/0015587X.1897.9720431.

Ryrie, Alec, *The Sorcerer's Tale: Faith and Fraud in Tudor England* (Oxford: Oxford University Press, 2010).

Saunders, Corrine, *Magic and the Supernatural in Medieval English Romance* (Cambridge: D. S. Brewer, 2010).

Scot, Reginald, *The Discovery of Witchcraft* (London, 1584). Reprint 1665. Wing 1129: 18. *Early English Books Online.*

The Several Notorious and Lewd Cozenages of John West and Alice West, Falsely Called the King and Queen of Fairies (London, 1613). *Early English Books Online.*

Shakespeare, William, *The Norton Shakespeare*, ed. Stephen Greenblatt, 2nd edition (New York: Norton, 2008).

Sisson, C. J., 'A Topical Reference in *The Alchemist*', in *Joseph Quincy Adams Memorial Studies*, ed. James McManaway et al. (Washington, DC: The Folger Shakespeare Library, 1948), 739–41.

Spicksley, Judith M., 'Women, "Usury" and Credit in Early Modern England: The Case of the Maiden Investor', *Gender & History* 27, no. 2 (August 2015): 267–92.

Spyra, Piotr, 'Ben Jonson's *The Alchemist*: The Essential Guide to Early Modern Fairy Belief', *Folklore* 128, no. 3 (2017): 292–313.

S. S. *The Honest Lawyer* (London: Printed by George Purslowe for Richard Woodroffe [etc.], 1616).

Strong, Roy, *Gloriana: The Portraits of Queen Elizabeth I* (London: Randonhouse, 2003).

Swann, Marjorie, 'The Politics of Fairlore in Early Modern English Literature', *Renaissance Quarterly* 52, no. 2 (2000): 449–73.

Uszkalo, Kirsten, 'Cunning, Cozening and Queens in *The Merry Wives of Windsor*', *Shakespeare* 6, no. 1 (2010): 20–33. https://doi.10.1080/17450911003643084.

Walker, Julia, ed., *Dissing Elizabeth: Negative Representations of Gloriana* (Durham, NC: Duke University Press, 1998).

Wall, Wendy, 'Why Does Puck Sweep? Fairylore, Merry Wives, and Social Struggle', *Shakespeare Quarterly* 52, no. 1 (2001): 67–106.

Willard, Thomas, 'Pimping for the Fairy Queen: Some Cozeners in Shakespeare's England', in *Crime and Punishment in the Middle Ages and Early Modern Age: Mental-Historical Investigations of Basic Human Problems and Social Responses*, ed. Albrecht Classen and Connie Scarborough (Berlin: De Gruyter, 2012), 491–508.

Wilson, Jean, *Entertainments for Elizabeth I* (Totowa, NJ: D. S. Brewer, 1980).

The Wisdome of Doctor Dodypoll (London, 1600).

Woodcock, Mathew, *Fairy in The Faerie Queene: Renaissance Elf-Fashioning and Elizabethan Myth Making* (Aldershot, England: Ashgate, 2004).

Wright, Celeste Turner, 'Some Conventions Regarding the Usurer in Elizabethan Literature', *Studies in Philology* 31, no. 2 (1934): 176–97.

4

The sign of Abel Drugger: Fake news, finance and flattery in Ben Jonson's 'dotages'

David Hawkes

Against *eikonodulia*

He shall have a *bell*, that's *Abel*;
And by it standing one whose name is *Dee*,
In a *rug* gown, that's D and *Rug*, that's *drug*;
And right anest him a dog snarling *Er*;
There's *Drugger*, Abel Drugger. That's his sign.
— Ben Jonson, *The Alchemist* (2.6.14-18)[1]

In this speech, Ben Jonson's alchemist Subtle applies his expertise to designing the sign for Abel Drugger's shop. As an alchemist, Subtle assures Drugger that he can turn signs into money. As we know well today, he is quite correct: the skilful manipulation of images in advertising can indeed produce wealth. As George Soros has pointed out,[2] today's financialized capitalism is itself a form of alchemy, which creates value where none previously existed. Furthermore, the nature of Drugger's business parallels the technique by which he publicizes it. He runs a drug store and, as Jacques Derrida reminds us, the *pharmakon* has been acknowledged as analogous to *ecriture* since antiquity.[3] Like rhetorical sophistry, drugs invade the mind from outside and influence it by non-rational means. Plato and his Sophist opponents agree that, in the words of Gorgias of Leontini's *Encomium of Helen*: 'The power of discourse stands in the same relation to the soul's organization as the pharmacopoeia does to the physiology of bodies.'[4] Drugs and sophistry are analogous departures from reason.

As a result, drugs and sophistry were also considered analogous to the rituals performed by the Elizabethan *magus* John Dee and his ilk, as Subtle indicates by depicting Dee in Drugger's sign. Ritual magic attempts to influence both the subjective *psyche* and the objective environment by the manipulation of images, and the people of Renaissance England were convinced that they were experiencing a palpable growth in the power of 'black' magic. Jonson spent much of his career pondering the nature of magic, its connections to theatrical representation and its relationship to the blossoming field of finance. These interests deepened as he aged. *The New Inn* (1629) opens with another discussion of a commercial sign. The Host of the Light-Heart Inn considers himself skilled at manipulating visual emblems:

> The Sign o' the Light-Heart. There you may read it;
> So may your Master too, if he look on't.
> A Heart weigh'd with a Feather, and out weigh'd too:
> A Brain-child o' my own! and I am proud on't!
>
> (1.1.2-6)[5]

Yet the Host's conception of the sign as his 'Brian-child' indicates a confusion of semiotic with natural reproduction. To Jonson, we gather, the use of visual representation to entice customers into purchasing commodities seemed morally reprehensible. Visual representation easily usurps the rule of *nous* in the *psyche*, by-passing the faculty of reason, appealing directly to the senses, stimulating irrational passion and carnal appetite. Submission to the power of visual signs involved an alienation of the will, a delegation of volition to symbolic forces prior to the self. The Host's sign depicts the influence of money on the 'heart', translating from verbal into visual images:

> *A heavy Purse makes a light Heart.*
> There 'tis exprest! first, by a Purse of Gold,
> A heavy Purse, and then two Turtles, makes,
> A Heart with a Light stuck in't, a Light-heart!

(1.1.15-18)

Like Subtle working on Drugger's sign, the Host takes a craftsman's pride in his ability to adapt aesthetics to commercial ends. In late sixteenth-century London, the power of symbolic exchange-value was beginning to exercise an obvious cultural influence. Jonson was particularly fascinated with the impact of exchange-value on aesthetics, and several of his plays feature Prologues or Inductions in which audience members quibble about the price of admission and its effects on their reception of the spectacle on stage.[6] Jonson's philosophical objection to commodification was Aristotelian: the production of art for profit constituted a violation of art's natural *telos*. The necessity of appealing to a paying audience involved concessions to popular taste that he found (almost) intolerable.

Jonson's later work was shaped by the tension between his moralistic denunciation of commercialized aesthetics and his need to make a living. Economic exigencies meant that he was no more able to take his own advice and 'leave the loathed stage' than he was able to escape the 'more loathsome age'.[7] His epigram 'To My Bookseller' grudgingly allows the merchant to divert his work to the alien *telos* of profit, while implicitly likening retail exchange to usury: 'Thou that mak'st gain thy end, and wisely well, / Call'st a book good, or bad, as it doth sell, / Use mine so too' (1-3). However, he denies permission to employ such 'vile arts' (11) as placing the book prominently in the shop's window or advertising it on 'posts or walls' (7). Rather than resort to such subterfuge, he declares, he would prefer that its pages be used to wrap fish. Jonson's rejection of commodification approached the phobic in its intensity, but only in principle. In practice he was compelled to compromise, and his dismay at what he perceived as the consequent degradation of his art echoes throughout his late work.

Jonson's last complete plays – *The Staple of News* (1626), *The New Inn* (1629) and *The Magnetic Lady* (1632) – took a long time to recover from John Dryden's dismissal of them as 'dotages'. There are no performances of them at all recorded between 1660 and 1776.[8] But what made them inaccessible to the Enlightenment is precisely what renders them prescient of postmodernity. In this final comic trilogy, Jonson provides an extended critique of the autonomous power of representation, as it is manifested across the totality of social life. Because he precedes the Enlightenment 'dissociation of sensibility',[9] which divided experience into such mutually exclusive categories as 'economics', 'ethics' and 'aesthetics', Jonson conceives of creation as a macrocosm, whose individual 'spheres' are inseparable from the whole. A development in what today we call the 'economy' was for him necessarily paralleled by developments in ethics, in aesthetics and even in what we call 'gender' and 'sexuality'.

Jonson's last plays strain with the effort of discovering a coherent pattern in a disintegrating world. In their plots, as Samuel Jonson observed of the 'conceits' prevalent in seventeenth-century poetry, 'heterogeneous ideas are yoked by violence together'.[10] In particular, Jonson's 'dotages' insist on the homology between financial and verbal manifestations of the performative sign. In cultures accustomed to think of money and language as entirely discrete discourses, his point may seem obscure. But to Jonson the homology between linguistic and financial representation was axiomatic, and its figural expression came instinctively:

> *Custome* is most certaine Mistrese of Language, as the publicke stamp makes the current money. But wee must not be too frequent with the mint, every day coyning.... Letters are, as it were, the Banke of wordes, and restore themselves to an Author, as the pawnes of Language.[11]

As Douglas Bruster observes, early modern English literature had recourse to a vast range of 'well-established metaphors glossing representation itself as part of the system of economic exchange'.[12] In postmodernity, the determining power of representation is once again evident in the abstract, symbolic forms taken by financial value. The economy has become 'financialized', to the extent that it is now dominated by figurative exchanges among various forms of pecuniary symbol. Furthermore, the assumption that signs are efficacious extends far beyond economics, into linguistics and semiotics, and ultimately into the last redoubts of nature, such as gender and sexuality. The late twentieth and early twenty-first centuries have been defined by the financialization of the economy and the legitimization of non-procreative sexualities – that is to say, by forms of limitless (*ateleological*) and self-referential *(autotelic)* desire. Each of Jonson's last plays personifies the object of such desire in the form of an unattainable, irresistible and fabulously wealthy woman pursued by a posse of salivating men: Lady Pecunia in *The Staple of News*, Lady Frampul in *The New Inn* and Lady Loadstone in *The Magnetic Lady*.

Aristotelian and scholastic morality objected to all forms of *autotelic* desire because, lacking *telos*, such desire was endless and therefore unnatural. It lacked essence; it was endlessly malleable because essence consists in *telos*. The error reflected in unnatural desire or *cupiditas* was basically semiotic. Since the body was the visible representation of the soul, an erotic fixation on the body was a form of idolatry. The liturgical, linguistic, financial and erotic forms of fetishization all attribute efficacy to symbols. That is the transgression committed by ritual magic and, from the Protestant perspective, in the Catholic Sacraments. Jonson's last plays, which looked like 'dotages' to Enlightenment sensibilities, actually constitute a sophisticated critique of performativity across its various forms of appearance. As *The Magnetic Lady*'s Captain Ironside observes:

> to wise
> And well experience'd men, words do but signifie;
> They have no power, save with dull grammarians,
> Whose souls are nought, but a syntaxis of them.
>
> (1.1.79-82)[13]

Wise men understand that words are referential: they 'do but signifie'. The only people who regard them as possessing performative 'power' are those whose souls are constructed out of representation. Jonson's ethical commitment to ontological essentialism and his moralistic revulsion from spectacular appearances reach their climax as his career draws to a close, and the thematic concerns of his final works suggest that his views developed in response to the contemporary rise in the practical power of money. The trade in money followed the same fundamental principles in Jonson's day as in our own. *The Magnetic Lady*'s personification of usury, Sir Moth Interest, is presented as a financial genius, a derivatives trader who employs sophisticated logarithms to determine the prices of the stocks in which he deals. Compass the Steward emphasizes that these investments are purely abstract and that, as with all financial derivatives, Interest's rate of profit is independent of any underlying commodity:

> There's within,
> Sir *Interest,* as able a Philosopher,
> In buying and selling! Has reduc'd his thrift,
> To certain principles, and in that method,
> As he will tell you instantly, by *Logorythms,*
> The utmost profit of a stock imployed:
> (Be the commodity what it will) the place,
> Or time, but causing very, very little,
> Or, I may say, no paralax at all,
> In his pecuniary observations!
>
> (1.6.31-40)

Like today's speculative derivatives, the stocks in which Interest deals are performative rather than referential signs: they do not derive their value from reference to any underlying commodity. Interest justifies his opinion that 'the love of Money' is 'a Vertue' with a brazen inversion of Aristotle's description of usury as unnatural reproduction: 'My Monies are my Blood, my Parents, Kindred / And he that loves not those, he is unnatural' (2.6.39-40). From the perspective of Interest, the reproduction of money appears to be a *natural* process, and its fruits naturally evoke the same emotions as those of human reproduction. Interest consolidates his position as the anti-Aristotle when he commits the classic philosophical error of treating 'Wealth' as if it were an end-in-itself like knowledge or honour. Because he conceives of 'Wealth' as abstract exchange-value, as opposed to substantial use-value, he imagines it as infinite and comparable to the soul:

> [W]e all know the Soul of man is infinite
> In what it covets. Who desireth knowledge,
> Desires it infinitely. Who covets Honour,
> Covets it infinitely: It will be then

No hard thing for a coveting man to prove,
Or to confess, he aims at infinite Wealth.

(2.6.50-55)

Interest sees limitless desire as a moral good because he evaluates
abstract qualities like knowledge and honour in quantitative terms.
He regards them as comparable to 'Wealth', which is the only kind
of value he understands. Interest also asserts that it is 'natural' to
'set a price on Money' (2.6.71-72). He thus collapses nature (*phusis*)
into custom (*nomos*), deconstructing the binary and subverting
the idea of nature as distinct from custom. But Interest's clinching
rationalization of 'Wealth' is its performativity: 'it doth inable him
that hath it, / To the performance of all real Actions' (2.6.82-83). To
confirm his point, when 'Wealth' finally makes its appearance, it is
personified as 'Lady Pecunia Do-all'.

The trope of personification, or *prosopopeia*, dominates literary
depictions of money from Aristophanes to Defoe because it captures
the reversal of subject and object that occurs when independent
agency is attributed to symbols. Jonson's emblematic incarnations
of money lack consistency – in *The Staple of News* Penniboy Senior
addresses gold as 'Lord Piece' and also as 'Lady Pecunia' – because
the figural process of personification is the whole point. Once the
medium of exchange is treated as a commodity, once it is attributed
its own exchange-value, it inevitably acquires performative power:

> [*He shows a piece [of gold]* Here's a piece, my good *Lord*
>   Piece, doth all;
> Goes to the butchers, fetches in a mutton;
> Then to the bakers, brings in bread, makes fires,
> Gets wine, and does more real courtesies
> Than all my lords, I know: My sweet *Lord* Piece.

(2.4.108-11)[14]

Physical gold can do none of these things; symbolic exchange-
value can do all of them. The actions performed by money are
more efficacious – more 'real' as Jonson puts it – that the actions of
human beings. Jonson dwells constantly on his age's displacement
of qualitative, ethical or aesthetic value into quantitative, financial
value. He understands this process as part of a more general
conquest of essence by appearance and thus of the soul by the body

(in his quarrels with Inigo Jones, Jonson describes Jones's spectacles as the 'body' of the masque, while his words form its 'soul'). In *The Staple of News*, the usurer Penniboy Senior contrasts the efficacy of money with the impotence of personified 'merit': '*Merit* will keep no House, nor pay no House-rent. / Will Mistris *Merit* go to Market, think you, / Set on the Pot, or feed the Family?' (2.4.131-34). Perhaps the full resonance of such lines is only audible in societies, like Jonson's and our own, where the usurious power of financial signs exerts an obvious, inescapable influence on quotidian culture. Until the late twentieth century few critics appreciated the point of *The New Inn* or *The Magnetic Lady*,[15] and *The Staple of News* fared even worse.[16] But as Anthony Parr points out in his 1988 Introduction to the Revels edition of *The Staple*:

> In recent years critics have started to perceive that the play is not really about cupidity and avarice in the same way that (say) *Volpone* is; but the extent to which Jonson has shifted from a single satiric focus in earlier plays to exploration of a series of related trends has not been fully appreciated.
>
> (13)

Over the three decades since Parr wrote, this vague critical awareness that the play is 'not really about cupidity and avarice' so much as the 'related trends' provoked by such vices has developed into a solid consensus. In fact, all three of Jonson's last plays are concerned with the common elements that unite the financial and the linguistic manifestations of the performative sign. They offer a sustained reflection on the mutual influences of usury and sophistry. They warn against the fetishization of either financial or verbal symbols. Above all, they expose the intimate connections between what appeared to be disparate forms of *eikonodulia*: the worship of images.

Enjoying the news

As Don E. Wayne notes, *The Staple of News* 'emphasizes the proper circulation and reproduction of money regulated by contract. A central metaphor for such reproduction under lawful regulation is marriage'.[17] By the same logic, Jonson's central metaphor for the improper, unnatural reproduction of money is non-procreative sexuality, which he usually designates by the synecdoche of 'bawdry' or pimping.[18] One of his epigrams observes that usury and bawdry share the same *telos*: 'If, as their ends, their fruits were still the same, / Bawdry and usury were one kind of game.'[19] Although their empirical manifestations or 'fruits' are different, bawdry and usury are essentially identical because they share the same purpose: the substitution of a sterile surrogate for natural reproduction. In *The Staple of News* Penniboy Cantor remarks that '[a] *Money-Bawd*, is lightly a *Flesh-Bawd* too' (2.5.99-100). His immediate target is his brother, Penniboy Senior, who is indeed Pecunia's 'flesh-bawd', but he is not alone. Penniboy Cantor's prodigal son, Penniboy Junior, is also guilty of 'prostitut[ing] his mistress' (4.2.126). He circulates Pecunia among his friends, exclaiming 'kiss, kiss 'em, princess' (4.2.69) and '[k]iss 'em all, dear madam' (4.2.122). We see here the distinctive blend of lust and avarice displayed throughout Renaissance literature by the complaisant cuckold or 'wittol'. Corvino, who pimps his wife to Volpone, or Thomas Middleton's Allwit, who organizes his wife's prostitution in *A Chaste Maid in Cheapside*, are only the best-known instances of this familiar figure.

Jonson's last plays borrow heavily from Aristophanes, especially the *Plutus*, with its paradigmatic personification of money, and the *Clouds*, whose protagonist attempts to evade his debtors by paying to learn sophistry at the 'Thinking Shop'. Following Aristophanes, Jonson connects usury to sophistry by combining the pursuit of Pecunia with a critique of linguistic performativity. Pecunia's suitors all attempt to win her favour by founding institutions devoted to the systematic inculcation of sophistry. The play features three separate attempts to institutionalize false or misleading verbal discourse: the Staple of News, the Canter's College and the Society of Jeerers. Well into the twentieth century, critics were puzzled by this juxtaposition of seemingly unrelated themes. David Kay criticized *The Staple*'s 'divided focus on wealth and on news',[20] while Cobrun Gum found it an 'unfortunate conglomeration of conflicting elements'.[21] Richard Levin noted that

> most critics have objected … to what they regard as the unfortunate combination of this generalized 'allegory' of the use and abuse of wealth with the 'realistic' and topical satire of the News Office, and to the resultant loss of unity in the play as a whole.[22]

Today, however, Jonson's analysis of the intercourse between money and language may be easier to understand. The titular 'Staple of News' is a shop (or perhaps a warehouse) where current events are packaged and marketed in the form of 'news', which is then sold at a profit to consumers. Jonson had already outlined his critique of commodified current events in the anti-masque to *News from the New World* (1621), when the Factor announces: 'I have hope to erect a Staple for News ere long, whither all shall be brought and thence again vented under the name of Staple-news.'[23] In the same masque, a Printer declares:

> Indeed I am all for sale, gentlemen, you say true: I am a printer, and a printer of news; and I do hearken after 'em wherever they be, at any rates; I'll give anything for a good copy now, be it true or false, so't be news.
>
> (2.16-19)

In *The Staple,* both the retailers and the consumers of 'news' have lost the ability to discriminate on a qualitative basis; their only criterion is quantity, which is expressed in terms of financial value. The first customer we meet is a generic 'Country Woman' who demands: 'A *Groatsworth* of any *News*, I care not what, / To carry down this *Saturday*, to our *Vicar*' (1.4.11-12). The avaricious owners of the Staple are quick to draw their conclusions:

FITTON
    Though it be ne're so false, it runs *News* still.
PENNIBOY JUNIOR
    See divers Mens Opinions! Unto some,
    The very printing of them makes them *News;*
    That ha' not the Heart to believe anything,
    But what they see in print.

> (1.2.50-54)

Emboldened in their wooing of Pecunia by the success of their business, the Staple's investors are driven to exaggerate and invent sensational falsehoods (the Grand Turk has turned Christian, etc.), which are eagerly credited by their customers. The 'Master of the Staple and Prime Jeerer' is named Cymbal. This alludes to 1 Corinthians 13.1: 'Though I speak with the tongues of men and

THE SIGN OF ABEL DRUGGER

of angels, and have not charity, I am become as sounding brass, or a tinkling cymbal.' It also puns on 'symbol', emphasizing his role as personification of the efficacious sign. Cymbal declares himself Pecunia's 'Servant', invoking her as the 'wonder, / Of these our Times', and lauding her ability to 'dazzle the vulgar Eyes, / And strike the People blind with admiration' (3.2.239-40).

In response, Penniboy Cantor, the wise, disguised father of the play's prodigal, laments the malign influence of money on public opinion: 'How hath all just true Reputation fall'n, / Since Money, this base Money 'gan to have any!' (3.2.247-48). This is also Jonson's complaint about his own profession. He parallels the 'Country Woman's' commodified attitude to 'news' with the commentary of four 'Gossips' who play the roles of audience members, evaluating the play in the terms of a housewife addressing a shopkeeper: 'Look your News be new and fresh, Mr. Prologue, and untainted; I shall find them else, if they be stale, or fly-blown, quickly' (1.Int.28-30). Gossip Mirth reports cancelling a visit to the theatre due to criticism of the stage as a mixture of magic and pornography:

> Mrs. Trouble Truth dissuaded us, and told us, he was a profane Poet, and all his Plays had Devils in them: That he kept School upo' the Stage, could conjure there, above the School of Westminster, and Doctor Lamb too: Not a Play he made, but had a Devil in it: And that he would learn us all to make our Husbands Cuckolds at Plays.
>
> (1.Int.43-47)

We may laugh at the Gossip's credulity, but Jonson's objections to the 'shows' of Inigo Jones were not dissimilar. He complained that they appealed to the senses rather than to the intellect. They were mere appearances, depthless simulacra, that tempted the audience into fetishism of every kind. By the end of his life, Jonson was sure that this generalized idolatry resulted from commercialization. In *The Staple* he takes special pains to ensure that the financial motive is not missed. The Prologue to Act 3 laments that 'the Allegory, and purpose of the Author hath hitherto been wholly mistaken', warns against the commentary offered by 'these ridiculous Gossips that tattle between the Acts', and insists that the audience focus on the commercial motive behind the Staple's sophistry: 'do the Author and your own Judgment a Courtesie, and perceive the Trick of alluring Money to the Office, and there coz'ning the people' (3.Int.7-8).

The owners and patrons of the Staple spend their spare time among 'the Jeerers', a society dedicated to the art of verbal abuse. The stage directions identify its members by their professions – Doctor, Sea-Captain, Poetaster – each with the addition: 'and jeerer'. Keenly aware of the power of words to wound, the Jeerers subject everyone around them to vicious mockery. They wield words as weapons, exploiting their performative power for social advantage and forming a collective identity based on what today we might call 'hate speech'. However, the play's most ambitious project to advance sophistry is Penniboy Junior's educational institution: 'I'll build a *Colledge,* I and my *Pecunia,* / And call it *Canters Colledge:* sounds it well?' (3.4.81-82). The prospect of youth being systematically instructed in 'canting' is the last straw for Penniboy Cantor, who finally throws off his disguise and prevents his son's pernicious proposal.

The staff of the Staple, the society of Jeerers and the faculty of the proposed College are mostly composed of the same individuals, and the three institutions share the purpose of promoting sophistry. Penniboy Cantor is their sole opponent. Like Compass in *The Magnetic Lady*, he regards signs in terms of their use-value, not their exchange-value. In this he is contrasted with his brother, Penniboy Senior. Described as 'a Slave, and an Idolator to Pecunia', Penniboy Senior is one of Jonson's archetypal 'money-bawds'. He laments that '[t]he Trade of Mony is fal'n two i' the Hundred' and deplores the tendency of debtors to 'not pay the Use; / Bate of the Use? I am mad with this time's manners' (3.4.58-59). The two Penniboys engage in a heated debate about the nature of money. Cantor, who is disguised as a beggar, observes that 'you are near as wretched as myself, / You dare not use your Money, and I have none' (2.5.24-25). Senior assumes that 'use' means 'loan at interest': 'Not use my Money, cogging *Jack!* who uses it / At better Rates?' (2.5.26-27). But Cantor has in mind the money's use-value, which can only be realized by spending it: 'Sir, I meant / You durst not to enjoy it' (2.5.31-32). Like the beggar, the miserly usurer effectively has no money, since the only 'enjoyment' it gives him is the spectacle of its own reproduction.

In the parlance of the day, to 'enjoy' something was to realize its 'worth' or use-value. To 'value' something, on the other hand, was to translate it into exchange-value. As Marx points out on the first page of *Capital*: 'In English writers of the seventeenth century we still often find the word "worth" used for use-value and "value" for exchange-value.'[24] The Prologue to *The New Inn* deplores Lord Frampul's neglect of his aristocratic wife 'whose worth (though he truly enjoy'd) he never could rightly value' (2-3). Although proud of his wife's noble birth, that is to say, Frampul has failed appropriately to profit from it in financial terms. Thus, Jonson raises the portentous problem of the widening polarity, which was beginning to look like a contradiction, between 'value' and 'worth'. With the legitimization of usury, 'value' achieved the capacity of autonomous reproduction, threatening to obscure and displace everything's natural 'worth'. Jonson's last plays expatiate in fine detail on the infinite, unnatural fertility of compound interest. In *The Magnetic Lady*, the lawyer Practise congratulates Sir Moth Interest:

> But here's a mighty gain, Sir, you have made
> Of this one Stock! the Principal first doubled,
> In the first Seven year; and that redoubled
> I' the next Seven! beside Six thousand pound,
> There's threescore thousand got in Fourteen year,
> After the usual Rate of Ten i' the Hundred,
> And the Ten thousand paid.
>
> (2.6.29-35)

For Interest and Practise, money is an infinitely self-reproducing symbol. In *The Staple of News,* by contrast, Lady Pecunia styles herself 'the Infanta of the Mines', which suggests that she identifies herself with gold bullion. She is sufficiently concerned about her lineage to employ a 'Herald' named Piedmantle to confirm this genealogy:

> PIEDMANTLE
> I have deduc'd her ——
> BROKER
> From all the *Spanish Mines* in the *West Indies,*
> I hope: for she comes that way by her Mother,
> But by her Grand-mother, she's *Dutches* of *Mines.*
>
> (2.2.12-15)

Pecunia even claims some Welsh blood, in what appears to be a mocking reference to John Dee's claim to have discovered gold in Wales. Jonson's ridicule links her bullionist conception of financial value to the pretension that led low-born 'new men' to claim noble blood. Pecunia's belief in her own inherent worth is contradicted by Penniboy Senior's notion of money as a mere sign, endlessly reproducible through the magic of compound interest. When his Porter admits to having spent sixpence on a pint of beer, the usurer explodes with indignation:

> Varlet! Know'st thou what thou hast done?
> What a consumption thou hast made of a *State?*
> It might please Heaven, (a lusty Knave, and young)
> To let thee live some *seventy* Years longer,
> Till thou art *fourscore and ten,* perhaps a *hundred.*
> Say *seventy* Years; how many times *seven* in *seventy?*
> Why *seven* times *ten* is *ten* times *seven,* mark me,
> I will demonstrate to thee on my Fingers.
> *Six-pence* in *seven* Year, (Use upon Use)
> Grows in that first *seven* Year to be a *Twelve-pence;*
> That, in the next, *Two shillings;* the third, *Four shillings*
> The fourth *seven* Year, *Eight shillings;* the fifth, *Sixteen;*
> The sixth, *Two and thirty;* the seventh, *Three pound four;*
> The eighth, *Six pound and eight;* the ninth, *Twelve pound sixteen;*
> And the tenth *seven, Five and twenty pound*
> *Twelve shillings.* This thou art fall'n from, by thy Riot!
> Should'st thou live *seventy* Years, by spending *Six-pence*
> Once i' the *seven:* But in a Day to waste it!
> There is a *Sum* that *Number* cannot reach!
>
>   (5.4.17–35)

As such speeches show, Jonson saw compound interest as comically absurd, but he nevertheless feared its effects. The reproduction of financial value, like semiotic significance in general, is endless and therefore belongs to custom rather than to nature. Everything natural has an end. Whether financial or linguistic, signs are part of *nomos*, not of phusis: they do not naturally reproduce. At the end of *The Staple of News*, Penniboy Cantor lectures his usurious sibling on Pecunia's true nature, advising him:

To use her like a Friend, not like a Slave,
Or like an *Idol*. Superstition
Doth violate the Deity it worships,
No less than Scorn doth. And believe it, *Brother*,
The Use of things is all, and not the *Store*.

(5.6.22-26)

Cantor's pun pointedly advocates the 'Use' of money in the sense
of its 'enjoyment', the realization of its natural, inherent use-value,
rather than the usurious fetishization of its artificial exchange-
value. Pecunia herself concurs. She aspires to utility, not adoration,
when she hopes '[t]hat she may still be Aid unto their Uses, / Not
Slave unto their Pleasures, or a Tyrant / Over their fair Desires'
(5.6.61-63).[25] After all, no one could understand the dangers of
attributing 'tyrannical' power to symbolic exchange-value better
than Lady Pecunia – with the possible exception of her creator.

Cookery and flattery

Jonson dedicated the last years of his life to composing lengthy,
didactic protests against the tyrannical power of symbols. This helps
to explain the otherwise incongruous presence of 'Master-Cooks' in
many of his late works. Although the connection Jonson repeatedly
draws between cookery and poetry has been traced to Athenæus
of Naucratis's third-century CE *Deipnosophista*,[26] it is surely just
as apposite to note that Plato uses cookery as his main example of
κολακεία, which English translators rendered as 'flattery'. In Plato
the concept of 'flattery' is generalized to mean any use of artificial
representation to disguise or replace natural essence. In the *Gorgias*,
Socrates points out that the natural *telos* of food is nutrition, so
that by adding non-nutritious colourings and seasonings that
appeal to the senses, 'cookery' ignores the *telos* of food and is thus
a form of 'flattery'. He describes 'personal adornment' as a similar
kind of 'flattery', since it seeks to simulate by artifice the physical
beauty that only 'gymnastics' can achieve in reality. Thus, 'flattery'
is Socrates's general term for the deceptive power of appearances:

I sum up its substance in the name flattery. This practice, as
I view it, has many branches, and one of them is cookery; which

appears indeed to be an art but, by my account of it, is not an art but a habitude or knack. I call rhetoric another branch of it, as also personal adornment and sophistry – four branches of it for four kinds of affairs.[27]

Socrates and the Sophists agree on this point. In his vindication of Helen of Troy, the Sophist Gorgias draws an analogy between the power of sexual attraction and the force of verbal rhetoric. Like magic, both of them can influence the human will with such irresistible force that the individual subjected to them is absolved of responsibility for their actions. 'If it was love that brought all these things to pass,' declares Gorgias, Helen 'escapes without difficulty from the blame for the sin alleged to have taken place' (ibid.). She was equally defenceless against the seductive force of Paris's rhetoric: 'if persuasive discourse deceived her soul, it is not on that account difficult to defend her and absolve her of responsibility, thus: discourse is a great potentate, which by the smallest and most secret body accomplishes the most divine works'.[28]

In Plato's *Gorgias*, Socrates constructs an analogy between rhetoric and cookery, claiming that they are 'parts of the same practice' and that 'rhetoric is the counterpart of cookery in the soul' (465d). If it were up to the body, Socrates explains, cookery would be judged preferable to nutrition, since its appeal is specifically to physical pleasure (465c-d). It follows that cookery is an essentially *banausic* or servile art, a mere 'knack'. Jonson focused closely on this argument towards the end of his career. In the anti-masque for the cancelled *Neptune's Triumph for the Return of Albion* (1624) a Cook informs a Poet:

[T]here is a palate of the Understanding as well as of the Senses. The Taste is taken with good relishes, the Sight with faire objects, the Hearing with delicate sounds, the Smelling with pure sents, the Feeling with softe and plump bodies, but the Understanding with all these.[29]

This Cook is a transparent surrogate for Inigo Jones, whose 'spectacles' were for Jonson the most immediately obvious and objectionable form of 'flattery'. As Richard Finkelstein observes: 'Jonson's masques repeatedly associate spectacle not just with greater power, but with increased risks to reason.'[30] The Cook impudently addresses the Poet as 'Brother' and insists that his own art is in every way poetry's equal:

> [Y]ou shall see I am a *Poet*,
> No lesse then *Cooke,* and that I find you want
> A speciall service here, an *Antimasque,*
> Ile fit you with a dish out of the Kitchin,
> Such, as I thinke, will take the present palates,
> A *metaphoricall* dish!

(325)

Jonson evidently alludes here to Petronius's *Satyricon*, where the former slave Trimalchio, a hideous parody of Epicurean gluttony, holds a feast of inconceivable vulgarity, during which he infuriates a genuine poet by repeatedly insisting on their 'brotherhood'. The exalted self-image of Trimalchio and the Cook in *Neptune's Triumph* is shared, in *The Staple of News*, by the cook Lickfinger.[31] As the poet Madrigal reports:

> He holds no Man can be a *Poet*,
> That is not a good *Cook,* to know the Palats,
> And several *tastes* o' the time. He draws all *Arts*
> Out of the *Kitchin,* but the *Art* of *Poetry*,
> Which he concludes the same with *Cookery.*

(3.3.21-25)

Like the play's sophists, Lickfinger is full of projects to institutionalize his art. He plans to found 'a Colony of Cooks' to 'convert the Cannibals' of America '[i]n one six Months, and by plain Cookery, / No Magick to't' (3.3.171-72). He protests too much, of course, since Jonson, following Plato, has already exposed cookery as magic continued by other means. Any deployment of human 'art' to alter or obscure 'nature' was, for Jonson as for Plato, to be denounced as 'flattery'. The cooks who wander through his 'dotages', like the 'money-bawds' who accompany them, illustrate the effects of 'flattery' across every aspect of Caroline culture.

An emblematic 'Master-Cook' (4.2.19) also features prominently in *Rollo, Duke of Normandy* (*c.* 1629), a collaboration between Jonson, George Chapman, John Fletcher and Phillip Massinger. As in Jonson's solo plays, this Cook indulges in absurd braggadocio about his culinary prowess, but he is eventually hanged for attempting to poison the Duke. As he is led to the gallows, a Boy in the crowd expresses disappointment at the spectacle's inadequacy: 'Are there no more?'[32] Far from taking offense, the jovial Cook jokes about the commodification of his own death: 'My Friend, if you be unprovided of a hanging / You look like a good Fellow, I can afford you / A reasonable penny-worth' (3.2.10-12). He then sings a lengthy ballad of his own composition: 'we have it here, Sir; / And so must every Merchant of our voyage, / He'll make a sweet return else on his Credit' (3.2.47-49). The lament concludes with a mordant reference to the Cook's reification as a spectacle for the audience: 'That I who at so many a Feast have pleased so many Tasters, / Should I My self come to be dress'd, a dish for you, my Masters' (3.2.86-89).

The demise of so fascinating a figure could only be temporary, and almost the first words from the Prologue in *The New Inn* (1629) assure the audience that 'we ha' the same Cook / Still' (3-4). The Prologue goes on to pre-empt the 'sick Palate' and 'nice Stomach' of potential critics, denouncing them as symptoms of the age's more general elevation of appearance above essence:

Beware to bring such Appetites to the Stage,
They do confess a weak, sick, queasie Age;
And a shrew'd grudging too of Ignorance,
When Clothes and Faces 'bove the Men advance.

(17-20)

To prefer flavour over nutrition is to judge essence by appearance, in a manner analogous to evaluating the body by the clothes, or the soul by the body. *The New Inn* is Jonson's most didactic play and, like most English didacticism from Langland to Bunyan, it resorts to allegorical personification to convey its lessons. By the third scene the Host and his permanent guest Lovell are engaged in debate about the influence of money on education. Their metaphors are invariably culinary – 'You're tart, mine Host, and talk above your seasoning' (1.3.92) – as Lovell suggests that the Host's son might train to be a page in one of England's 'Nurseries of Nobility'. In response the Host laments that 'nobility', which was once defined by inherent 'virtue', has been undermined by market forces:

Aye, that was when the Nurseries self was Noble,
And only Vertue made it, not the Market,
That Titles were not vented at the Drum,
Or common out-cry.

                                              (1.3.52-55)

Complaints against the commodification of nobility date at least
from Aristophanes's *Frogs*, where the displacement of aristocracy
by oligarchy is compared to the driving of pure gold coins out of
circulation by clipped or mixed currency, whose value was more
symbolic than inherent.[33] In 1605 Jonson had been imprisoned for
mocking James I's 'thirty-pound knights',[34] and he evidently found
the degradation of nobility by commodification of an attractive
theme. In *The Staple of News* Penniboy Senior reacts to hearing his
nephew described as 'noble' with amazement: 'Noble! how Noble!
who hath made him Noble?' The youth answers truthfully: 'Why,
my most noble Money hath, or shall' (4.3.27-28). In contrast to
the sordid Penniboys, the moral hero of *The New Inn* – Lovell –
expounds the Platonic, idealist conception of *caritas*. He condemns
the *autotelic* fetishization of the body:

My End is lost in loving of a Face,
An Eye, Lip, Nose, Hand, Foot, or other part,
Whose all is but a Statue, if the Mind
Move not, which only can make the return.

                                              (3.2.149-53)

Jonson comments on the contemporary decline of such idealism
by casting Lovell into a profound melancholy. In fact, he considers
leaving the inn altogether. As the Host has already indicated, the
'Light-Heart Inn' represents both the macrocosm of the world and
the microcosm of the individual *psyche*. Rather than allow Lovell to
leave his 'heart', the Host resolves: 'I'll pull my Sign down!' But the
power of signs cannot be dismantled so easily. When Lady Frampul
dresses the Host's adopted son as a girl, he enthusiastically urges the
lad to 'use' this new identity: 'Make your use of it ... *Frank*, become
/ What these brave Ladies would ha' you' (2.2.38-40). The play's
denoument forces the audience to ask whether this transformation
in Frank's appearance also constitutes a transubstantiation of his
essence. Is a biological man who 'presents' as a woman essentially

male or female? In J. L. Austin's terms, is Frank's announcement of his female gender a 'felicitous performative statement' or a 'false referential statement?' While disguised as a girl, Frank is married to Lord Beaufort, who is already established as an archetype of male lust – 'Gi' me the Body, if it be a good one' (3.2.156) – and of robust heterosexuality. Beaufort celebrates his sexual tastes with a classical reference:

> I have read somewhere, that man and woman,
> Were, in the first Creation, both one piece,
> And being cleft asunder, ever since,
> Love was an appetite to be rejoin'd.
>
> (3.2.79-83)

It is left to Lovell to remind him: 'It is a Fable of *Plato*'s, in his *Banquet*, / And uttered there by *Aristophanes*' (3.2.87-88). The myth of the hermaphrodite, as recounted by Plato's Aristophanes in the *Symposium*, is symbolically central to Jonson's play. As Patrick Cheney remarks: 'the New Inn at the "sign" of the Light Heart is a hermaphroditic rebus (or sign or symbol) in which male and female meet to create the required wholeness'.[35] Frank's male gender is soon revealed, to Beaufort's amusing horror, and a typical Renaissance comedy might have ended there. Jonson gives the plot an additional twist, however, with the further revelation that Frank is in reality Laetitia, Lady Frampul's long-lost sister. Frank's female gender, which the audience has been led to assume is merely a disguise, turns out to be true. Or does it? After all, the audience remains aware that the actor playing Frank is in reality a boy. The multiple layers of appearance and reality leave Frank's essential gender undecidable. In postmodernist parlance, we have entered the condition of *hyper-reality* and the demise of natural gender among the first consequences. Lovell still doggedly follows Plato, maintaining that love's proper *telos* is spiritual union:

> And where it starts or steps aside from this,
> It is a meer degenerous appetite,
> A lost, oblique, deprav'd affection,
> And bears no mark or character of Love.
>
> (3.2.166-69)

With equal predictability, Lady Frampul plots to win the argument by 'flattery'. She pretends to be won over by Lovell's Platonism, prompting Pru the Chambermaid to exclaim: 'Well feign'd, my Lady: now her Parts begin!' (3.2.177). In her comic ignorance, however, Lady Frampul alleges her conversion in precisely the terms most likely to offend Platonic sensibilities. She extols the magical effects of Lovell's rhetoric, his 'Alchimy / Of Love, or Language' (3.2.170-71). She relishes his words in blatantly sensual terms: 'let min' ear / Be feasted still, and filled with this Banquet! / No sense can ever surfeit on such truth!' (3.2.201-03). She conceives of Lovell's *caritas* as a religious idol: 'What Penance shall I do to be receiv'd, / And reconcil'd to the Church of Love? / Go on Procession, bare-foot, to his Image' (3.2.218-20).

Unsurprisingly she fails to deceive Lovell, who denounces her for practising 'the art of flattery', noting that she is an 'actor' and that 'all is personated, / And counterfeit comes from her!'(3.2.265-66). Over the course of Lady Frampul's apparently heartfelt speeches, however, some observers have started to have their doubts. Lord Latimer asks: 'But do you think she plays? ... Sure she is serious!' (3.2.214 ... 3.2.260). Just as Frank turns out to be female in biology as well as in presentation, it eventually transpires that Lady Frampul has indeed been sincerely converted by Lovell's preaching. Once again, what seemed to be false turns out to be true – or rather, the polarity between truth and falsehood collapses. Lady Frampul reproaches Pru for adhering to their original deception:

LADY FRAMPUL
    You'll let a Lady wear her Masque, Pru.
PRUDENCE
    But how do I know, when her Ladiship is pleas'd
    To leave it off, except she tell me so?
LADY FRAMPUL
    You might ha' known that by my looks, and language,
    Had you been or regardant, or observant.

                                        (4.4.297-301)

Jonson's point is that in a world of performative signs, where appearance is systematically confounded with essence, there is no effective difference between acting and sincerity. Pru is unwilling to give up her belief in the distinction: 'I swear, I thought you had dissembled, Madam, / And doubt you do so yet' (4.4.312-13). Lady Frampul's furious response – 'Dull, stupid, Wench!' (4.4.314) – shows how violently she deplores Pru's stubborn differentiation between her 'looks, and language' and her interior intention. For Lady Frampul has no interior intention: performance, she insists, is everything. The London public's uncomprehending response to *The New Inn* convinced Jonson that Lady Frampul's self-conception was fast becoming universal. In the 'Ode to Himself', written as consolation for the play's hostile reception, Jonson returns to his favourite culinary metaphors:

> Say that thou pour'st them Wheat,
>   And they will Acorns Eat:
> 'Twere simple Fury still thy self to wast
>   On such as have no tast.
> To offer them a surfeit of pure Bread,
>   Whose Appetites are dead!
> No, give them Grains their Fill,
>   Husks, Draff to drink and swill.
> If they love Lees, and leave the lusty Wine,
> Envy them not their Palats with the Swine.
>
> (11-20)

Although Cordelia Zuckerman is right to find 'something important in the failure [of *The New Inn*] itself that Jonson wanted to emphasize',[36] Jonson had been describing his art in the vocabulary of the kitchen at least since the Prologue to *Epicene* (1609): 'Our wishes, like to those make public feasts, / Are not to please the cook's taste, but the guests' (8-9). If sophisticated critics with 'cunning palates' attend the play, Jonson asks that they indulge his appeal to lower tastes: 'to present all custard, or all tart, / And have no other meats, to bear a part. / Or to want bread, and salt, were but course art' (16-18). Twenty years and many disappointments later, the embittered poet deploys the same metaphor to opposite effect. No longer does the 'cook' claim that his main aim is the pleasure of his 'guests'. In the Prologue to *Epicene* Jonson was happy to envisage the audience feasting from a metaphorical doggie-bag: 'you shall eat / A week at ord'naries, on his broken meat' (27). In the 'Ode to Himself', by contrast, the same metaphor is used to show that the guests are no longer worthy of the feast: 'who the Relish of these Guests will fit, / Needs set them but the Alms-basket of Wit' (29-30). Jonson 'loathed' his 'age' because he despised its taste. As his 'dotages' demonstrate, however, he never ceased exhorting his audience to demand more than table-scraps.

Notes

1   Ben Jonson, *The Alchemist* ed. Alvin B. Kernan (New Haven, CT: Yale University Press, 1974).

2   See Introduction, 1–2.

3   See Jacques Derrida, 'Plato's Pharmacy', in *Dissemination*, trans. and ed. Barbara Johnson (Cambridge University Press, 1981), 61–171.

4   Gorgias of Leontini, *Encomium of Helen*, trans. Brian R. Donovan (1999). Retrieved 31 October 2021 from https://faculty.bemidjistate.edu/bdonovan/helen.html.

5   Ben Jonson, *The New Inn* (1.1.3-6) (Folio 1692). Retrieved 4 February 2022 from https://hollowaypages.com/jonson1692inn.htm. Subsequent references are to this edition.

6   In *Bartholomew Fair* a Scrivener opens the action by announcing that 'it shall be lawful for any man to judge his sixpen'worth, his twelvepen'worth, so to his eighteen-pence, two shillings, half a crown, to the value of his place' (Ben Jonson, *The Alchemist and Other Plays*, ed. Gordon Campbell, Oxford University Press, 1995, 330). At the start of Act 2 in *The Magnetic Lady* the critic Damplay complains that 'I see no reason, if I come here, and give my eighteen pence, or two shillings for my seat, but I should take it out in censure, on the stage'. Speaking for the players, a Boy responds: 'Your two shilling worth is allow'd you: but you will take your ten shilling worth, your twenty shilling worth, and more' (2.Int.59-64).

7   Ben Jonson, 'Ode to Himself', in *Complete Poems*, ed. George Parfitt (London: Penguin Classics, 1988), 1–2, 160.

8   Larry S. Champion, *Ben Jonson's Dotages: A Reconsideration of the Late Plays* (University of Kentucky Press, 1967), 4.

9   T. S. Eliot, 'The Metaphysical Poets' (1917) in *Selected Essays, 1917–1932* (New York: Harcourt, Brace and Co., 1932), 242. Although the phrase is Eliot's, the idea that modernity institutes a fragmentation of experience can be traced at least as far back as Hegel, and arguably to seventeenth-century English 'political economy', which first erected a moral cordon sanitaire around self-interested or 'economic' behaviour.

10   Samuel Jonson, *Lives of the Most Eminent English Poets*, vol. 1
      (London: J. Ferguson, 1819), 19.
11   Ben Jonson, *Discoveries* in *Critical Essays of the Seventeenth
      Century*, vol. 1, ed. J. E. Spingarn (Clarendon Press: Oxford,
      1908), 49.
12   Douglas Bruster, 'The Representation Market of Early Modern
      England', *Renaissance Drama* 41, no. 1/2 (2013): 1–23, 13.
13   Ben Jonson, *The Magnetic Lady* (Folio 1692). Retrieved 4 February
      2022 from https://www.hollowaypages.com/jonson1692magnetic.
      htm. Subsequent references are to this edition.
14   Ben Jonson, *The Staple of News* (Folio 1692). Retrieved 4 February
      2022 from https://hollowaypages.com/jonson1692news.htm.
      Subsequent references are to this edition.
15   As late as 1960 Jonas Barish claimed that Jonson's 'resumption of
      old-fashioned themes' in *The New Inn* and *The Magnetic Lady*
      'testifies either to a decline in his experimental energy or to a more
      aggressive wooing of his dwindling audience'. *Ben Jonson and the
      Language of Prose Comedy* (Harvard University Press, 1960), 241.
      Champion (1967) was among the first to recognize *The Magnetic
      Lady* as 'a dramatic portrayal of his *ars poetica* ... a remarkable
      summary of Jonson's comic technique' (105). Yet four years
      later Ronald McFarland took issue with him, finding the play 'of
      little interest in terms of plot or character delineation'. 'Jonson's
      Magnetic Lady and the Reception of Gilbert's De Magnete',
      Studies in English Literature, 1500–1900 11, no. 2 (1971):
      283–93, 288.
16   In 1906 W. W. Greg declared it 'little more than a cento made up
      of borrowings from earlier works'. 'Jonson's "Staple of News",'
      The Modern Language Review 1, no. 4 (1906): 327.
17   Don E. Wayne, '"Pox on Your Distinction!" Humanist Reformation
      and Deformations of the Everyday in *The Staple of News*', in
      Renaissance Culture and the Everyday, ed. Patricia Fumerton and
      Simon Hunt (University of Pennsylvania Press, 1999), 67–91, 70.
18   David Hawkes, 'Bawdry, Cuckoldry and Usury in Early Modernity
      and Postmodernity', *English Literary Renaissance* 50, no. 1 (Winter,
      2020): 61–9.
19   Ben Jonson, Epigram LVII, 'On Bawds and Usurers'. Retrieved
      4 February 2022 from http://www.luminarium.org/sevenlit/jonson/
      epigram57.htm.
20   David Kay, *Ben Jonson: A Literary Life* (London: Macmillan, 1995),
      166. See also Jane Rickard, 'A Divided Jonson?: Art and Truth in
      The Staple of News', *English Literary Renaissance*, 42, no. 2 (2012):
      294–316.

21   Cobrun Gum, *The Aristophanic Comedies of Ben Jonson: A Comparative Study of Jonson and Aristophanes* (De Gruyter, 1969, 2015), 190.

22   Richard Levin, '"The Staple of News," the Society of Jeerers and the Canters' College', *Philological Quarterly* 44, no. 4 (1965): 445.

23   Ben Jonson, *News from the New World* (1621). Retrieved 4 February 2022 from https://math.dartmouth.edu/~matc/Readers/renaissance.astro/9.1.Moon.html. Subsequent references are to this edition.

24   Karl Marx, *Capital*, vol. 1, trans. Ben Fowkes (London: Penguin, 1990), 126n4.

25   See Stephen Deng, 'Global Economy: Ben Jonson's The Staple of News and the Ethics of Mercantilism', in *Global Traffic*, ed. Barbara Sebek and Stephen Deng (New York: Palgrave Macmillan, 2008), 245–6.

26   See Don K. Hedrick, 'Cooking for the Anthropophagi: Jonson and His Audience', *Studies in English Literature, 1500–1900* 17, no. 2 (1977): 233–45, 236.

27   Plato, *Gorgias*, 463a-b. Retrieved 11 January 2021 from Perseus: http://www.perseus.tufts.edu/hopper/text?doc=Perseus%3Atext%3A 1999.01.0178%3Atext%3DGorg.%3Apage%3D463.

28   Georgias of Leontini, 'Encomium of Helen' trans. Brian Donovan. Retrieved 5 January 2022 from https://faculty.bemidjistate.edu/bdonovan/helen.html. As Matthew Gumpert comments, Gorgias 'seeks to justify the seductive power of appearance and to equate it with the persuasive power of language'. *Grafting Helen: The Abduction of the Classical Past* (University of Wisconsin Press, 2001), 21.

29   Ben Jonson, 'Neptune's Triumph for the Return of Albion', in *Ben Jonson's Masques and Entertainments*, ed. Henry Morley (London: Routledge, 1890), 320. Subsequent references are to this edition.

30   Richard Finkelstein, 'Ben Jonson on Spectacle', *Comparative Drama* 21, no. 2 (1987): 103–14, 107.

31   See Bruce Boehrer, *The Fury of Men's Gullets: Ben Jonson and the Digestive Canal* (University of Pennsylvania Press, 1997), 138.

32   Ben Jonson, Phillip Massinger, John Fletcher and George Chapman, 'The Tragedy of Rollo, Duke of Normandy', in *The Dramatic Works of Ben Jonson and Beaumont and Fletcher* (London: John Stockdale, 1811), 3.2.8.

33   Since the seventeenth century this has been known as 'Gresham's Law'. See David Hawkes, 'Thomas Gresham's Law, Jane Shore's Mercy: Value and Class in the Plays of Thomas Heywood', *English Literary History* 77, no. 1 (Spring 2010): 25–44.

34   George Chapman, Ben Jonson and John Marston, *Eastward Ho*
      (1605), 4.1.173.
35   See Patrick Cheney, 'Jonson's "The New Inn" and Plato's Myth of
      the Hermaphrodite', *Renaissance Drama* 14 (1983): 173–94.
36   Cordelia Zuckerman, 'Not Clothes but Brains: Display, Status and
      Reading in Ben Jonson's *The New Inn*', *Philological Quarterly* 93,
      no. 4 (Fall 2014), 483–506, 483.

Works cited

Barish, Jonas. *Ben Jonson and the Language of Prose Comedy*. Harvard
    University Press, 1960).
Boehrer, Bruce. *The Fury of Men's Gullets: Ben Jonson and the Digestive
    Canal*. University of Pennsylvania Press, 1997.
Bruster, Douglas. 'The Representation Market of Early Modern England.'
    Renaissance Drama 41, no. 1/2 (2013): 1–23.
Champion, Larry S. *Ben Jonson's Dotages: A Reconsideration of the Late
    Plays*. University of Kentucky Press, 1967.
Cheney, Patrick. 'Jonson's *The New Inn* and Plato's Myth of the
    Hermaphrodite.' *Renaissance Drama* 14 (1983): 173–94.
Deng, Stephen. 'Global Œconomy: Ben Jonson's *The Staple of News* and
    the Ethics of Mercantilism,' in Barbara Sebek and Stephen Deng (ed.)
    Global Traffic. Palgrave Macmillan: New York, 2008.
Derrida, Jacques. *Dissemination*, trans. and ed. Barbara Johnson.
    Cambridge University Press, 1981.
Eliot, T.S. *Selected Essays, 1917–1932*. New York: Harcourt, Brace and
    Co., 1932.
Finkelstein, Richard. 'Ben Jonson on Spectacle', *Comparative Drama* 21:2
    (1987): 103–14.
Gorgias. *Encomium of Helen*, trans. Brian R. Donovan (1999). Retrieved
    31 October 2021: https://faculty.bemidjistate.edu/bdonovan/helen.html.
Greg, W.W. 'Jonson's "*Staple of News*."' *The Modern Language Review*
    1:4 (1906): 327.
Gum, Cobrun. *The Aristophanic Comedies of Ben Jonson: A Comparative
    Study of Jonson and Aristophanes*. De Gruyter, 1969, 2015.
Gumpert, Matthew. 'Grafting Helen: The Abduction of the Classical Past.'
    University of Wisconsin Press, 2001.
Hawkes, David. 'Thomas Gresham's Law, Jane Shore's Mercy: Value and
    Class in the Plays of Thomas Heywood', *English Literary History* 77:1
    (Spring, 2010), 25–44.
Hawkes, David. 'Bawdry, Cuckoldry and Usury in Early Modernity and
    Postmodernity.' *English Literary Renaissance* 50:1 (Winter, 2020), 61–69.

Hedrick, Don K. 'Cooking for the Anthropophagi: Jonson and His Audience.' *Studies in English Literature, 1500–1900* 17:2 (1977), 233–45.

Johnson, Samuel. *Lives of the Most Eminent English Poets* vol.1. London: J. Ferguson, 1819.

Jonson, Ben *The New Inn* (Folio 1692). Retrieved 04 February 2022 from https://hollowaypages.com/jonson1692inn.htm.

Jonson, Ben. *The Alchemist and Other Plays* ed. Gordon Campbell. Oxford University Press, 1995.

Jonson, Ben. *Complete Poems* ed. George Parfitt. London: Penguin Classics, 1988.

Jonson, Ben. 'Discoveries' in *Critical Essays of the Seventeenth Century* vol. 1, ed. J. E. Spingarn. Clarendon Press: Oxford, 1908.

Jonson, Ben. *The Magnetic Lady* (Folio 1692). Retrieved 04 February 2022 from https://www.hollowaypages.com/jonson1692magnetic.htm.

Jonson, Ben, Phillip Massinger, John Fletcher and George Chapman, *The Tragedy of Rollo, Duke of Normandy*, in *The Dramatic Works of Ben Jonson and Beaumont and Fletcher*. London: John Stockdale, 1811.

Jonson, Ben. *The Staple of News* (Folio 1692). Retrieved 04 February 2022 from https://hollowaypages.com/jonson1692news.htm.

Jonson, Ben. *News from the New World* (1621). Retrieved 04 February 2022 from https://math.dartmouth.edu/~matc/Readers/renaissance.astro/9.1.Moon.html.

Jonson, Ben. 'Neptune's Triumph for the Return of Albion', in *Ben Jonson's Masques and Entertainments*, ed. Henry Morley. London: Routledge, 1890.

Kay, David. *Ben Jonson: A Literary Life*. London: Macmillan, 1995.

Levin, Richard. '"The Staple of News," the Society of Jeerers and the Canters' College', *Philological Quarterly* 44:4 (1965).

Marx, Karl. *Capital*, vol. 1, trans. Ben Fowkes. London: Penguin, 1990.

McFarland, Ronald. 'Jonson's *Magnetic Lady* and the Reception of Gilbert's *De Magnete*.' *Studies in English Literature, 1500–1900* 11:2 (1971): 283–93.

Rickard, Jane. 'A Divided Jonson?: Art and Truth in *The Staple of News*.' *English Literary Renaissance* 42:2 (2012), 294–316.

Wayne, Don E. '"Pox on Your Distinction!" Humanist Reformation and Deformations of the Everyday in *The Staple of News*', in *Renaissance Culture and the Everyday*, ed. Patricia Fumerton and Simon Hunt. University of Pennsylvania Press, 1999, 67–91.

Zuckerman, Cordelia. 'Not Clothes but Brains: Display, Status and Reading in Ben Jonson's *The New Inn*.' *Philological Quarterly* 93:4 (Fall 2014), 483–506.

5

Coins, counterfeit and queer threat in *The Comedy of Errors*

Melissa Vipperman-Cohen

*O villain, thou hast stolen both mine office and my name; /
The one ne'er got me credit, the other mickle blame.*

(3.1.44-45)

Queering the *Comedy*

By exploring the conflation of illicit sex and dubious economics through 'queer' practices such as sodomy and counterfeiting, Shakespeare's *The Comedy of Errors* warns against the precariousness of credit culture and its reliance on reputation. In coding affective relationships and sexual experiences through economic language, Shakespeare conflates them, so that the threats of improper economics and unnatural sexuality grow ever more entangled and intertwined. Despite the Syracusans' insistence on the threats posed by Ephesian 'dark-working sorcerers' and 'soul-killing witches', who deceive citizens and strangers alike, the true threat to Ephesian society is the transformative, even demonic magic of the city's emergent representation-based economy with its sinister ability to replicate, and even to replace the human individual (1.2.99-100).

The play highlights the promise and peril of a money-based economy, while prioritizing the male, affective homosocial relationships upon which such an economy is predicated. It reveals how moneylending and the culture of credit supersede the affective bonds of the heterosexual family structure, prioritizing instead the homosocial production of male wealth signified by figurative gold 'progeny' and coinage. The threat of the counterfeit coin, and by extension the counterfeit character, is recognized as a danger to both the burgeoning credit economy and familial stability. Despite the seeming levity of the play's finale, *The Comedy of Errors* challenges the growing significance of credit culture through its treatment of the different kinds of wealth made possible by such a system.

The Antipholi's arrival at the thriving trade city of Ephesus, and their farcical yet crucial disruption of its economy, bring to light the hidden connections between counterfeiting, conjuring and queerness. The twins form a particularly queer anomaly that goes beyond the heterosexual/homosexual binary. Described through the metaphor of counterfeit coins circulating in and disrupting the Ephesian credit economy, they present an unnatural form of generation, which is revealed through the growing threat of the city's dark, sodomitical witchcraft, and culminates in the figure of the sinister Doctor Pinch. The play gestures towards the tenuousness of credit and reputation, suggests the folly of basing identity on possessions that can be taken away, and generally emphasizes the simultaneous difficulty and danger of the Delphic Oracle's instruction to 'know thyself'. Is there even a self to know?

Money, magic and the world as marketplace

The Comedy of Errors (1594) is concerned with the construction of selfhood in a commodified world created by credit, defined by money, and filled with false copies of both. The play opens in the city of Ephesus, a historical centre of Greek commerce and trade noted for its exceptional wealth.[1] The city was situated on several vital maritime and land trade routes, connecting the east with the west, and the north with the south.[2] Ephesus was rich in coin specie, and its location on the Aegean Sea made it a thriving trade hub. In fact, modern coinage originated in Ephesus's neighbour city of Lydia in the seventh century BCE.[3] The city carries deep biblical significance as a place of religious and mystical power. It was one of the wealthiest and most powerful centres of Asia Minor in the second and first centuries BCE and CE. Its wealth was evident in the famous prominence of gold and silver statues and images, many dedicated to the goddess Artemis, and the city was deeply committed to its identity as the keeper and protector of the Artemis cult.[4]

To Christians, Ephesus became infamous for its association with idolatry and with powerful pagan magic in general. The Apostle Paul visited the city in an attempt to turn the citizens away from Artemis in the first century CE. Although he convinced some of his audience to abjure their magic, Acts 19 details how 'many also of them [...] used curious arts' to practise sorcery with the aid of expensive books worth 'fifty thousand pieces of silver' (Acts 19.19-20). Acts describes how a prominent silversmith named Demetrius, whose profession dominated the city through the manufacture of icons of Artemis, disdained Paul's work and encouraged his compatriots to reject the Christian's teachings. Paul's denunciation of the worship of icons, 'the works of men's hands', directly threatened the local economy, which was completely dependent on the Artemis cult. Ephesians knew that their skill and their art had power to bring in money, and this automatically placed them in opposition to Christian iconoclasm.

The characters in Shakespeare's play describe themselves and their relationships in strikingly numismatic language, evidently understanding their social standing, if not their very identities, as profoundly connected to financial value. From the opening scene, it is made clear that gold and money are vital to the city, its larger trade networks and its citizenry. An aged merchant, Egeon, has travelled from the rival city of Syracuse seeking his long-lost wife, one of his twin sons, and a slave, who coincidentally is also a twin. However, Syracuse and Ephesus are locked in deadly conflict, and it is illegal for citizens to travel between them. When they attempt to pass through Syracuse, Ephesians are put to death if they lack coins or 'guilders to redeem their lives' in the amount of 'a thousand marks' (1.1.8, 21).[5] Despite its comedic, at times farcical nature, *The Comedy of Errors* presents a nuanced portrait of a trading merchant's precarious social and financial status. The consequences of failure are dire. They include loss of family, financial ruin and death. Kent Cartwright notes that

> the play's mysterious circulation of words and objects is matched by the market economy's circulation of obligations and goods. *Errors* is saturated with merchants ... the comedy's backdrop is a trade war; a luxury commodity plays a key role in the plot; and an international trader's urgency to collect a debt spurs the action into crisis.
>
> (39)

Critics such as Colette Gordon, Curtis Perry, Douglas Bruster, Shankar Raman and Thomas Cosgrove have pointed out the play's interest in such economic matters as specie, value, money, mercantilism, exchange, credit, liquidity and commodification. The character of the counterfeit is subjected to an especially complicated and contradictory analysis, which forms the main subject of this chapter.

The culture of credit and reputation

Much like the English economy of the sixteenth century, the world of Ephesus relies on credit. The issue of money begins and ends the play; from Egeon's mercantile ventures and his desperation to find someone to loan him a thousand marks, through the constant movement and confusion of gold pieces across the stage, to the Duke's final pardon. Much critical work has already been done to establish how *Errors* negotiates the market's reliance on lending and credit. By incorporating a queer theoretical lens to supplement these economic approaches, I intend to show that the play expresses anxiety regarding not only the new social relationships shaped by credit, but also the sexual practices implicated in these processes. In addition to building on Will Fisher's conceptualization of the connections between illegitimate money (such as counterfeit coins) and illicit sexual practices (such as sodomy), my argument is influenced by Christine Varnado's account of the construction of queerness as the object of one's deepest fears. In her exploration of witch-hunt literature, Varnado conceptualizes queerness as 'an affectively supercharged cycle ... projective and attributive; it constructs queerness in another, and by the paranoid logic of implication, it reveals its own secret investments'.[6] This suspicion of otherness, paranoid projection and recognition of oneself in one's opposite all recall the counterfeiting twins' behaviour in *The Comedy of Errors*. There is more to commodification than alienation and circulation. Antipholus of Syracuse alludes to a yet greater danger, one that threatens to spread 'queer' conceptions of identity throughout society: the notion of the individual as *its own counterfeit*.

By tracing the circulation of gold in the forms of both jewellery and coins, the play reveals the irreconcilable tension between the necessity of engaging with the capitalist credit economy and the moral and practical peril of involvement in trade and usury. Antipholus of Ephesus purchases a gold chain for his wife in order to ameliorate their tense marriage and, as it moves from hand to hand, the chain reveals the complicated role played by specie in the Ephesian (and by implication the English) economies. More importantly, however, the chain underscores the new bonds of obligation that undergird capitalist exchange – and its progress shows how violating those obligations can disrupt a socio-economic system that prioritizes figurative, homosocial chains of friendship and economic connection.

Through its farcical, repeated cases of mistaken identity, *The Comedy of Errors* explores how the Ephesian economy (and by extension the broader Mediterranean market) is predicated on surprisingly unstable credit exchanges. These financial exchanges turn out to be more important to the city's social and affective systems than relations of marriage or biological family. In his foundational work on 'the culture of credit', Craig Muldrew argues that English capitalism expanded rapidly in the sixteenth century, thanks to a new kind of socio-economic value, predicated on an individual or household's reputation and credit, which allowed people to lend with trust in both small, informal exchanges and much larger, international transactions.[7] To be a 'creditor' in early modern England was to occupy a position with significant social, economic and legal weight. Like Muldrew, Laura Kolb argues that, because specie was so limited in the face of rapidly expanding commerce, credit was the only abundant currency. Yet it was also an extremely individualized method of evaluation, which varied greatly from person to person, and needed to be constantly renegotiated. Kolb claims that borrowing and lending practices based on credit and reputation reified interpersonal relationships. The extension of credit had to be mediated through affective, intimate social structures among friends and acquaintances.[8] One's credit became a currency as valuable as specie, except that it was outwardly facing, public and highly vulnerable to damage. Indeed, the very concept of 'reputation' was intended to express creditworthiness.

The practice of extending one's credit and reputation to another man was imbued with emotional, even erotic significance, due to its connection with homosocial friendship, which in turn was coded with significant romantic and sexual undertones. Early modern male friendship was so deeply immersed in emotion as to be associated with marriage. Alan Bray traces the imbrication of eroticism, both physical and emotional, throughout the bonds of male, homosocial friendship, pointing out that such friendship was profoundly public, deeply codified, and psychologically significant. It both influenced and was influenced by myriad social, political, religious and economic structures that extended well beyond what modern culture regards as the erotic sphere.[9] Bray stresses that friendship was not a solely private or personal relationship but a public exchange, constructed through performative rituals, oaths, emotional and physical intimacy and mutual obligations: much like marriage.[10] It was crucial that both parties maintained a perceived lack of self-interest or transactional advancement, as well as a hospitable demeanour. A friend's financial, social and political interests were inextricably intertwined with one's own, and committing to a friendship held the potential for significant financial and social profit or loss.[11]

The chain

Shakespeare fuses affective with economic relations using the plot device of the gold chain. Antipholus of Ephesus engages the aptly named goldsmith Angelo to make a 'carcanet' for his wife Adriana, supposedly as an apology for his infidelity (3.1.4). The ornament is more than just jewellery, however; the chain's greater significance lies in its revelation of the credit exchanges involved in its creation and distribution. This credit mechanism was vital to the Ephesian social and economic spheres. Paralleling the figurative chains of economic obligation that characterize the Ephesian economy, Antipholus's chain moves through the play as the physical expression of abstract market interactions. The irony is that, during this process, the metaphorical chains of obligation that produced the chain are repeatedly disrupted, resulting in severe consequences and punishment for several characters – both those that lend money or goods to others and those who seek to take advantage of the trust that others have placed in them.

Antipholus extends a highly stylized invitation to Angelo and the merchant Balthazar to join him for dinner, thus ostentatiously demonstrating his humility and friendship, before realizing that he is locked out of his house. Not knowing that his twin is inside with Adriana, and furious at finding his home sealed against him, Antipholus threatens to bestow the chain he is about to receive on 'a wench of excellent discourse' in order to 'spite' Adriana (3.1.109,118). In farcical fashion, however, the merchant Angelo accidentally bestows the chain on a bewildered Antipholus of Syracuse, indicating that he will accept payment for it in the future, thus putting his trust in Antipholus of Ephesus's credit-worthiness. Although Antipholus of Syracuse begs him to 'receive the money now', Angelo insists on deferred payment, so that Antipholus of Syracuse ultimately accepts what he thinks of as a 'golden gift' (3.2.181,188). Angelo simply respects the tenets of what he believes to be their credit relationship, yet Antipholus of Syracuse takes advantage of another's reputation (not realizing that it is his twin's). It is not surprising that Angelo does not require immediate repayment for his commodity – Antipholus of Ephesus's reputation is so valuable in the city that he himself has borrowed against it.

As it moves between characters and around the stage, the chain comes to signify the increasingly precarious chains of credit and obligation that bind Ephesian society together. At the beginning of Act 4, we find that Angelo has borrowed money from a second merchant, a sum so great that he is threatened with imprisonment if he does not repay it. He has taken out this loan because Antipholus of Ephesus maintains a 'very reverend reputation' and 'credit infinite', so great that '[h]is word might bear [Angelo's] wealth at any time' (5.1.5, 6, 8). Yet to Angelo's eyes Antipholus refuses to satisfy his debts, jeopardizing his own position. Even as Angelo pleads with Antipholus of Ephesus to '[c]onsider how it stands upon [his] credit' when he refuses to pay for the chain, noting that it 'touches [him] in reputation' as well, he is finally forced to request his arrest (4.1.68, 71). As soon as one link in the chain of credit breaks, as when Antipholus of Ephesus refuses to live up to his good name and pay his debts, the whole system collapses. A confused and angry Ephesian Antipholus pays the usual penalty for disobeying the rules of the credit culture: he is sent to debtor's prison.

Counterfeit – 'The One So Like the Other / As Could Not Be Distinguished but by Names'

The twins' names and appearances do more than cause amusing cases of mistaken identity. Their doubleness mirrors the double nature of commodities and money. As Cosgrove puts it, the concept of the 'double body … is the key to understanding the magical nature of money in The Comedy of Errors' (153). Furthermore, the confusion that the Antipholi bring to the play functions as a physical embodiment of the social anxiety surrounding coining and counterfeit money, the replication and altering of specie. The circulation of gold specie and numismatic signs in the sixteenth century gave rise to an expanded understanding of exchange-value and created an opportunity to redefine or 'queer' value itself.

Their persistent inability to define gold as either use-value for its worth as metal, or as exchange-value for its capacity to represent other commodities, troubled many economists struggling to understand the new 'status of representation'.[12] David Hawkes argues that '[t]he change in the attitude toward money … was part of a shift in the status of representation in general, and it was understood as such by the people of the time'.[13] For example, Francis Bacon believed that the world as it was perceived by the senses was true and knowable, but also that man's words do not accurately represent it. The expression of experience through systems of signification is inherently flawed, and to imagine otherwise is idolatrous:

> For man is but the servant and interpreter of nature: what he does and what he knows is only what he has observed of nature's order in fact or in thought; beyond this he knows nothing and can do nothing.... Men believe that their reason governs words, but it is also true that words react upon the understanding; and this it is that has rendered philosophy and the sciences sophistical and inactive.[14]

For Bacon, then, language possessed the power to act upon, and to distort, the rational 'understanding'. His recognition of the abstract power of verbal signs coincided, historically and conceptually, with symbolic exchange-value's acquisition of a practical power that was independent of the precious metal in which it was embodied. Stephen Deng points out that, although early modern money primarily took the form of material specie, the question of whether money's power consisted in intrinsic worth or extrinsic value was widely prevalent.[15] Hawkes describes how the prospect of financial value's independence brought deep discomfort to many early modern minds:

> [F]or most literate Englishmen, the autonomy of value was one manifestation of the same tendency that could be observed in religious idolatry and carnal sensuality in all its forms. It is this totalizing perspective that allows the thinkers of the early modern period an insight into the spiritual and ethical implications of commodity fetishism that has largely been lost to our own epoch.[16]

For example, the commodification of coins caused severe political and economic frustration. Since English gold coins were more valuable and rarer than silver in international trading, they were highly sought after and even purchased as commodities. Akinobu Kuroda reminds us that, although the influx of both gold and silver increased 'interregional trade', gold was clearly more valuable and more limited in quantity.[17] Under Elizabeth, the English mint was relatively successful in regulating silver coin and bullion production, although the country's stores of gold specie were at an historic low.

There were large quantities of foreign gold coins in circulation, however, and it was particularly problematic that many looked remarkably similar to the English gold coins known as 'Angels'. Between 1558 and 1603, growing numbers of English merchants complained that the foreign gold coins in circulation looked too much like Angels to differentiate between them, and that they were therefore losing profit on counterfeit coins.

Shakespeare's twins are the living embodiments of one of the crown's greatest economic and political problems: counterfeiting. The twins are counterfeits of one another, at once interchangeable and entirely different. Their internal selves are unknowable, and external appearance is their only legible value. When Antipholus of Syracuse worries that he 'confounds himself', he is akin to the virtually identical coins in his purse; he cannot distinguish himself from another, and he is therefore in danger of losing his own self. Following Aristotle's association of usury with reproduction, Elizabethans often connected children with coining, as analogous forms of generation. Just as the crown could legitimize metal and transform it into money, so a man was thought to stamp his essence and legitimacy on his children. Egeon's twin sons epitomize the analogy. They are 'the one so like the other / As could not be distinguished but by names' (1.1.51-2). Yet the plot depends on the point that the twins are *not* essentially the same, though they may be outwardly indistinguishable – much like the Angel coins so often counterfeited that Elizabeth was forced to issue multiple edicts against them for debasing financial value. Although the twins are truly Egeon's biological children, their symbolic role as counterfeits circulating in the Ephesian social marketplace has dire implications. As they soon discover, the market demands that the individual subject voluntarily relinquish the notion of itself as unique, and instead agree to lose itself, like coins being rubbed against one another in a purse, 'sweating' until they are diminished and intermingled.[18]

Queer threat: Counterfeiting as sexual crime

While the onstage exchanges of the gold chain demonstrate the complexity and precariousness of the credit economy, the Antipholi embody a queer threat to both the social and the economic spheres.

Like counterfeit coins, their unregulated circulation is perceived as a devilish magic, whose influence grows as the play progresses, and their distinct identities remain unacknowledged. As these counterfeits circulate, they 'queer' the Ephesian economy and affect those that participate in it through the connections among counterfeiting, sodomy and demonic magic. Ephesian exchanges become unnatural, and the credit system that should be their foundation is undermined.

By analogy with the creation and circulation of false coins, the twins also personify production without procreation, a queer concept that disrupts the play's economies by introducing unnatural and unacceptable financial and sexual possibilities. As Fisher notes in his work on 'queer money', 'unnatural sexualities and unnatural economics were coded through each other' in early modernity.[19] The queering of Ephesian commerce is reflected in the Syracusans' growing fear of magic. They believe that the sorcery surrounding them is becoming stronger and more dangerous, as Antipholus receives gifts that seem too good to be true, while Dromio receives the attentions of a mysterious kitchen maid. The frantic Dromio demands: 'Am I Dromio? Am I your man? Am I myself?' after declaring that 'she, being a very beastly creature, lays claim to me' (3.2.72-3, 85). Dromio describes the woman as a globe encompassing the foulest foreign lands, who knew 'what privy marks I had about me' so intimately that he fled her 'as a witch' (3.2.147, 149). Witches were often thought to have knowledge of a person's intimate body parts, and Dromio is terrified of a woman who is not a woman, but either a monstrous man or a witch, who seems to know everything about him without his understanding how. He experiences the witch's sexual claim to his body as a challenge to his very identity.

Fisher observes that the language of minting coins was highly sexualized, as it was thought to involve male form being imprinted or 'stamped' on female matter.[20] The production of counterfeit coins was described in similarly sexualized terms. The authority to grant value to coins was supposed to rest solely with the monarch and to usurp that power by counterfeiting was nothing short of treason.[21] The punishment for counterfeiting also involved highly physical, arguably sexualized acts – those who coined falsely were often castrated.[22] Similarly the play conflates the confusion of the Antipholi with cuckoldry. When Dromio returns home after failing to convince his master to accompany him, he reveals that Antipholus of Ephesus is 'horn-mad'. He alludes to the wrong Antipholus returning and threatening to cuckold the real one with Adriana, who accuses Antipholus of Syracuse of lying to her for sport: 'How ill agrees it with your gravity / To counterfeit thus grossly with your slave' (2.2.174-5). As living embodiments of the counterfeit, the twins constitute a clear and present danger to the sexual, economic and even the linguistic stability of Ephesus.

Sodomy and witchcraft

The Aristotelian connection between usury and sodomy is well known. Both are deemed unnatural forms of procreation, conjuring artificial generation out of acts that are naturally non-reproductive. Since both sodomy and usury were considered as generalized transgressions, with ramifications far beyond what today we call the 'sexual' and 'economic' 'spheres', their emergence was instinctively connected to the violation of other societal taboos, including the practice of witchcraft.[23] Hawkes describes how 'counterfeiting and coin clipping [were] conceptually akin to both magic and usury' because they privilege the efficacious power of representational symbols.[24] In the *Basilikon Doron*, James warns his son 'never to forgive' a number of crimes, including witchcraft, sodomy and counterfeiting. If money is the source of the apparent magic of the marketplace, however, money can also magically challenge the market's profitability. As Cosgrove observes: '*The Comedy of Errors* is not only motivated by the inability of money to circulate and the magical confusion this produces, but also that the play understands money *as* magical to such an extent that magic itself will take on qualities of the monetary.'[25] The looming threat of witchcraft culminates in the conjuror Doctor Pinch, who makes manifest the dangers of the counterfeiting that the Antipholi have brought to Ephesus. When the market functions correctly it can work beneficent magic, but when 'queer' money begins to circulate, the magic turns dangerous, and the Antipholi find themselves surrounded by witches, demons and sorcerers.

The Syracusans perceive a convergence between their wildly fluctuating economic fortunes and the magic that they believe lurks all around them. When he first meets Adriana, who speaks to him as if to her husband, Antipholus of Syracuse asks in terror, 'What error drives our eyes and ear amiss?' Dromio believes that '[t]his is the fairy land' and fears that 'goblins' will 'suck our breath or pinch us black and blue' (2.2.195, 198). Yet the Ephesians bear the brunt of the Syracusans' fortunes. When the Ephesian pair encounter locked doors at home, Dromio exclaims, 'O villain, thou hast stolen both mine office and my name; / The one ne'er got me credit, the other mickle blame' (3.1.44-5). We are confronted with what Kent Cartwright terms 'the disturbing possibility that different characters might share the same identity'.[26]

Doctor Pinch is the epitome of the collapsed distinction between performative magic and the economy. Although Pinch is a schoolmaster, and a respectable member of the Ephesian community, he is also referred to as a 'conjurer' whose task is to exorcise the demonic possession apparently afflicting Antipholus of Ephesus and Dromio. Antipholus articulates the collapse of sexual and economic norms when he demands of Adriana 'wherefore didst thou lock me forth today?' and 'why dost thou deny the bag of gold?' (4.4.96-7). Adriana inadvertently tells the truth when she rails at him: 'Dissembling villain, thou speak'st false in both' (4.4.101). Pinch's presence elides the distinction between magic and Catholic 'popery' (also associated with sodomy in Protestant England), by performing an exorcism and embodying a 'living dead man' (5.1.241). Kent Cartwright argues that Pinch is in fact a material incarnation of Antipholus of Syracuse's anxieties about 'nimble jugglers' and 'prating mountebanks' who visits not him but his twin (they describe Pinch in almost identical language) (1.2.98, 101).[27] Thus, Syracusan Antipholus's worst fears are experienced by Ephesian Antipholus in a magical exchange. Magical exchange is, in fact, fast becoming normal practice in Ephesus.

Final act

Despite the reunion of the Antipholus and Dromios with their respective twins and parents/masters, Ephesus has been transformed by queered coin and counterfeit individuals. It is impossible to revert to innocence. Instead, the play's finale reinforces the tension between use- and exchange-value. When the brothers have been correctly identified, the Duke attempts to restore the Ephesian economy to its previous state: surprisingly, Egeon is pardoned, but Angelo receives recognition for making the chain, which goes to its rightful owner. Yet even though both the Antipholi have been discovered, the Duke must still ask, '[W]hich is the natural man / And which the spirit?' He is unable to 'decipher' or differentiate between them (5.1.332-4). Colette Gordon points out that the chain's recovery constitutes 'an essential recovery of identity'.[28] She argues that it is bonds of credit, not of blood, that bind the characters back together at the end of the play. The Dromios embrace, walking offstage together as Dromio of Ephesus, remarks:

We came into the world like brother and brother;
And now let's go hand in hand, not one before another.
(5.1.425-426)

This familial affection might be a cheerful ending to a play that has treated these two as little more than cattle to be beaten at the whims of their masters. Instead, however, Shakespeare reinforces their interchangeability, reflecting what Cartwright calls the play's 'anxieties about identity and the dissolution of the self'.[29] The two human commodities are reunited and indistinguishable once again so that they can continue to serve their masters, like the gold coins circulating in the marketplace.

The threat of queer money lingers in the repeated inability of even the twins' most intimate friends and family to identify them, just as Elizabeth's merchants and governors struggled to identify counterfeit coins, thus devaluing the political power of the sovereign, and sapping the economic strength of the market. At the play's end we are left to assume that the queer counterfeits will continue to circulate and to disrupt the credit of Ephesus. It cannot be otherwise, for sexuality is intricately intertwined with the economy, in ancient Ephesus, Shakespeare's England, and the postmodern Anglosphere alike. To trace the homology between sexual and economic counterfeits in *The Comedy of Errors* is, therefore, also to suggest ways in which sexual and economic values can be re-evaluated, re-created – 'queered' in short – in our own societies.

Note

I am sincerely grateful to David Hawkes for his guidance and suggestions on early drafts of this piece. I thank the participants in the Shakespeare Association of America seminar who read the first iteration of this chapter and provided welcome critique, and I thank the anonymous reviewers for their feedback.

Notes

1   Thomas Cosgrove, 'The Commodity of Errors', *Shakespeare* 14, no. 2 (2018): 150; Kent Cartwright, 'Introduction', in *The Comedy of Errors*, ed. Kent Cartwright (New York: Arden, 2016), 50–2.

2   Paul Trebilco, *The Early Christians in Ephesus from Paul to Ignatius* (Grand Rapids: Wm. B. Eerdmans Publishing, 2007), 17.

3   Stephen Deng, *Coinage and State Formation* (New York: Palgrave Macmillan, 2011), 51; Cosgrove, 'The Commodity', 150.

4   Trebilco, *The Early Christians*, 29.

5   Sandra K. Fischer, *Econolingua* (Newark: University of Delaware Press, 1985), 170.

6   Christine Varnado, *The Shapes of Fancy* (Minneapolis: University of Minnesota Press, 2020), 147.

7   Craig Muldrew, *The Economy of Obligation* (New York: St. Martin's Press, 1998), 2–4.

8   Laura Kolb, *Fictions of Credit* (Oxford: Oxford University Press, 2021), 2.

9   Alan Bray, *Homosexuality in Renaissance England* (New York: Columbia University Press, 1995); Alan Bray, *The Friend* (Chicago: University of Chicago Press, 2003).

10 Bray, *The Friend*, 9–10.

11 Ibid., 61.

12 David Hawkes, *Idols of the Marketplace* (New York: Palgrave, 2001), 32.

13 Ibid., 32–3.

14 Francis Bacon, *Novum Organum* (1878).

15 Deng, *Coinage and State Formation*, 1.

16 Hawkes, *Idols of the Marketplace*, 22.

17 Akinobu Kuroda, *A Global History of Money* (New York: Routledge, 2020), 119–20.

18 'Sweating' was a form of counterfeiting in which coins were put in bags and shaken hard to slough off metallic shavings. Valerie Forman, 'Marked Angels: Counterfeits, Commodities, and *The Roaring Girl*', *Renaissance Quarterly* 54, no. 4 (2001): 1538, 10.2307/1262161.
19 Will Fisher, 'Queer Money', *ELH* 66, no. 1 (1999): 15.
20 Ibid., 8.
21 Ibid., 10.
22 Ibid.
23 Jonathan Goldberg, *Sodometries* (Stanford: Stanford University Press, 1992); Valerie Traub, *Thinking Sex with the Early Moderns* (Philadelphia: University of Pennsylvania Press, 2016); David Hawkes *The Reign of Anti-Logos* (Palgrave Macmillan, 2020); Fisher, 'Queer Money'.
24 Hawkes, *The Reign*, 156.
25 Cosgrove, 'The Commodity of Errors', 150.
26 Kent Cartwright, 'Language, Magic, the Dromios, and "The Comedy of Errors"', *Studies in English Literature, 1500–1900* 47, no. 2 (2007): 332.
27 Ibid., 341–2.
28 Gordon, 'Crediting Errors', *Shakespeare* 6, no. 2 (2010): 180.
29 Cartwright, 'Language', 332, 345.

Works cited

Bacon, Francis, *Bacon's Novum organum*, Clarendon Press series (Oxford: Clarendon Press, 1878).

Bray, Alan, *Homosexuality in Renaissance England*, Morningside ed. Between Men–between Women (New York: Columbia University Press, 1995).

Bray, Alan, *The Friend* (Chicago: University of Chicago Press, 2003).

Bruster, Douglas, *Drama and the Market in the Age of Shakespeare*, Cambridge Studies in Renaissance Literature and Culture (Cambridge: Cambridge University Press, 1992). https://doi.org/10.1017/CBO9780511553080.

Cartwright, Kent, 'Language, Magic, the Dromios, and "The Comedy of Errors"', *Studies in English* Literature, *1500–1900* 47, no. 2 (2007): 331–54.

Chitty, Christopher, *Sexual Hegemony* (Theory Q. Durham: Duke University Press, 2020).

Cosgrove, Thomas, 'The Commodity of Errors: Shakespeare and the Magic of the Value-Form', *Shakespeare* 14, no. 2 (3 April 2018): 149–56. https://doi.org/10.1080/17450918.2018.1455735.

Degenhardt, Jane Hwang and Henry S. Turner, 'Between Worlds in Shakespeare's Comedy of Errors', *Exemplaria* 33, no. 2 (3 April 2021): 158–83. https://doi.org/10.1080/10412573.2021.1914990.

Deng, Stephen, *Coinage and State Formation in Early Modern English Literature – UC San Diego* (New York: Palgrave Macmillan, 2011). https://search-library.ucsd.edu.

Anonymous, England and Wales Sovereign (1558–1603: Elizabeth I), *By the Queene. The Queenes Maiestie Hauyng Not Long since Geuen Her Louyng Subiectes Knowledge by Proclamation, of Certayne Forrayne Coynes of Golde Brought into This Realme, of Muche Lesse Value Then Angels of Golde of This Realme, and yet Stamped so like to the Same Angels, as It Was Harde without Diligent Markynge Therof* … (London: England, 1565), https://www.proquest.com/eebo/docview/2240906369/citation/70FE7A9112914FAEPQ/3.

Finkelstein, Richard, '"The Comedy of Errors" and the Theology of Things', *Studies in English Literature, 1500–1900* 52, no. 2 (2012): 325–44.

Fischer, Sandra K., *Econolingua: A Glossary of Coins and Economic Language in Renaissance Drama* (Newark: University of Delaware Press, 1985).

Fisher, Will, 'Queer Money', *ELH* 66, no. 1 (1999): 1–23.

Forman, Valerie, 'Marked Angels: Counterfeits, Commodities, and *The Roaring Girl*', *Renaissance Quarterly* 54, no. 4 (2001): 1531–60. https://doi.org/10.2307/1262161.

Goldberg, Jonathan, *Sodometries: Renaissance Texts, Modern Sexualities* (Stanford, CA: Stanford University Press, 1992).

Gordon, Colette, 'Crediting Errors: Credit, Liquidity, Performance and *The Comedy of Errors*'. *Shakespeare* 6, no. 2 (1 June 2010): 165–84. https://doi.org/10.1080/17450911003790232.

Grav, Peter F. *Shakespeare and the Economic Imperative: 'What's Aught but as 'tis Valued?'* Studies in Major Literary Authors (New York: Routledge, 2008).

Greene, Jody, '"You Must Eat Men": The Sodomitic Economy of Renaissance Patronage', *GLQ: A Journal of Lesbian and Gay Studies* 1, no. 2 (1 April 1994): 163–97. https://doi.org/10.1215/10642684-1-2-163.

Hawkes, David, *Idols of the Marketplace: Idolatry and Commodity Fetishism in English Literature, 1580–1680*, 1st edition, Early Modern Cultural Studies, 1500–1700 (New York: Palgrave, 2001).

Hawkes, David, *Reign of Anti-Logos: Performance in Postmodernity* (New York: Palgrave Macmillan, 2020).

Hawkes, David, *Shakespeare and Economic Theory*, Arden Shakespeare and Theory (London, [England] and New York: Bloomsbury Arden Shakespeare, 2015).

Huffer, Lynne, '*The Comedy of Errors*: In Praise of Error', 10 January 2011. https://doi.org/10.1215/9780822393337-007.

Jones, Norman L., *God and the Moneylenders: Usury and Law in Early Modern England* (Oxford, UK: Blackwell, 1989).

Kolb, Laura, *Fictions of Credit in the Age of Shakespeare* (Oxford: Oxford University Press, 2021).

Kuroda, Akinobu, *A Global History of Money*, Electronic resource. 1st edition. Routledge Explorations in Economic History (New York: Routledge, 2020). https://www.taylorfrancis.com/books/9781003016205.

Lehnhof, Kent R., 'Twinship and Marriage in *The Comedy of Errors*', *SEL Studies in English Literature 1500–1900* 60, no. 2 (2020): 277–98. https://doi.org/10.1353/sel.2020.0012.

Madhavi Menon, *Shakesqueer: A Queer Companion to the Complete Works of Shakespeare*, Series Q (Duke University Press, 2011). https://doi.org/10.1215/9780822393337.

Marx, Karl, 'The Power of Money in Bourgeois Society', in *Economic and Philosophic Manuscripts of 1844* (Mineola, New York: Dover Publications, Inc, 2007).

Marx, Karl and Friedrich Engels, *Capital: A Critique of Political Economy. Volume 1* (Digireads.comPublishing, 2010).

McEnery, Tony and Helen Baker, 'The Public Representation of Homosexual Men in Seventeenth-Century England – a Corpus Based View', *Journal of Historical Sociolinguistics* 3, no. 2 (1 October 2017): 197–217. https://doi.org/10.1515/jhsl-2017-1003.

Muldrew, Craig, *The Economy of Obligation: The Culture of Credit and Social Relations in Early Modern England*, Early Modern History (New York: St. Martin's press, 1998).

Perry, Curtis, 'Commerce, Community, and Nostalgia in The Comedy of Errors', in *Money and the Age of Shakespeare: Essays in New Economic Criticism*, ed. Linda Woodbridge, Early Modern Cultural Studies (New York: Palgrave Macmillan, 2003), 39–51. https://doi.org/10.1057/9781403982469_3.

Raman, Shankar, 'Marking Time: Memory and Market in "The Comedy of Errors"', *Shakespeare Quarterly* 56, no. 2 (2005): 176–205.

Reeser, Todd W., 'How to Do Early Modern Queer History', *GLQ: A Journal of Lesbian and Gay Studies* 26, no. 1 (1 January 2020): 183–96. https://doi.org/10.1215/10642684-7929229.

Reeves, Eileen, 'As Good as Gold: The Mobile Earth and Early Modern Economics', *Journal of the Warburg and Courtauld Institutes* 62 (1999): 126–66. https://doi.org/10.2307/751385.

Shakespeare, William, *The Comedy of Errors: Third Series*, ed. Kent Cartwright, 3rd edition (London and New York: The Arden Shakespeare, 2016).

Shakespeare, William, *The Comedy of Errors: With New and Updated Critical Essays and a Revised Bibliography*, ed. Harry Levin (Signet Classic, 2002).

Traub, Valerie, *Thinking Sex with the Early Moderns*, Haney Foundation Series (Philadelphia: University of Pennsylvania Press, 2016).

Trebilco, Paul, *The Early Christians in Ephesus from Paul to Ignatius* (Grand Rapids, MI: Wm. B. Eerdmans Publishing, 2007).

Varnado, Christine, *The Shapes of Fancy: Reading for Queer Desire in Early Modern Literature* (Minneapolis: University of Minnesota Press, 2020). https://doi.org/10.5749/j.ctv10rrc4x.

Zurcher, Andrew, 'Consideration, Contract, and the End of *The Comedy of Errors*', *Law and Humanities* 1, no. 2 (1 January 2007): 145–65. https://doi.org/10.1080/17521483.2007.11423732.

6

The magic of bounty in *Timon of Athens*: Gold, society, nature

Hugh Grady

The opening scene of Shakespeare and Middleton's *Timon of Athens* presents us immediately with the social and civic life surrounding the legendary patron of the arts and giver of gifts Lord Timon – whose entrance, however, is delayed some 95 lines into the scene. This pause allows us to take in the extraordinary 'draw' that Timon's presence exerts. The Poet – one of four purveyors of goods hoping to entice a purchase or sponsorship of their work by Timon – surveys the confluence of people and apostrophizes the spirit he sees as, in effect, conjured up by Timon through the magic of his wealth and generosity:

> See,
> Magic of bounty, all these spirits thy power
> Hath conjured to attend.[1]

The 'magic of bounty' is a major theme in the play's two contrasting parts, and it is linked to the larger cultural connections explored in this anthology between magic and money. Shakespeare and Middleton[2] (though in different ways and with different emphases) explore and explode that connection, using the play to show the social structure of 'bounty' as both a social process that ruins Timon and morally bankrupts Athens and as an economic one that is prescient of Karl Marx's analysis of money and capital. Marx saw money as an alienated power of human society that takes on a life of its own and ends up as a destructive force unintentionally transforming the lifeworld of human society – and in many ways destroying it. This is an effect the play explicitly stages for us. The 'magic' power of money is shown in the play to work above all as disruptive – potentially catastrophically so – of the human lifeworld, the culturally formed social context in which ordinary humans live life and create meaning.[3] The play demonstrates how the power of wealth contrasts with a natural world of beneficial exchanges and fecundity, which Timon begins to appreciate once he is in his exile in the play's second half. But these are brief moments and come late. Most of the play works in a socially critical, satirical mode. The revelation of the money economy's social destruction makes up much of the first half of this diptych-like play and continues into the second.

In the first scene, an attractive surface of urban liveliness is presented. Athenian civil life appears bustling and appealing, with the 'magic' of bounty dazzling all in attendance. The Merchant, for example, speaks of Timon in highly idealizing (and as later events will show, ultimately ironic) tones:

A most incomparable man, breathed, as it were,
To an untirable and continuate goodness.

(1.10-11; 1.1.10-11)

But he is the object of sycophancy, and he is clearly being taken advantage of because of his kindness and the 'bounty' he owns, as portrayed in the series of supplicants that the play's first scene presents. Timon grants all the requests – paying the substantial debt of his friend Ventidius, bestowing a large financial gift upon his old servant Lucilius to enable his marriage to the daughter of a wealthy man, even suggesting to the Painter and Jeweller that he will later purchase their products. This is either the generosity of a saint, the indifference of a holder of limitless wealth or the foolish profligacy of an egoistic spendthrift.[4] The ambiguous quality of the character Timon – his susceptibility to these and other interpretations – is a marked and very Shakespearean characteristic of the play, which resists any simple or one-sided interpretation. In what follows I will attempt to do justice to this complexity while recognizing how the play also directs scorn and disapprobation to certain of the social realities it depicts, in a classical satirical manner. While *Timon* is set in ancient Athens and developed out of stories found in Plutarch and Lucian, it has clear relevance to the social life of Shakespeare's London. Beyond that, it is a play which has found new audiences in our own time of economic disasters and increasing dissatisfaction with a capitalist society that the play manages to reference and critique in the earliest stages of its development.

What is magic?

The Poet had told us early in the play's first scene that the crowd drawn to see Lord Timon had been 'conjured' by the 'magic of bounty'. But what in Shakespeare's culture was understood by the term 'magic'? There were myriad interpretations, with differences especially between learned and popular viewpoints. What they had in common was the idea of the operation of 'occult' or hidden powers used to manipulate the world. This notion of magic flourished in late antiquity, waned in the Middle Ages, but experienced something of a renaissance in the fifteenth century. Italian fifteenth-century Neoplatonists Marsilio Ficino (1433–99) and Pico della Mirandola (1463–94) had made a large impression on the learned with the argument that some forms of magic were the result of natural processes based in the occult connections among the different objects and relations of nature (the stars and jewels were important for these arguments). The Neoplatonists held that learning in the occult traditions founded by the (mythical) Hermes Trismegistus allowed one to practise magic through occult knowledge without the intervention of demons or spirits.[5]

To be sure, they believed in the existence of magic-performing demons and spirits as well, and such traditions were exhibited on Elizabethan and Jacobean stages in Marlowe's *Dr Faustus*, with its demonic magic, and in Shakespeare's *The Tempest*, in which Prospero relies on 'natural spirits' like Ariel to effect his magical acts. These 'natural spirits' were also the invention of Renaissance Neoplatonists who drew on various Platonic philosophers from late antiquity for the idea. Shakespeare also referenced other supposed sources of magic in both English folklore and classical literature for the magic exhibited in *A Midsummer Night's Dream*, allowing Robin Goodfellow and Oberon to perform wondrous deeds. And of course he drew on demonology and accounts of witchcraft in *Macbeth*.

These dramatic enactments of magic by Shakespeare and his contemporaries provide their own cultural evidence for a popular as well as learned knowledge of the idea of magic – though of course they tell us nothing about degrees of belief or scepticism concerning the various kinds of magic described in cultural documents, whether in the minds of the authors or the audiences. Enough documents have survived, however, to show that there were arguments for and against the reality of magic in Shakespeare's day. Perhaps because of the ambiguity surrounding the subject, magic clearly made for very good theatre, whatever belief for or against it worked within authors and spectators.

Timon of Athens is, of course, not in the same category as *The Tempest*, *Macbeth* or *A Midsummer Night's Dream* in depicting magic in the world. In those plays, the fiction of representation involves an aesthetic acceptance of occult phenomena at work in the world impacting characters in significant ways. In other words, they are plays in which magic is (fictionally) presented as real. In *Timon*, in contrast, magic is one of the terms of a metaphor, explicitly presented in the Poet's proclamation in the play's opening that I quoted above. Later in the play we will see that what had appeared a kind of magic to the Poet in scene 1 has various 'natural' explanations, the revelation of which constitutes much of the thematic work of the play. It follows a strategy of first presenting the illusion of limitless, 'magic' bounty in which Timon (and apparently his friends and receivers of his gifts) lived, then depicting the collapse of the illusion.

The illusion is both social and economic, but these categories are interconnected in the play. Both aspects of the illusion, hinted at in scene 1, are plainly developed in scene 2 and thereafter. Timon is a character of a type we have seen much of in our own time, a person able to create his own reality in defiance of all sorts of counter-acting messages and impactful acts from the larger social and natural worlds in which he exists. He clearly believes in an idealistic and even beneficent set of suppositions about the qualities of community, friendship and obligations to mutual support which he upholds. As the play progresses, however, it becomes clear that he is mistaken in the belief, and he gets no support from old friends when his own finances collapse. His idealism is particularly clearly expressed in scene 2, written by Middleton, in which Timon (before his bankruptcy) refuses to accept any payments by those he has helped, asserting that giving is better than receiving:

> Why, I have often wished myself poorer, that I might come nearer to you. We are born to do benefits; and what better or properer can we call our own than the riches of our friends? O, what a precious comfort 'tis to have so many like brothers commanding one another's fortunes! O, joy, e'en made away ere't can be born: mine eyes cannot hold out water, methinks. To forget their faults, I drink to you.
>
> (2.96-103; 1.2.90-96)

Some of Timon's followers, like the First Lord, take this at face value and praise Timon for his generosity: 'The noblest mind he carries / That ever governed man,' he says (1. 284-85; 1.1. 279-80). A bit earlier, he had praised Timon as one who 'outgoes / The very heart of kindness' (1. 277-78; 1.1.274). But others see foolishness in Timon's free hand. We hear something of this in the Second Lord's reply to the First Lord's praise just quoted:

> He pours it out. Plutus the god of gold
> Is but his steward; no meed but he repays
> Sevenfold above itself; no gift to him
> But breeds the giver a return exceeding
> All use of quittance.
>
> (1. 279-83; 1.1.275-79)

In this characterization of Timon's gift-giving habits, there is an indirect allusion to the practice of usury that, as we will soon see, is afflicting Timon without his being aware of it. Aristotle had famously proclaimed usury as unnatural because it was an instance of a dead thing acting like a live one by reproducing itself, or as it was often put, by 'breeding'. In the diction of the Second Lord here, Timon is already a victim of usury, but a willing one, turning gifts rather than loans to interest-bearing economic exchanges – becoming his own usurer, as it were.

We could assess this behaviour (as several critics in the past have done), as a case of Timon operating in a 'gift economy', that is, an economy (like some of the Native American cultures of the Pacific Northwest as described by anthropologist Marcel Mauss) in which wealth is accumulated only in order to be given away in celebrations of the potlach.[6] These are profoundly anti-capitalist societies in which the concept of ownership around which capitalist society is founded is turned on its head: these societies are structured through a completely different set of norms and customs. For their members, an accumulation of wealth is shameful, and social status is gained only by giving it away.

Timon shares something of this ethos, inasmuch as he clearly experiences much pleasure in giving away his wealth. But the analogy between these social customs breaks down when we examine the evaluations of Timon's actions by other citizens of Athens. Instead of applauding his charity unreservedly (as in a gift economy) many of the minor characters are given lines in the opening scenes that express apprehension or distaste for his actions. We see such an attitude, for example, in the Second Lord's speech (1. 279-83; 1.1. 275-79) given above.

Above all, a negative critique of Timon's gift-giving is voiced by and theatrically embodied in a dialogical antagonist who acts as Timon's critic but comes from a completely different cultural tradition from that of gift economies: one of the play's most significant secondary characters, the Cynical philosopher Apemantus.[7] He becomes the voice of much of the play's satirical, biting discourse, and he takes a 'plague on both your houses' position, criticizing both Timon and his supplicants – and seeing the whole 'confluence, this great flood of visitors' (1.42; 1.1.43) that the poet had early ascribed to the 'Magic of bounty' as nothing but a spectacle exhibiting the foolishness and corruptness of humanity in general:

That there should be small love amongst these sweet knaves,
And all this courtesy! The strain of man's bred out
Into baboon and monkey.

                              (1.253-55; 1.1.249-51)

He is most struck by the hypocrisy of the guests whom he sees as pretending love and admiration to cover over their avaricious exploitation of Timon's foolish generosity. Middleton's development of this character makes this judgement even more explicit.

Diagnosing the magic (1)

In the next scene of the play (written by Middleton), the earlier hints of disapproval of Timon's profligacy turn into explicit condemnations with various emotional gradations from grief to scorn. Middleton's Apemantus in scene 2 is continuous with Shakespeare's, but he is more explicit in his criticisms of Timon's role in the foolishness than was Shakespeare's version in the previous scene:

> O gods, what a number of men eats Timon, and he sees 'em not! It grieves me to see so many dip their meat in one man's blood; and all the madness is, he cheers them up, too.
>
> (2.39-42; 1.2.39-41)

In short, the opening two scenes of the play present us with a portrait of a well-meaning but deceived Timon and an opportunistic coterie of friends willingly exploiting his foolishness. This situation is further developed in Middleton's scene 2 in Timon's extravagant (and, as it turns out, completely unrealistic) praise of friendship and the obligations of friends to be generous to those in need, following directly those quoted previously:

> 'O you gods,' think I, 'what need we have any friends if we should ne'er have need of 'em. They were the most needless creatures living, should we ne'er have use for 'em, and would most resemble sweet instruments hung up in cases, that keeps their sound to themselves.'
>
> (2.91-96; 1.2.86-90)

These lines are the prelude to the following several scenes which depict Timon's friends turning their backs on the pressing needs of their supposed friend.

If, then, Timon's social life is soon exposed to be a kind of living lie, a bubble of self-delusion abetted by those taking financial advantage of the situation, the play also reveals the deceptive economic underpinning of the situation through the character of Timon's steward Flavius, who becomes the voice of economic reality making explicit what we might have guessed: that Timon is in fact limited in financial resources, and his profligate generosity is undoing his fortune.

Flavius, though critical of Timon's profligacy, seems genuinely to esteem his master, essentially seeing him as more sinned against than sinning:

> When all our offices have been oppressed
> With riotous feeders, when our vaults have wept
> With drunken spilth of wine, when every room
> Hath blazed with lights and brayed with minstrelsy,
> I have retired me to a wasteful cock
> And set mine eyes at flow.
>
> (4.153-58; 2.2.153-57)

There is clearly material in the play to justify the portrait of a noble and generous Timon given by G. Wilson Knight among others.[8] These traits cannot be merely dismissed because in a context of worldly wisdom they seem foolish, any more than the gifts of a potlach can be regarded as insignificant, or the teachings of Jesus on wealth and charity can be ridiculed as naive.

But it is this worldly framework that Timon's creditors evoke as they provide lessons on the brutal economic reality in which Timon has – foolishly or nobly or both – immersed himself. He is in debt to usurers, and they are demanding payments for outstanding loans. Timon, loath to step out of his illusions, approaches several friends to whom he has dispersed his bounty, and he says to Flavius:

> No villainous bounty yet hath passed my heart.
> Unwisely, not ignobly, have I given.
> Why dost thou weep? Canst thou the conscience lack
> To think I shall lack friends? Secure thy heart.
> If I would broach the vessels of my love
> And try the argument of hearts by borrowing,
> Men and men's fortunes could I frankly use
> As I can bid thee speak.
>
> (4.168-175; 2.2.167-174)

And then he adds, 'You shall perceive how you/Mistake my fortunes. I am wealthy in my friends' (4.178-79; 2.2.177-78).

Apemantus Again: Outsider and Seer

In the play's complex structure of conflicting views of the life and character of its protagonist Timon, no character is given more stage time and speeches than Apemantus, already discussed above and appearing both early and late in the play. Although some critics see him as an almost wholly negative character, I think he has important positive features as one of those 'outsider' figures who populate Shakespeare's plays from early to late in his career – characters like the many versions of Fools – but also others who share some of their qualities, like Mercutio, Jacques, Falstaff, Autolycus and Caliban. They function dramatically as foils to more central ones and are most valuable for what they reveal in their relations with others rather than as fully developed figures in their own right. But they perform a critical and dialogic role in the plays they appear in, providing an outsider's 'take' on the main action depicted in the larger stories being dramatized. And the nearest relative to Apemantus among these is undoubtedly the scurrilous satirist Thersites, from that other Shakespearean tragedy set in ancient Greece, *Troilus and Cressida*.

As I pointed out in earlier writings on *Troilus*, the Greek setting manifests the lesser status of Greece compared to Rome in English Renaissance culture. Ancient Greece was generally seen as less culturally central and substantially politically weaker than Rome in Shakespeare's time,[9] and this is reflected in the atmospheres of the locales in *Troilus and Cressida* and *Timon of Athens*. Both of these plays contain much bitter, snarling, and disillusioned satirical material, and both take a very jaundiced view of the human lives and actions they portray.[10] Until Timon himself begins to employ this style in his denunciatory poetry of the play's second half, Apemantus is its main voice. In this play above all perhaps, the style is the man.

This background is helpful to a modern reader because without it Apemantus might be dismissed as simply an unpleasant, oral-aggressive and thoroughly unlikeable troll. He is all of these things, but in addition he is a truth-teller, a character who sees through the illusion in which Timon has ensconced himself and which is reinforced by his many followers and exploiters. He is essentially correct if very impolitic in his assessment of Timon's guests arriving for the banquet scene quoted in part earlier:

> Achës contract and starve your supple joints!
> That there should be small love amongst these sweet knaves,
> And all this courtesy! The strain of man's bred out
> Into baboon and monkey.
>
> (1.251-55; 1.1. 248-51)

It is precisely Timon's social delusions that Apemantus punctures. Timon believes himself, as we have seen, to be a beloved figure surrounded by friends as selfless as himself. Apemantus sees through this into the completely instrumental, exploitative mindsets of these guests, and he says so clearly. His insight as to the supposed friends' true motives is clearly corroborated in the events portrayed in the middle sections of the play, as they desert Timon after he has lost all his money to usurious creditors.

The outcome, of course, perfectly fits in with the bitter satirical mode the play exhibits in much of its discourse. Timon's friends fail him in a series of brief dramatic vignettes of rampant ingratitude towards him. Timon's sunny disposition leaves him, and he plots one last banquet, in which he serves his creditors bowls of water and curses them.

In the middle parts of the play, then, Timon's intertwined illusions (the social one of a benevolent communalistic loving society, the economic one of boundless wealth) are exposed as errors of perception and assumption, and Timon's benevolence gives way to rage and hatred. The violent oscillation of states of mind does not go without choral commentary, however. And it is the philosopher Apemantus who provides a diagnosis:

> The middle of humanity thou never knewest, but the extremity of both ends. When thou was in thy gilt and thy perfume, they mocked thee for too much curiosity; in thy rags thou know'st none, but art despised for the contrary.
>
> (14.302-06; 4.3.307-310)

But Timon is steadfast in his conversion to misanthropy, and the play goes on to explore his new state of mind. Indeed, much of the second half of the play is given over to a series of visits to Timon in his exile by various interlocutors from the first half, each in effect contextualizing and contrasting their own worldviews against Timon's nihilism. It is a tribute to the depth of this play's explorations that Timon's case is by no means easily overcome, however much it is finally revealed as a philosophical dead end whose ultimate outcome can only be the suicide that Timon in fact undertakes at the play's end. In that way, Timon's disillusion in the second half of the play is itself exposed as a new kind of illusion.

Timon *Misanthropos*

The 'new' Timon of this diptych-like play's second half sounds oddly familiar. There seems to have been a migration of discourse, from the Cynic Apemantus to Timon *Misanthropos*. 'Men report / Thou dost affect my manners, and dost use them,' Apemantus says in greeting to Timon in his first encounter with the new man (14.199-200; 4.3.200-01). But the discourse migration had begun in the play's second banquet scene (11; 3.6), a more theatrical event than the first one in which Timon feigns contentment and friendship with his guests – before covers are removed from the offered dishes, and they are revealed to be plates of warm water. Here for the first time in the play, the disillusioned Timon embraces Apemantus's bitter, biting and railing style – but adds an intense rage which Apemantus lacked:

> Live loathed and long,
> Most smiling, smooth, detested parasites,
> Courteous destroyers, affable wolves, meek bears,
> You fools of fortune, trencher-friends, time's flies,
> Cap-and-knee slaves, vapours, and minute-jacks!
> Of man and beast the infinite malady
> Crust you quite o'er.
>
> (11.92-98; 3.6.80-86)

And then he adds, after aiming a few stones at his guests:

> Henceforth be no feast
> Whereat a villain's not a welcome guest.
> Burn house! Sink Athens! Henceforth hated be
> Of Timon man and all humanity.

(11.101-04; 3.6.89-92)

The illusions of the play's opening are now shattered. Timon has taken in the reality that his beloved community is actually composed of a collection of sycophants and parasites who deserve scorn. And his illusions about the magic of his bounty are gone as well, as the bounty is revealed to have been propped up through a series of usurious loans that have now come due, impoverishing him.

The next scene (12; 4.1) finds Timon outside the walls of Athens, which he addresses, calling on them (and later in the speech, on the gods) to curse Athens's institutions and inhabitants. It is the first of a number of such curses pronounced by Timon in the play's second half, as he confronts friends like Alcibiades, Flavius and Apemantus; symbolic figures like the bandits and prostitutes; and officials including the senators from Athens. The universal negative judgements which Timon imposes on all of them, regardless of their specific merits and demerits, hints at one of the play's thematic points in its evaluation of Timon's misanthropy. He has created that 'night in which ... all cows are black' described by Hegel in his critique of Friedrich Schelling in his Preface to *The Phenomenology of Mind*.[11] Like Schelling according to Hegel, Timon is guilty of using categories so broad as to deprive him of the ability to make necessary distinctions at moral, practical and even ontological levels. As the scenes with his visitors unroll, it is clear he is unable to distinguish his loyal friends from those who are visiting merely to get his money or otherwise use him instrumentally. The shock of his experience of betrayal and abandonment has caused a kind of madness, bracing in its critical view of a corrupt world, but clearly deficient in its abstract universality. Although both Apemantus and Flavius give him some telling advice, it is Alcibiades who recognizes the madness for what it is, takes what is of value in it and turns his hand towards the task of challenging the corrupt world rather than simply abandoning it as Timon has done in his black despair.

I will return to him below, but first it will be necessary to explore how far Timon gets in his understanding of the world in his newly misanthropic state.

Diagnosing the magic (2): The social function of bounty

As Timon digs for roots to eat, very ironically, he strikes gold and cries:

> Gold? Yellow, glittering, precious gold?
> No, gods, I am no idle votarist:
> Roots, you clear heavens. Thus much of this will make
> Black white, foul fair, wrong, right,
> Base noble, old young, coward valiant.
> Ha, you gods! Why this, what, this, you gods? Why, this
> Will lug our priests and servants from your sides,
> Pluck stout men's pillows from below their heads.
> This yellow slave
> Will knit and break religions, bless th' accursed,
> Make the hoar leprosy adored, place thieves,
> And give them title, knee, and approbation
> With senators on the bench. This is it
> That makes the wappered widow wed again;
> She whom the spittle house and ulcerous sores
> Would cast the gorge at, this embalms and spices
> To th' April day again. Come, damned earth,
> Thou common whore of mankind, that puts odds
> Among the rout of nations; I will make thee
> Do thy right nature.
>
> (14.24-44; 4.3.26-45)

The trope of apostrophe, as often in other Shakespearean soliloquies, helps emphasize the way in which the speech envisions gold (a synecdoche here standing for all forms of wealth and money) as a powerful social agent – in fact a kind of revolutionary one – but also one that in its levelling mission destroys both beneficial traditions and human solidarity and community. It is a force stronger than religion, able to both 'knit' (i.e. unify) and 'break' (destroy). It can reverse common human aversions to a disease like leprosy or ulcers and ennoble and empower thieves with titles and reverence. It is the 'common whore of mankind' that turns all other values into mercantile ones. It operates as an object of envy that brings disorder to the relations between the different nations of the earth.

As spectators of the play, we have already been witnesses to the corrosive moral effects of the desire for money in the form of the subversion of friendship and fellowship it has facilitated, as Timon has reduced his relation to his companions to one of economic largesse. The depth of such friendship was revealed in the cool reactions of Timon's friends to his financial troubles. 'I am wealthy in my friends,' he had mistakenly told his servants before turning to those friends for the kind of financial help he had himself provided them in happier days. The results, of course, constituted a powerful puncturing of Timon's illusion bubble. In this fictional Athens, money is far from the means of displaying the compassion and brotherhood fantasized by Timon. Instead, money is the goal, not the means, of upper-class civic life.

The play also connects the socially corrosive effects of a proto-capitalist economy to a number of other dubious social practices, including the spread of sexually transmitted diseases through prostitution and the prostitution of artists in search of patronage for their creations. Political corruption and injustice are also effects of money's 'magic', as illustrated in the plot concerning Alcibiades and the Senate (largely written – and none too clearly, as we will see below – by Middleton).

Timon and Usury

In linking a money-centred social life to these other social ills, Shakespeare was drawing on a network of ancient and medieval discourses focused on the issue of usury – the lending out of money in loans requiring additional repayments through interest. As mentioned previously, Aristotle had famously condemned the

practice as unnatural and therefore as unethical, and there were
passages in Deuteronomy which, although leaving more scope for
exceptions, were largely interpreted by medieval and much early
modern Christianity as condemning the charging of interest in
loans. The issue was quite alive in Shakespeare's time as David
Hawkes points out in his groundbreaking *The Culture of Usury in
Renaissance England*:

> Once attuned to the nuances and vocabulary of the issue, it is
> impossible to avoid noting figurative, illustrative, and allusive
> deployments of the usury debate in thousands of texts ostensibly
> devoted to other matters. Usury, in its multifarious incarnations,
> was far more important to the people of early modern England
> than one might imagine from a survey of twentieth- or twenty-
> first century studies of the period.[12]

Now usury is, of and in itself, a major issue in the play *Timon*.
The collapse of Timon's personal fortune, we are explicitly told, has
resulted from the calling in of usurious loans that have been made
to him, as we learn when Apemantus sums up the proceedings at
the end of a dinner party we have witnessed, when three financial
agents demand immediate payment of loans past due from Timon.
Apemantus describes the agents as 'Poor rogues' and usurers'
men, bawds between gold and want' (4.57-58; 2.2.62-63). In the
banter that follows, the minor character the Fool – presented as
servant to the mistress of a brothel – links usury to prostitution
and venereal disease much as occurs in the dark comic scenes of
Measure for Measure.

What makes *Timon* distinctive from much of the discourse of
usury circulating in early modern England, however, is that in this
play Shakespeare enlarges the social critique of usurious loans
so that usury is itself a kind of synecdoche for a systematically
organized money economy of the kind later to be called capitalism.
Like *Troilus and Cressida*, *Timon* acts as Shakespeare's thought
experiment to envision a modernity that, in his own day, existed only
as certain tendencies within a still largely medieval social polity.[13] It
reveals Shakespeare as a keen and insightful participant in and critic
of modernity, establishing in this play a critique of the capitalist
economic system which was developing in the London around
him in its pre-industrial stage. The "magic of bounty" is revealed

to derive from the paradoxical, delusive properties of financial interest, which becomes in Marx's sense no longer simply money but capital, that is, money expended not for tangible commodities but for profits. For any post-Marxist reader, the 'magic of bounty' is, as John Jowett puts it, 'a figuration of capitalism itself'.[14]

The first critic who saw this clearly was Karl Marx, who wrote that Shakespeare had presciently discerned 'the real nature of money', giving us a description not just of his own day's financial follies, but of the logic of any economy following the sway of capitalist principles. Marx refers to the 'divine power of money' rather than the 'magic of bounty', but the two concepts are nearly identical. Marx wrote of Timon's apostrophe to gold and of a later, related passage (14.387-93; 4.3.382-92):

> Shakespeare excellently depicts the real nature of money.... Shakespeare stresses especially two properties of Money: (1) It is the visible divinity – the transformation of all human and natural properties into their contraries, the universal confounding and overturning of things; it makes brothers of impossibilities. (2) It is the common whore, the common pimp of people and nations.
>
> The overturning and confounding of all human and natural qualities, the fraternization of impossibilities – the divine power of money – lies in its *character* as men's estranged, alienating, and self-disposing *species-nature*. Money is the *alienated ability of mankind.*[15]

Marx also alluded to the ideas about money contained in Timon's soliloquy at a strategic moment of *Capital* (using a more popular language than before – but very similar concepts):

> Since gold does not disclose what has been transformed into it, everything, commodity or not, is convertible into gold ... Just as every qualitative difference between commodities is extinguished in money, so money, on its side, like the radical leveller that it is, does away with all distinctions. But money itself is a commodity, an external object, capable of becoming the private power of private persons. The ancients therefore denounced money as subversive of the economic and moral order of things.[16]

Here clearly, Marx is a Shakespearean in his analysis.[17] For both of them, money is the central organizing principle of societies of morally inverted values, putting money – supposedly a medium of exchange – ahead of anything else. The young Marx categorized money as embodying an alienation of human species-being – one that is given control over every individual and of society as a whole. The older Marx wrote of the private expropriation of a universal human capability. But both passages are essentially explications of Timon's speech.[18]

How does this prescient critique of emerging capitalist modernity relate to other aspects of this singular work, particularly its strongly asserted discourse of nihilism? Much of the dialogue on nihilism occurs in the darkly comic encounter between the newly misanthropic Timon and the Cynic Apemantus, and while each one scores some important points, the debate ends in mutual taunting and schoolboy antics – a conclusion which greatly weakens its force as a philosophical resolution. Timon's only other real friends, Alcibiades and the faithful steward Flavius, in contrast, treat Timon's misanthropy as a madness that well exhibits the final effects of Athenian corruption but is in itself a mental degeneration to be pitied. Thus, the ending movement of the play reinforces the diagnosis of profound corruption in Athens, but it undermines Timon's misanthropy as an adequate response. We hear this diagnosis in Alcibiades's pleas to Timandra to disregard Timon's insults as the mad thoughts of a once noble mind (14.88-89; 4.3.89-90). We hear them again in his reaction to Timon's misanthropic epitaph: 'These well express in thee thy latter spirits' (17.75; 5.4.74), he says, just before invoking Timon's final seaside resting place as carrying instead a message of 'faults forgiven' (17.80; 5.4.79).

The role of Alcibiades

Alcibiades is able at the play's end to distinguish Timon's mad misanthropy from his quite rational, and highly painful, sense of having been betrayed and exploited. In effect, Alcibiades fulfills the paradoxical prayer of Timon to enact justice through 'plague and infection' with a conceptual shift – into political terms – in Timon's absence. As the Messenger explains to two of the Senators, Alcibiades has taken Timon's cause as his own, proclaiming 'fellowship i'th' cause against your city, / In part for his sake moved' (15.12-13; 5.2.11-12). What is it that the military man Alcibiades has in common with the now bankrupt civilian Timon? The first part of the answer, enigmatic as it is, lies in the scene of Alcibiades at the Senate (10; 3.5) – a frustrating portion of the text, clearly written by Middleton, and raising as many questions as it answers. Indeed, the scene has been a primary piece of evidence in the case, most substantially argued in 1942 by Una Ellis Fermor, that the playtext as we have it is unfinished and faulty in a number of ways[19] – and ended up in the 1623 Folio only to fill in the then blank place left by the last-minute removal of *Troilus and Cressida* due to temporary copyright issues.[20]

The chief problem with the scene is that it centres on an action and a character otherwise completely absent from the play. It begins with one senator agreeing with another that an (unidentified) perpetrator of a crime deserves the death penalty. Then Alcibiades speaks as 'an humble suitor' to the Senate in favour of the accused. He asks for mercy for his unnamed friend, not as innocent of the crime, but as deserving clemency on a number of grounds: that putting this deed aside, he was a man 'of comely virtues'; that in the killing he was defending his reputation and good name in a kind of trial by combat; that he showed courage in doing this and that he had fought bravely for Athens as a soldier in past battles. When these arguments are gainsaid by the Senators, he asks for mercy again on grounds that soldiers are prone to anger and their anger is necessary to the state, so that this friend should be pardoned for the sake of soldiers and the state alike. And when these arguments are denied, he asks that the friend be pardoned because of Alcibiades's own great deeds. In effect he argues that the Senate owes him the favour.

The senators are not pleased, and after a very brief warning, they banish Alcibiades for refusing to be silenced. The scene ends with Alcibiades in soliloquy. He accuses the Senate of practising usury while he was receiving wounds in Athens's defence (and thus obliquely allying them with the destroyers of Timon but otherwise not mentioning him) and vows to employ his army against Athens (10.104-13; 3.5.107-16).

As John Jowett noted in his groundbreaking edition of the play, critics and directors have often felt the need to supplement this enigmatic scene with various additions – verbal and visual – to help integrate it with the rest of the play.[21] Of course, if we think ahead to the play's conclusion and the central role played by Alcibiades in it, it is clear that there needs to be motivation for his attack on Athens and for his taking on Timon's cause. But this Senate scene remains an unsatisfactory portion of a play that is otherwise fairly clear in its implied judgements and social criticisms. Alcibiades's arguments seem shaky – or based on a concept of aristocratic privilege that was suspect even in Shakespeare's day. In other words, Alcibiades's cause is far from clearly deserving of readers' and viewers' support – especially since we are completely ignorant of the characters of those involved or of the concrete circumstances and particulars of the case in question. As Jowett argues, there is a parallel with Timon's situation when Alcibiades employs commercial and financial terms in arguing his case that the Senate and city owe him a favour.[22] But this parallel strikes me as double-edged, as easily implying a critique of Timon and Alcibiades as it does an argument that they have been wronged. Is this an artistic failing or a piece of intended ambiguity? It is impossible to decide.

On the other hand, we do witness the events leading up to Alcibiades's banishment by the senators and a response that this punishment is grossly disproportionate to the deeds presented is virtually inevitable – especially given his past great military services to the state. It seems clear that the senators' personal pique leads to a life-altering, unjust punishment for Alcibiades. He seems guilty of nothing more than pleading passionately for his cause and disregarding the Senate's sense of decorum. The banishment seeks to align Athens's political structure with that of its corrupt and venal commercial and social one and thus to justify Alcibiades's subsequent actions as a salutary revolt aimed at reforming the state and society. The intention of the scene is clear, if the execution of the intention is problematic – and as Jowett argues, probably a product of conceptual differences between Middleton and Shakespeare on Alcibiades's motivation and character.[23]

Timon of Athens's utopian moments

Nevertheless, the final moments of this dark play make surprisingly affirmative if brief counter-statements – in the context, to be sure, of the impressively massive nihilistic vision articulated by Timon himself to which the affirmative elements are in dialectical relation. I discussed this dynamic in an earlier essay, adducing as evidence the environmental work of art and gravesite constructed by Timon as his final resting place.[24] In addition, as briefly outlined above, there is Alcibiades's forgiving framing of Timon's nihilism as merely his 'latter spirits', to be reintegrated into a more inclusive view of the life and spirit of 'noble Timon'. In this context, I want to turn to a reinforcing, similar passage of the play occurring earlier but getting at the same combination.

The passage (made famous by Vladimir Nabokov's use of one of its phrases for the title of his novel *Pale Fire*) occurs in the midst of the visits from personifications of the social ills of Athens that make up much of the play's second half. In this case, it is part of the dialogue Timon has with a visiting group of bandits or Banditti, who had heard that Timon retained some of the gold he was famous for. Timon uses the occasion for more of his misanthropic, universalizing discourse, urging his visitors to pursue their vocations because they do honestly what all other men do surreptitiously. He even finds a parallel of their craft in nature:

> I'll example you with thievery.
> The sun's a thief, and with his great attraction
> Robs the vast sea. The moon's an arrant thief,
> And her pale fire she snatches from the sun.
> The sea's a thief, whose liquid surge resolves
> The moon into salt tears. The earth's a thief,
> That feeds and breeds by a composture stol'n
> From gen'ral excrement. Each thing's a thief.
> The laws, your curb and whip, in their rough power
> Has unchecked theft.
>
> (14.435-444; 4.3.428-37)

It's an extraordinary passage, and quite different in its affect and conceptions from the ancient text sometimes seen as its source, Anacreon's Ode 19. The similarity resides in the way both compositions use the interconnected cycles of the sun, moon, evaporation and the water cycle as allegories for human activity. Anacreon interprets the similarities as an inducement to drinking: nature does it, why not we? But Shakespeare labels the natural cycles as theft, images of a corrupt society in which there are no honest men, only mutual robbers.

And Shakespeare's poetry is more complex in other ways. The passage works like one of the baroque images identified by Walter Benjamin in his study of seventeenth-century German *Trauerspiele* in his *The Origin of German Tragic Drama*.[25] It projects two opposing but dialectically connected meanings, one socially critical, the other utopian, but in a specific sense connected to the socially critical reading.

This critical moment of the image is not far to seek. It is one more vivid image of a world corrupted by money, delineating the central position occupied by money in a nascent capitalist economy. It is a vision reminiscent of some recent, anti-Adam Smith theories of capitalism that see every transaction as an attempt by both parties to get the better of each other, in effect to swindle. In Timon's speech, however, the vision is universal and indicts the universally corrupt cosmos perceived by the greatly injured Timon.

The utopian meaning of the passage finds its semantic sources largely in the poetic affect and associations of the description's lyrical language, as well as resonance with other moments of this complex play – above all in Timon's last 'gift' to humanity in the form of his environmental gravesite, and in the turn to nature, just politics, and art in the concluding speech of Alcibiades.

The images of the natural world, in this reading, stand in contrast to the universal theft constituted by capitalist society. Timon first alludes to this contrast in the soliloquy accompanying his digging for roots in the wilderness. He refers to nature as a 'Common mother – thou / Whose womb unmeasurable and infinite breast / Teems and feeds all' (14.178-80; 4.3.179-81). In contrast to the human lifeworld, we perceive in nature cycles of mutual support and regeneration, especially in the lines, 'That feeds and breeds by a composture stol'n/ From gen'ral excrement' (14.441-43; 4.3. 433-35). Timon's great denunciations of gold had seen it as a form of dirt and of excrement, and these lines evoke that association. Only here the earth and dung become means of renewing compost, of regeneration and ultimately redemption. Both of the images' meanings remain in force; neither cancels out the other. Instead, as Benjamin wrote, their relation is one of two extremes dialectically connected but separate: 'dialectics at a standstill'.[26]

The idea describes, in its way, a kind of magic, an interconnected web of natural entities transforming into each other in a perfect cycle, not unlike the occult connections among the different objects and relations of nature underlying 'magic' as argued for by Ficino and Pico della Mirandola (briefly discussed above). But in this satirical play there are two systems of exchange referenced: most prominently the exchanges of usurious capitalism leading to Timon's misery and tragic end of life. The first references the society of destructive hypocrisy and sycophancy described by Apemantus and the later Timon: a society of universal thievery. The second exchange system referenced, however, is that of the natural world, in the brief but key passages enunciated by Timon quoted above, describing exchanges creative of a natural world of harmony and interconnection – and providing the underlying utopian alternative implied by all satire. Timon alludes to these natural rhythms twice, here as well as in his description of the gravesite by the sea he has constructed for himself, which takes advantage of natural tides to form what Alcibiades later describes as a 'rich conceit' or conception:

> Timon hath made his everlasting mansion
> Upon the beachèd verge of the salt flood,
> Who once a day with his embossèd froth
> The turbulent surge shall cover.
>
> (14.750-53; 5.1.205-08)

Here, as discussed above, the process of natural metamorphosis, of turning apparent evil into good, is described, injecting a faint element of redemption into the misery of his end and evoking death as a termination point for social evil:

> What is amiss, plague and infection mend.
> Graves only be men's works, and death their gain.
> Sun, hide thy beams. Timon hath done his reign.
>
> (14.756-58; 5.2.211-13)

Timon has ended his reign. But the corrupt city that the play has implicitly made its chief collective villain and satirical target, the city which formed him and in which he had attempted to live a virtuous if deluded life, remains. Timon's misanthropic vision, while understandable, can do nothing to reform Athens. That would take a utopian virtuous politics, and Alcibiades – quite against the grain of his treatment by Plutarch as something of an unreliable and even treacherous louche and bon vivant – steps forward in his own and in Timon's name to undertake a virtuous and practical reform of the city, dispensing justice and mercy as he sees fit:

> Bring me into your city,
> And I will use the olive with my sword,
> Make war breed peace, make peace stint war, make each
> Prescribe to other as each other's leech.
> Let our drums strike.
>
> (17.82-86; 5.4.82-84)

This dark, satirical play, which explores the depths of human nature and finds it capable of immense injustice and hypocrisy, produces at its very end a counter-discourse that proclaims justice possible through a harmony with nature as a foundation for a truly human life. In its own way, it looks forward to *The Winter's Tale* and the other utopian late plays while linking as well with the earlier dark tragedies like *Hamlet* and *King Lear*. We could term it a Shakespearean *Lehrstücke* or learning-play – a Brechtian dramatic fable that punctures the prevailing illusions of its social context while hinting at possible solutions to them. The 'magic of bounty' is the illusion; political reform (in a utopian, unspecified form) is the needed reality in this often unjustly deprecated philosophical play.

Notes

1   William Shakespeare and Thomas Middleton, *Timon of Athens*, ed. John Jowett, The Oxford Shakespeare (Oxford: Oxford University Press, 2004), 1.5-7. This edition numbers the play's scenes consecutively, omitting the traditional division of a play into acts – a change from the usual editorially supplied act divisions in use since

the re-editing of Shakespeare in the eighteenth century. The text of *Timon* in the 1623 First Folio (the only extant textual source of the play) designates the first scene as 'Actus Primus. Scoena Prima' but then discontinues act or scene divisions for the remainder of the play – so that subsequent editors have had to supply them following what they considered best editorial practice. Therefore, in order to accommodate readers using texts with act-and-scene divisions, the first citation from Jowett's edition will be followed by an act-scene-line citation of the same passage from another edition using act divisions: Karl Klein, ed. *Timon of Athens*, by William Shakespeare (Cambridge: Cambridge University Press, 2001), 1.1.5-7. I ignore minor differences between the readings of the texts, relying on Jowett's.

2   There is now a virtual critical consensus that the play was jointly written by William Shakespeare and Thomas Middleton around 1606 or a bit later. They each wrote individual scenes, though many scholars believe they may have entered some additions to each other's scenes. Speaking roughly, Shakespeare wrote the beginning and end of the play comprising about 2/3 of the total text; Middleton wrote scene 2 and the middle scenes. For details, see Jowett, ed., introduction to *Timon of Athens*, 1–11.

3   Habermas borrowed this concept from phenomenological philosophy and set it up in a dialectical relation to the series of reified systems – the capitalist system above all, but including state bureaucracy and aspects of instrumental reason; see Jürgen Habermas, *The Theory of Communicative Action*, 2 vols., trans. Thomas McCarthy (Boston: Beacon, 1984, 1987).

4   All of these positions can be found in the critical literature on *Timon*. See my earlier citations of examples of these differing interpretations in Hugh Grady, *Shakespeare and Impure Aesthetics* (Cambridge: Cambridge University Press, 2009), 111–13.

5   For an excellent summary of these developments, on which I draw here, see Brian P. Copenhaver, 'Magic', in *The Cambridge History of Science: Vol. 3, Early Modern Science*, ed. Katherine Park and Lorraine Daston (Cambridge: Cambridge University Press, 2006), 518–40.

6   Marcel Mauss, *The Gift: The Form and Reason for Exchange in Archaic Societies*, trans. W. D. Halls (New York: Norton, 1990). One memorable use of Mauss to help illuminate Timon's motivation (combined with psychoanalytic theory) is Coppélia Kahn (1987), '"Magic of Bounty": *Timon of Athens*, Jacobean Patronage, and Maternal Power', *Shakespeare Quarterly* 38, no. 1: 34–57. See also Michael Chorost, 'Biological Finance in Shakespeare's *Timon of*

Athens', *ELR* 21 (1991): 349–70; and Ken Jackson, '"One wish" or the Possibility of the Impossible: Derrida, the Gift, and God in *Timon of Athens*', *Shakespeare Quarterly* 52, no. 1 (2001): 34–66, as well as my earlier treatment of the play in Grady, *Shakespeare and Impure Aesthetics*, 90–129.

7   The term 'Cynic' derives from the Greek word for dog, which in turn was either a reference to a gymnasium where the sect developed or the nickname of its best-known figure, Diogenes of Sinope (412?–323 BCE), who disdained worldly pleasures and had no fixed domicile. Diogenes was generally admired in the classical world for his principled consistency. Our own most common associations with the term 'cynic' – in the sense of a person who believes that other people are motivated in all their actions by selfishness – seem to come to prominence later. The main uses of the term from Shakespeare's era given in the OED link cynicism with asceticism or the disdaining of pleasure, with railing against society and those accepting its ordinary customs, and with an unpleasant disposition or churlishness.

8   G. Wilson Knight, *The Wheel of Fire: Interpretations of Shakespearian Tragedy with Three New Essays* (London: Methuen, 1949), 210–11 and throughout the chapter on *Timon*.

9   See Hugh Grady, *Shakespeare's Universal Wolf: Studies in Early Modern Reification* (Oxford: Oxford University Press, 1996), 58–94. Two important sources for this conception of the early modern view of ancient Greece were Robert Miola, 'Timon in Shakespeare's Athens', *Shakespeare Quarterly* 31, no. 1 (1980): 21–30; and T. J. B. Spencer, '"Greeks" and "Merrygreeks": A Background to *Timon of Athens* and *Troilus and Cressida*', in *Essays on Shakespeare and Elizabethan Drama in Honor of Hardin Craig*, ed. Richard Hoslely (Columbia: University of Missouri Press, 1962), 223–33.

10   This is a stance of much Roman satirical verse, and Shakespeare probably learned from the satirical style of Latin satirists like Horace or Juvenal – and their English imitators.

11   G. W. F. Hegel, *The Phenomenology of Mind*, trans. J. B. Baillie (New York: Harper and Row, 1967), 79.

12   David Hawkes, *The Culture of Usury in Renaissance England* (London: Palgrave, 2010), 1.

13   I discussed this in Grady, *Shakespeare's Universal Wolf*, 26–57.

14   John Jowett, 'Shakespeare, Middleton, and Debt in *Timon of Athens*', Presentation, Annual Meeting, Shakespeare Association of America, Miami, April 2001.

15   Karl Marx, *The Economic and Philosophic Manuscripts of 1844*, ed. Dirk Struik (New York, International Publishers, 1964), 167–8.

16 Karl Marx, *Capital: A Critique of Political Economy, Vol. 1: The Process of Capitalist Production* (New York: International, 1967), 132–3.
17 For a much more detailed and extensive account of Shakespeare's influence on Marx, see Christian A. Smith, *Shakespeare's Influence on Karl Marx: The Shakespearean Roots of Marxism* (New York: Routledge, 2022).
18 This section of my chapter draws on arguments about the play and its critique of commodity fetishism that I made in Grady, *Shakespeare and Impure Aesthetics*, 114–17.
19 Una Ellis-Fermor, "'Timon of Athens': An Unfinished Play', *The Review of English Studies* 18 (1942): 270–83. In Jowett's 2004 edition, the case that the play is 'in some ways incomplete' is maintained – albeit not Ellis-Fermor's belief that the play is also an artistic failure (Jowett, ed., introduction to *Timon of Athens*, 1–11). Jackson, '"One Wish" or the Possibility of the Impossible', also argues that the two-authored play was not finished.
20 For a clear account of these issues, see Klein, 'Textual Analysis', in *Timon of Athens*, ed. Klein 181–2.
21 Jowett, ed., introduction to *Timon of Athens*, 70–4; 114–18.
22 Ibid., 51–2.
23 Ibid., 71.
24 Grady, *Shakespeare and Impure Aesthetics*, 124–9.
25 Walter Benjamin, *The Origin of German Tragic Drama*, trans. John Osborne (London: New Left Books, 1977), 159–235, especially the analysis of the double meaning of a visual emblem, 194.
26 Walter Benjamin, *The Arcades Project*, trans. Howard Eiland and Kevin McLaughlin (Cambridge, MA: Belknap Press of Harvard University Press, 1999), 462–3.

7

'An Antony that grew the more by reaping': The immeasurable bounty of the sharing economy in Cleopatra's Egypt

Kemal Onur Toker

This chapter seeks to analyse *Antony and Cleopatra* as the culmination of Shakespeare's thinking through of a closely intertwined set of poetic, economic and political themes.[1] The playwright had already begun exploring these ideas in *Romeo and Juliet* and *Troilus and Cressida*.[2] These three plays constitute Shakespeare's eponymous 'couples trilogy', and one of their central themes is indeed that of eponymy: the metaphorical process whereby proper names are translated into common predicates such that it becomes possible to talk about 'a Juliet' (*Romeo and Juliet*, 3. 3. 59) or 'an Antony' (*Antony and Cleopatra*, 1.3.91; 2.5.14; 4.2.18; 5.2.86; 5.2.98)[3] or 'Troiluses ... Cressids ... [and] Panders' (*Troilus and Cressida*, 3.2. 189-90). This translation of the 'proper' into the 'common' is a matter not just of stylistics or poetics but also of politics and economics. The New Economic Criticism of the past thirty years has served to reinforce New Historicism's already strong (albeit partially disavowed) tendency to construe all 'commonness' and 'generality' – and therefore also all discursiveness and sociability – in accordance with the exorbitantly privileged model of monetary capital. Drawing on recent work on the sharing economy of digital 'information goods' – alongside more traditional staples of Renaissance criticism such as Elyot's *Governour* and Cicero's *De Officiis* – I will provide a reading of *Antony and Cleopatra* that aims to loosen the monopolistic hold of the monetary model on our attempts to understand the general circulation of 'social energy' and 'cultural capital' in both Shakespeare's world and our own.

When Aristotle quipped that 'money is the measure of all things' (*Nicomachean Ethics* 1133a), he expected his readers to understand that this witticism is truly valid only within the restricted domain of the market. Cognizant of the fact that the most advanced mathematicians of his age were rapidly embracing the existence of incommensurability as a fundamental truth of their discipline,[4] Aristotle was openly contemptuous of those who imagined that genuine knowledge was a matter of reducing all things to the measure of this or that standard (cf. *Metaphysics* 986a, 1053a-b). The bleak magic of money consists in rendering actually incommensurable things perfectly commensurate to the same artificial quantitative standard[5] – so that, for instance, someone who toils for $15 per hour can know for sure that a whole day of their life is worth exactly $139 less than Apple's cheapest tablet computer. This impressive feat of Procrustean commensuration is, of course, a transparent performative political fiction[6] in which we all (more or less) willingly suspend disbelief so as to facilitate the orderly exchange of goods and services in the global marketplace. As Shakespeare recognized, the real danger with this pragmatic habit of acquiescing in what we know to be a convenient lie is that we might eventually come to adopt two corrosively cynical conclusions: truth itself is nothing but a performative political fiction, and the old philosophical doctrine that true value grows the more by sharing (cf. *De Officiis* 1.50-2) – 'The more I give to thee / The more I have' (*Romeo and Juliet* 2.1.176-7; cf. *Antony and Cleopatra* 5.2.86-7) – is nothing but a mystical piece of irrational magical thinking.

A new Timon or a new Juliet

An indefinite article modifies Antony's proper name on five separate occasions in the first edition of that play in which he shares the eponymic spotlight with Cleopatra. Elsewhere in his work, Shakespeare resorts to this peculiar type of catachresis – treating a proper name as if it were a common word, that is, a word denoting a quality that could be shared among many otherwise disparate entities – only very sparingly. We do indeed hear several times about 'a Richard' (*Richard III* 4.4. 37-41) – and just once about 'a Juliet' – but we never hear about 'a Hamlet', 'a Macbeth' or 'an Othello'. Enobarbus does perhaps come close to employing the proper name of Caesar as a common noun when he mimics Lepidus's obsequious flattery of his fellow triumvir: 'Would you praise [Octavius] Caesar? Say "Caesar." Go no further' (3.2.13). But neither Lepidus nor Enobarbus is frivolous enough to imagine that it would be appropriate to eulogize the young emperor as '*a* Caesar'. The quality of being Caesar – the quality of being 'the universal landlord' (3.13.72) – is not something that Octavius is able or willing to hold in common with anyone else, which is why he methodically eliminates all his actual and potential fellow 'world-sharers' (2.7.72). In the course of the play, it becomes increasingly obvious that the imperious 'boy' (3.13.17) is capable of relating to the world only through acts of command and exchange, never through acts of sharing. This Caesar knows only how to economize his financial and political capital so as to make sure he becomes and remains the one who rules over the many; he is utterly appalled (cf. 1.4.19-21) by the common touch of an Antony, who wishes himself to become the many and for the many to 'be clapped up together in / An Antony' (4.2.17-18).

Although he is no stranger to the economy of command and exchange, Antony's preferred mode of being in the world is that of sharing his bounty. In this regard, he is Shakespeare's attempt to imagine a new Juliet whose capacity for sharing knows no bounds. The young lover's 'the more I give to thee, / The more I have' (*Romeo and Juliet* 2.1.176-177) finds its moving counterpart in Cleopatra's eulogy of an Antony whose bounty was itself '[a]n Antony ... / That grew the more by reaping' (5.2.86-87). At the beginning of the play, Antony himself pays homage to Juliet by transposing her 'They are but beggars that can count their worth' (*Romeo and Juliet* 2.5.32) into his own 'There's beggary in the love that can be reckoned' (1.1.15). Antony shares with Juliet an exuberant affirmation of the sheer infinity of goods whose sharing makes human fellowship possible. But Antony is not only a new Juliet. He is constantly haunted by the prospect of becoming a new Timon.

In North's version of Plutarch's *Lives*, we read that Mark Antony decided to seclude himself on the island of Pharos after the disaster at Actium, 'saying that he would lead *Timons* life, because he had the like wrong offered him, that was affore offered vnto *Timon:* and that for the vnthankefulnes of those he had done good vnto, and whom he tooke to be his frendes, he was angry with all men'.[7] Like Timon, Antony comes to grief because of his feckless inability to restrain his appetite for affectionate companionship and conviviality. It is one of the glories of Shakespeare's play that his Antony soars far above the abyss of the ruined Timon's misanthropy, even at the very heart of his loss. And yet his two shocking flashes of misogynistic savagery towards Cleopatra – in act 3: 'I found you as a morsel cold upon / Dead Caesar's trencher ...' (3.13.116-7); and again in act 4: 'Triple-turned whore! [...] The witch shall die!' (4.13.13, 47) – are more than sufficient reminders of how close he comes to plumbing the depths of that abyss.

No matter how uncharacteristic these brief outbursts might seem, Antony had already been tutored in such unkindness by the 'Roman thoughts' that troubled him from the start of the play. In Rome and in the presence of his new wife Octavia and her bother Octavius, he seemed utterly resolved to renounce any further attachment to his Alexandrian life with Cleopatra:

> Good night, sir. – My Octavia,
> Read not my blemishes in the world's report.
> I have not kept my square, but that to come
> Shall all be done by the rule.

> (2.3.4-7)

As the Norton editors point out, 'keeping one's square' and doing things 'by the rule' are expressions derived from the arts of precise quantitative measurement. In this play, to 'square' is also to engage in a ruthless struggle for political power (cf. 2.1.46). In keeping his square and doing things by the rule, Octavia's Roman incarnation of Antony thus promises to adopt the calculating Machiavellian rationality of his new brother-in-law. Cleopatra's Alexandrian version of Antony, on the other hand, will remain the insouciant connoisseur of all that 'O'erflows the measure' (1.1.2) – at least until his reckless indulgence brings him to the brink of Timon's ruinous misanthropy.

This contrast between measured, dispassionate Roman rationality and reckless, impassioned Egyptian excess has, of course, been a commonplace of the critical literature.[8] It seems to me, however, that the fundamental clash of values that drives the plot of *Antony and Cleopatra* is not so much a conflict between dispassionate rationality and passionate excess as between two different conceptions of social and economic rationality. From Octavius Caesar's eminently 'square' Roman perspective, 'an Antony that grew the more by reaping' is, at best, a particularly hyperbolic example of the 'Asiatic' rhetoric for which Antony was already infamous before he set foot beyond the confines of Europe. At worst, this 'Asiatic' flight of fancy is the delusional and paradoxical watchword of the irrational Alexandrian prodigality whose upshot is the fate of Timon. But if Cleopatra's Antony emerges at the end of the play, not as a new Timon, but as a new Juliet – at his death he is very much a generous lover rather than a bitter misanthrope – this is because Shakespeare had at his disposal cultural resources that enabled him to discern in 'an Antony that grows the more by reaping' a formula that reveals the foundations of all human sociability and rationality. These cultural resources – which I will briefly discuss in the following section – have been obscured from our view, since the seventeenth century, by what I shall call a 'metric' conception of rationality. Recent scholarship on the economics of 'information goods' will also prove invaluable in uncovering the sort of rationality that animates Cleopatra's eulogy of an Antony who could fully share in Juliet's boast,

> My bounty is as boundless as the sea,
> My love as deep; the more I give to thee,
> The more I have, for both are infinite.
>
> (*Romeo and Juliet* 2.1.175-7)

The bounties of money and
Ratio et Oratio

The more I give of anything, the less I have left of it; therefore, I shall not give anything unless I get in exchange something of equal or greater value. Such are some of the most fundamental presuppositions of the metric type of rationality that guides the conduct of Octavius Caesar in its entirety. The young emperor 'gets money where / He loses hearts' (2.1.13-14), and he is quite happy with the bargain. It enables him to amass the 'coin' to buy the services of many a mercenary minister. Caesar is, of course, no stranger to the theatrics of the so-called 'gift economy'; nevertheless, his bounteous 'nobleness' is always 'well acted' (5.2.44) in exchange for greater power and authority. The sort of bounty that Cleopatra ascribes to Antony, on the other hand, aspires to undermine the very of axiom of scarcity (dearness = dearth) that underlies Caesar's mercenary bargains and royal gifts alike. If there was or ever could be such a thing, a bounty that 'grew the more by reaping' would undo the primordial condition of scarcity that makes the carefully measured reckonings of (gift or commodity) exchange necessary in the first place.

In Shakespeare's culture, there were several scriptural, liturgical and mythological *topoi* that served as models for such infinite bounty: the New Testament miracle of loaves and fishes, the sacrament of Holy Communion and the Arthurian legend of the Holy Grail all invoke a type of wealth that grows the more by sharing. In a more secular vein, scholars like Marc Shell[9] and Hugh Grady[10] discern in the financial markets of early modern capitalism the quotidian counterpart of such supernatural bounteousness. It is nevertheless crucial to note that the 'magic' of finance most certainly does *not* consist in generating a bounty that abolishes scarcity altogether. After all, the 'bounty' or profit that one can derive from financial investments – which Shakespeare's contemporaries still called 'usury' – is entirely a function of the relative scarcity of money in a given market: like any other commodity, money becomes cheap when it is abundant and dear when it is in dearth.[11]

Goods in the marketplace are, as Octavius Caesar himself puts it, 'deared by being lacked'[12] (1.4.44). This basic fact of market economics generates a strong antisocial incentive for profit-minded sellers to create artificial scarcities by means of hoarding, engrossing, monopolizing or enclosing so as to make their cheapened wares dear again. This tendency to incentivize the antisocial practice of 'making a famine where abundance lies' accounts for at least some of the anti-market sentiment that pervades ancient and medieval literature. After stating that 'the desire of money is the root of all evil', the biblical author of 1 Timothy goes on to enjoin those who are rich in the goods of this world to 'be rich in good works, and be ready to distribute, and communicate' (Geneva Bible, 1 Timothy 6: 10, 18). What the rich are urged to 'communicate' – *communicare*, to share, to make available for common use – is primarily their own private wealth. Christian 'communication' or 'communion' is thus, among other things, a process whereby private wealth is diverted from its various antisocial uses in the market and translated into commonwealth. As Tyndale would put it in a treatise first published in 1527, 'Amonge Christen men loue maketh all thinges commune'.[13] Christian writers since antiquity have frequently been troubled by the thought that worldly goods may not be conducive to such bounteous 'communication'. In Queen Elizabeth's translation of Boethius, we read:

> The fame [of a generous person] fills many men's ears, but riches, not distributed, may not pass to many: which, when it is done, they must make poorer whom they leave. O scant and needy riches, which all to gain is not lawful for many, and come not to anyone, without they beggar the rest.[14]

Before getting to grips with this complaint about the scantiness of earthly riches, let us note that Boethius's original Latin does not in fact say that the 'fame' of a generous person 'fills many men's ears'. What he does actually say is captured with less economy but more fidelity in a clumsy verse translation published in 1525: 'A voyce vniuersal (I may conclude) / At ones may without apeyrement [lessening, impairment] / Fulfylle the yeres [ears] of a multitude'.[15] Boethius thus prefaces his invective against the beggarliness of worldly wealth with an acknowledgement of the universal communicative bounteousness of human speech.

The true quotidian counterpart of the magical bounteousness of the Holy Grail is not money or finance but language. This, to be sure, might seem a moot point. The New Economic Criticism of the past thirty years has taught us to regard money and language as perfectly analogous information technologies that shape and structure social reality in fundamentally similar ways.[16] Yet Boethius calls attention to a crucial distinction between money and all other information goods – a distinction which has recently become a vital issue in the world of digital currencies. As Don Tapscott, the author of a book on the *Blockchain Revolution*, points out,

> On the Internet, people haven't been able to transact or do business directly [without the intermediation of various financial institutions] for the simple reason that money isn't like other information goods and intellectual property per se. You can send the same selfie to all your friends, but you ought not give your friend a dollar that you've already given to someone else. The money must leave your account and go into your friend's. It can't exist in both places, let alone multiple places.[17]

Money and language are analogous phenomena insofar as both may be described as a set of information goods and techniques. Money, however, is a rather odd type of information good since it is specifically *designed* to *lack* what is, according to modern economics, the chief distinguishing characteristic of information goods: 'infinite expansibility'.[18] The same poem (or computer program or selfie) can exist in a potentially infinite number of places at the same time. However, it is only through criminal fraud that the same dollar (or renminbi or bitcoin, etc.) can exist in more than one location (for example my wallet and your bank account) at any given time. Money is thus an information construct which is designed to function as what economists call a 'rivalrous' good – a good of which one can always say, 'the more I give, the less I have'. Even on the Internet, monetary riches 'must make poorer whom they leave … and come not to anyone, without they beggar the rest'.

It might be objected that there is a hidden fallacy in the assumption that non-monetary information goods can exist in multiple places at the same time. When I share a selfie, what my friends receive is not the *original* file on my phone but a set of digital *copies*. Yet as early as Plato's *Parmenides* (132d-133a), this seemingly sensible distinction between the original and its copies is shown to be wholly irrelevant to the realm of 'ideas' or non-monetary 'information goods'. A leather-bound edition of the original first folio is many times more valuable in monetary terms than the innumerable electronic copies of Shakespeare's works available on the Internet. Yet in terms of information content, free online copies and the pages of the original first folio have an equal share in the common title of *Antony and Cleopatra*. An 'information good' or 'idea' is a quintessentially *generic* thing with regard to which the original/copy difference is entirely indifferent. It is precisely this indifference that makes 'ideas' existentially 'universal' (in the jargon of Platonic philosophy) or 'infinitely expansible' (in the jargon of modern economics).

Cleopatra's seemingly perverse unwillingness to distinguish between the original source of a message and its current, deputized bearer – her apparent inability to heed the messenger's plea, 'I that do bring the news made not the match' (2.5.68) – is thus arguably a testament to how well attuned she is to this bounteous communicative indifference. Many critics have been appalled by the Queen's treatment of the messenger who brings her news of Antony's marriage to Octavia.[19] It should, however, be recalled that Cleopatra's offence here consists ultimately in this: she overlooks the fact that the messenger is a totally inconsequential intermediary rather than a full-fledged agent in the affairs of which he speaks. Something very much like a 'Roman thought' does indeed seize the Queen when she reflects on how she has perhaps dealt with this mere functionary not in too cruel but in too *familiar* a manner: 'These hands do lack nobility, that they strike / A meaner than myself' (2.5.83-4). What Octavius finds so scandalous in Antony's Alexandrian conduct is also this lack of 'nobility' – a 'lack' which issues forth in an overflow of cheerfully vulgar gregariousness: 'keep[ing] the turn of tippling with a slave', 'reel[ing] the streets at noon', 'stand[ing] the buffet / With knaves that smell of sweat' (1.4.19-21).

Octavius rattles off this catalogue of depravities to impugn Antony's good name. When Antony himself displays his Alexandrian common touch on stage, however, he gives the lie to the Machiavellian and mercantile adage (cf. *1 Henry IV*, 3.2.40-87) that 'familiarity breeds contempt':

> I wish I could be made so many men,
> And all of you clapped up together in
> An Antony, that I might do you service
> So good as you have done.

(4.2.16-9)

These words do not prompt contemptuous sneers but generous tears from Antony's plebeian audience. This is the only time in the play when Antony adopts Cleopatra's habit of speaking about 'an Antony'. In his more belligerent Roman moods, he tends to assume an altogether different style. Thus, 'I am / Antony yet' (3.13.93-4) is merely a turgid Senecan transposition of Enobarbus's farcically pompous, 'Would you praise Caesar? Say "Caesar." Go no further'. As Cleopatra knows very well, saying 'an Antony' goes much further than saying either 'Caesar' or 'I am Antony yet'. The latter statements merely assert an individual's claim to a particular title. Saying 'an Antony', on the other hand, transforms a proper name into a common noun that partakes of the infinitely shareable bounty of reason and speech.

It is a fitting irony that the Roman author who most famously celebrated the infinitely shareable bounty of 'reason and speech' in his writing was also among the most prominent victims of the second triumvirate: Marcus Tullius Cicero. In the words of a mid-sixteenth-century English translation of Cicero's *De Officiis*, it is 'reason, and speeche [*ratio et oratio*] which by teaching, learnig, conferring, reasoning, & iudging, winneth one man to an other, and ioineth them in a certein naturall feloutship [*societas*]'. 'And surelic', continues Cicero, 'this is the feloutship, that spreadeth moste largelie with men amonge themselues, and with all among all: in the which ther must be kept a commonnesse of all thinges' (*De Officiis* 1.50-1). Such 'commonnesse of all thinges' is made possible only through the infinite communicative bounty of *ratio et oratio*. Just as others can light their candles at ours without thereby leaving us any the less illumined,[20] what we share through speech becomes 'profitable to those, that receiue them, & nothing burdenous to the giuer' (*De Officiis* 1.52).[21]

The splendour and misery of metric rationality

The bounteous view of *ratio et oratio* that finds its canonical articulation at *De Officiis* 1.50-2 has been roundly dismissed by Pierre Bourdieu, the pre-eminent twentieth-century theorist of 'cultural capital', as 'the illusion of linguistic communism'. As Bourdieu sees it, this 'illusion' manifests itself in the tendency to misdescribe 'symbolic appropriation as a sort of mystical participation'.[22] We can assume that this allegedly 'illusory' and 'mystical' view of communication was predominant in Shakespeare's day, since we know Cicero's *De Officiis* occupied the pride of place in English public school curricula well into the seventeenth century.[23] Already in Sir Thomas Elyot's *Boke Named the Gouernour*, however, we find a rejection of the type of human fellowship 'in the which ther must be kept a commonnesse of all thinges'. As Elyot would have it, 'where all thynge is commune, there lacketh ordre'. And 'where there is any lacke of ordre [there] nedes must be perpetuall conflicte ... [and eventually] uniuersall dissolution'.[24]

It is this threat of 'uniuersall dissolution' that Hobbes would use to justify the rule of his 'universal landlord', the Leviathan. But we already find the theme deployed to legitimize political authority in Shakespeare's *Troilus and Cressida*. As the consummate politician Ulysses has it, the ultimate consequence of the Greeks' dangerous neglect of 'the speciality of rule' (*Troilus and Cressida* 1.3.77) is that

[f]orce should be right – or rather, right and wrong,
Between whose endless jar justice resides,
Should lose their names, and so should justice too.

(1.3.116-8)

Here, very near the climax of his famous 'degree speech', Ulysses is clearly not staking the 'conservative' claim that political hierarchy is somehow in accordance with the dictates of divine or natural justice. Nor is he making the naive 'Machiavellian' or 'Calliclean' mistake of simply equating 'right' with 'might'. His far more radical, proto-Hobbesian point is that it makes no sense to talk about 'right and wrong' in a world where 'degree' and the 'specialty of rule' are entirely neglected. It is as if the words 'right' and 'wrong' were worthless counterfeit currency in the absence of an authority that could define and determine their significance. In Ulysses's speech, the very possibility of sharing a common moral vocabulary is made contingent upon the imposed political geometry of 'degree' and 'the speciality of rule'.

The Octavius Caesar of *Antony and Cleopatra* – he who deals exclusively 'on lieutenantry' (3.11.39) – is a younger version of this Ulysses, who is also a master not of the chivalric arts of single combat but of the Machiavellian arts of 'policy'. To be more precise, Octavius and Ulysses are both Shakespearean attempts to imagine a new type of 'Machiavel': a competent bureaucrat-in-chief who is neither charismatically fiendish (like Richard III) nor racked with bouts of debilitating remorse (like Henry IV). As Harold Goddard remarks with regard to Octavius, 'He is cold, like Iago, but instead of taking delight in the evil he does, he doesn't even know that it is evil.'[25] This strange and culpable innocence might seem to set Octavius far apart from the politic knowingness of Ulysses. However, it is precisely his full participation in Ulysses's Hobbesian wisdom that accounts for Octavius's uncanny innocence of good and evil.

For Octavius as for Ulysses, 'right and wrong' are words whose import is entirely dependent upon the principle of 'the speciality of rule'. Indeed, the word 'rule' itself neatly encapsulates the two 'Roman' obsessions that govern the conduct of the young Caesar. In Shakespeare's English as in our own, 'rule' is a synonym for that most Roman of preoccupations, *imperium*. In Shakespeare's English more than in our own, however, a 'rule' is also a standard of measurement. Under Octavius's rule, 'right and wrong' are mere metric constructs whose precise meaning and value are determined in strict accordance with a set of 'rules' or standards of Octavius's choosing. Antony seems to be under the impression that the 'most narrow measure' (3.4.8) that Octavius metes out to him is in flagrant breach of objective standards of justice. But Ulysses and Octavius are right to believe that the objectivity of any given standard of measurement is entirely a function – and a fiction – of the sovereign will of political authority. A standard issue 'pint' in the United States contains significantly less liquid than a standard issue 'pint' in the United Kingdom.[26] Nevertheless, upon being served a US pint at an American bar, a British tourist cannot reasonably complain about being given 'most narrow measure'. In the United States, the sovereign prerogative to 'fix the Standards of Weights and Measures' is among the 'enumerated powers' of the US Congress listed in Article I, Section 8 of the US Constitution.

Such arbitrary fixing of metric standards might well occasion some minor – or, at any rate, entirely remediable – misunderstandings and inconveniences in international commerce.[27] But it is also the condition of possibility of any successful act of measurement. The task of measurement is to ascertain and quantify, not the conformity of our standards to the world, but the conformity of the world to our standards. In *An Anatomy of the World*, John Donne laments the fact that we make the stars 'obey our pace' and serve our merely sublunary purposes when we cast over the heavens an artificial and imaginary 'net' of 'Meridians, and Parallels'.[28] Other seventeenth-century authors were more favourably impressed with the fact that such imaginary metric constructs can grant us the very real power to enhance our technological capabilities. Especially in Hobbes, admiration for the civilizing benefits of measurement[29] manifests itself alongside a strident insistence that we can only know what we ourselves have made.[30] Instead of encouraging his readers to 'hold, as it were, the mirror up to nature', Hobbes enjoins them to construct systems of measurement that can impose some sort of artificial order on our otherwise haphazard and unruly experience of reality.

In a remarkable anticipation of Hobbes, Shakespeare's Octavius deploys ordinary language as if it were such a system of measurement. The particular metric construct that serves as his model is, perhaps unsurprisingly, money. As Aristotle noted in his *Nicomachean Ethics* (1133a10-1133b20), under certain circumstances, money quite appropriately functions as the universal measure of all things (μετρεῖται γὰρ πάντα νομίσματι). In the marketplace, money facilitates exchange by making otherwise entirely incommensurable things – the proverbial apples and oranges – equally commensurate to the same easily quantified metric. In ordinary language, we may speak endless volumes about the relative gustatory merits of apples and oranges. But it is money that enables us to determine with quantitative precision that, on a given day at a given market, one apple is worth no more and no less than half an orange. Enobarbus brilliantly exposes the monetary inspiration of Octavius's imperial anthropometrics when he ascribes to the young man the oddly mercantile boast that 'being twenty times of better fortune, / He is twenty men to one' (4.2.3-4).

Throughout *Antony and Cleopatra*, the measurement of 'fortune' in quantitative terms is a persistent theme whose variations range from high-spirited musings about the manly endowments of prospective lovers – 'Am I not an inch of fortune better than she?' (1.2.55) – through peevish reflections on gamblers' luck – 'his quails ever / Beat mine, inhooped, at odds' (2.3.36-7) – all the way down to grim calculations of 'try[ing] a larger fortune' (2.6.34) and slaughtering 'much tall youth' (2.6.7) in the imperial game of *Realpolitik*. While he shows absolutely no interest in excelling his 'great competitor' in the arts of love, Octavius is certainly many times more fortunate than Antony in both recreational and geopolitical blood sports. And yet Cleopatra still insists that it is 'paltry to be Caesar / Not being Fortune, he is but Fortune's knave' (5.2.2-3).

Whatever else he is, Octavius is certainly no starry-eyed 'Fortune's fool'. Although she has just cause to accuse him of knavishness, Cleopatra is not belabouring the obvious point that this Caesar is a self-serving schemer. She is making the far more interesting observation that his self-serving scheming is itself a form of servility. The universal landlord is but Fortune's knave in the sense that he is the unwitting yet utterly possessed servant of the goddess of rivalrous riches – which 'must make poorer whom they leave ... and come not to anyone, without they beggar the rest'. Octavius's knavish paltriness consists in his genuine ignorance that there are types of riches which do not diminish but grow the more by sharing. Under his rule, even the gifts of *ratio et oratio* are transformed into rivalrous commodities that enrich and empower the 'universal landlord' at the expense of all his would-be 'world-sharers'.

Sovereign states have almost always attempted to exercise monopoly powers over the supply of money within their territories, and there may be sound economic and political reasons behind this policy of 'seigniorage'.[31] Octavius clearly aims to exercise monopoly powers over the supply of information as well. Like the monopolists of the digital economy – the Amazons, Googles and Facebooks – the young Caesar runs an efficient 'information aggregation' network which can also be deployed for the purposes of propaganda. Soon after receiving news of Antony's death, he moves to ensure that his version of the story will become the standard official account of the conquest of the East:

> Go with me to my tent; where you shall see
> How hardly I was drawn into this war,
> How calm and gentle I proceeded still
> In all my writings.

> (5.1.73-6)

We, of course, know very well what these 'writings' will show: the noble and soon-to-be 'august' Octavius was assiduously promoting the cause of 'universal peace' (4.6.5), while his competitor Antony was 'levying / The king's o' the earth for war' in shameful cahoots with the 'whore' to whom he had given up his empire (3.68-9).

Cleopatra's immeasurable rationality

Shakespeare's 'couples trilogy' can be read as a sustained critique of the metric conception of rationality that animates such imperious discursive monopolies. In *Romeo and Juliet* it is the female protagonist's sheer, immeasurable generosity that overwhelms the discursive monopoly of the antifeminist 'rule' according to which women say 'yea' because they are promiscuous and 'nay' because they are not only promiscuous but also desperate to be wooed (*Romeo and Juliet*, 2.1.137-143). Cressida is no doubt very much a creature of this 'rule' (cf. *Troilus and Cressida* 1.2.260-273), and yet Shakespeare is adamant in his refusal to grant her ex-lover the metric serenity to 'square the general sex / By Cressid's rule' (*Troilus and Cressida* 5.2.132-3). If Troilus is unable to go through with such 'squaring', this is because he is forced to confront a truth which overflows the measure of his monomaniacal insistence on the metric principle of 'rule in unity':

> If there be rule in unity itself,
> This is not she. O madness of discourse,
> That cause sets up with and against itself! [...]
> Within my soul there doth conduce a fight
> Of this strange nature, that a thing inseparate
> Divides more wider than the sky and earth;
> And yet the spacious breadth of this division
> Admits no orifex for a point as subtle
> As Ariachne's broken woof to enter.
>
> (*Troilus and Cressida* 5.2.147-152)

As recent scholarship[32] has shown, these lines display Shakespeare's familiarity with the theory of what the Pythagoreans – those metric fanatics of the ancient world – had already fatefully miscalled 'irrational' numbers.[33] At least on the face of it, there is indeed something rather 'mad' about such numbers. After all, granting the existence of even the most workaday 'irrational' numbers – $\sqrt{2}$ and π – commits us to the astounding belief that there is an *immeasurable* infinity lurking in the tiny distance that separates 1.41421 from 1.41422 (in the case of $\sqrt{2}$) or 3.141592 from 3.141593 (in the case of π). That 'a thing inseparate / Divides more wider than the sky and earth' is indeed an assault on the principle of 'rule in unity' that misidentifies rationality with commensuration. This, however, is not an assault on rationality as such. So-called 'irrational' numbers – numbers which are *incommensurable* to the arithmetic unit – are absolutely crucial to the eminently rational enterprise of higher mathematics. In his *Laws* (819b-820c), Plato laments the shameful mathematical ignorance and patent irrationality of those Greeks who wrongly assume that all quantities must be commensurable to the basic arithmetic unit. He goes on to remark, no doubt with some exaggeration, that facts about mathematical incommensurability are well known even to children in Egypt.

From the very first scene of *Antony and Cleopatra*, a profound antipathy to incommensurability is shown to be a definitive feature of the Roman mind. Although this antipathy is undoubtedly an index of the Romans' lack of insight into the dizzying truths of higher mathematics, it would also seem to suggest their familiarity with the more sobering truths of political economy. The Roman science of imperial rule has no use for that which 'O'erflows the measure' (1.1.2), because it presides over a realm of rivalrous scarcity in which all things are 'deared by being lacked'. From this eminently 'square' imperial perspective, to imagine an alternative conception of value is to indulge in nothing but idle daydreaming – which is why Cleopatra initially presents her vision of Antony's immeasurable bounty as a 'dream' that a true Roman can only dismiss with scornful derision. I will quote the relevant passage as it appears in the second edition of the *Norton Shakespeare*:

> You laugh when boys or women tell their dreams;
> Is't not your trick? [...]
> I dream'd there was an Emperor Antony.
> O, such another sleep, that I might see
> But such another man! [...]
>   For his bounty,

There was no winter in't; an autumn 'twas
That grew the more by reaping.

(5.2.73-4, 75-8, 85-7)

In the penultimate line of this passage, the second edition of the *Norton Shakespeare* follows the widely accepted emendation of the eighteenth-century critic who replaced the first folio's '*an Anthony*' with his own entirely conjectural 'an autumn'. After all, the puzzled yet bold critic of the British 'Augustan' age asked, '[H]ow could an Antony grow the more by reaping?'[34] This Augustan emendation – which silences Cleopatra's transformation of Antony's proper name into a common noun – does indeed have the virtue of creating a pleasing resonance between 'winter' and 'autumn'. However, it entirely obliterates the resonance of 'an Antony that grew the more by reaping' with what Cleopatra goes on to say about whether 'there was, or might be, such a man / As this I dream'd of' (5.2.92-3). When her Roman interlocutor answers this question in the negative, Cleopatra shoots back (I again quote from the second edition of the *Norton Shakespeare*):

You lie, up to the hearing of the gods.
But, if there be, or ever were, one such,
It's past the size of dreaming: nature wants stuff
To vie strange forms with fancy; yet, to imagine
An Antony, were nature's piece 'gainst fancy,
Condemning shadows quite.

(5.2.94-9)

To imagine *an* Antony – that is to say, to imagine the bounteous transformation of the proper into the common – is not only 'past the size of dreaming' but it is also 'nature's piece 'gainst fancy'. Cleopatra is drawing upon mimetic theories of the emulous relationship between art and nature that were current in both Hellenistic Egypt and Renaissance England. As Aristotle noted in his *Physics*, human art or *technē* works by imitating not only nature's already existing products but also its general modes and principles of production. This latter, more 'fanciful' type of imitation often allows *technē* to *surpass* particular works of nature in certain regards (cf. *Physics* 199a).[35] Nevertheless, although the fancy of human art may often 'tutor', 'mend' or even 'outwork' nature – cf. *Antony and Cleopatra* (2.2.213), *Timon of Athens* (1.1.38), *The Winter's Tale*

(4.4.89-97) – it does so not arbitrarily but in accordance with nature's own generic principles. 'An Antony that grew the more by reaping' is Cleopatra's felicitous formula for celebrating the *generic* bounty of those gifts – the gifts of *ratio et oratio* – which constitute the *natural* foundation of all human imagination and creativity.

As William Flesch suggests, the motto of Octavius Caesar's metric art of imperial rule is captured in his careful command to Taurus: '*Do not exceed* / The prescript of this scroll' (3.8.4-5).[36] Unlike works of mimetic art, metric rules and standards are arbitrary political constructs. For this very reason, however, only those invested with sovereign power can alter them at will; the rest of us may not exceed the prescript of their writ. Anyone who decides to manufacture and distribute their own fancifully altered dollars or pints will soon feel the full coercive might of the sovereign state bearing down upon them. And the sovereign might will be entirely in the right: measurement as such would become entirely unreliable and therefore pointless if everyone is able to vary metric standards at will. However, in this very regard, metric units such as dollars and pints are radically different from most other information goods, which we quite rightly feel free to 'mend' and vary as we see fit – witness, for instance, the Augustan critic's misguided yet widely accepted 'mending' of 'an Antony that grew the more by reaping' or Shakespeare's own decidedly more felicitous 'outworking' of North's translation of a French adaptation of Plutarch's *Life of Mark Antony*. As the authors of an article in the journal *Ecological Economics* point out,

> Conventional market resources are rival, or subtractive: one person's use leaves everyone else less to use ... Information is a different type of resource. If information is used by one person, it does not leave less for anyone else to use ... However, the resource of information is not just non-rival, but actually improves through use. The term 'additive' can be used to describe a resource that improves through use, such as open-source software. After reading this paper you may develop new and better ideas from which we may all benefit in the future.[37]

As two distinguished professors of Harvard Law School[38] – an institution not otherwise known for its radicalism – have been reminding us for over a decade, it is precisely this 'additive' nature of information goods (also known as the 'on the shoulders of giants' effect) which makes it socially *irrational* to allocate them by means of market mechanisms that will inevitably favour rent-seeking monopolists such as Google and Facebook. It is true that metric standards are best provisioned by powerful monopolies that can ensure widespread uniformity. However, there is much more to the bounty of human rationality than the provision of uniform metric standards. As Cleopatra rightly insists, there are certain socially constitutive goods – the generic goods of *ratio et oratio* – that do not diminish but grow the more by reaping.

In the first chapter of his *Shakespearean Negotiations*, Stephen Greenblatt reminds us that '[m]oney is only one kind of cultural capital'. However, in the final chapter of the same book, we see that Bourdieu's notion of 'cultural capital' will not allow Greenblatt to grant any exemptions from the monopoly of the monetary logic of value that equates 'dearness' with 'dearth': 'aesthetic value, like all other value, actively depends upon want, craving, and absence ... [A]rt itself – fantasy ridden and empty – is the very soul of scarcity'.[39] In *Antony and Cleopatra*, this quintessentially monetary conception of value finds its true advocate in Octavius Caesar who announces it as a fact 'taught us from the primal state' that all things are 'deared by being lacked'. Yet the play also presents us with an alternative conception of value – encapsulated in the phrase 'an Antony that grew the more by reaping' – which is not only 'fanciful' but also pre-eminently *rational*. Imperious monopolists such as Caesar and Microsoft will no doubt always insist that the gifts of *ratio et oratio* are best cultivated within the protective enclosure of a strong private property rights regime, in which all things are 'deared by being lacked'. Such a regime does have the effect of increasing the monetary value of what the monopolist has enclosed. But it also has the well-documented effect of stifling not only the diffusion but also the creation of new knowledge which, unlike money, is just the kind of 'cultural capital' that grows the more by sharing.[40]

Notes

1   This research was assisted by a Mellon/ACLS Dissertation Completion Fellowship from the American Council of Learned Societies.
2   Unless otherwise noted, all references to Shakespeare's works are to William Shakespeare, *The Norton Shakespeare*, ed. Stephen

Greenblatt et al., 3rd edition (New York: W. W. Norton & Company, 2016).

3   Further parenthetical references to Shakespeare's works will include a title only when a play other than *Antony and Cleopatra* is being cited. In the case of works other than *Antony and Cleopatra*, the title will be omitted from the parenthetical reference only when the immediate context clearly indicates the title of the referenced work.

4   The truth of incommensurability was first demonstrated with regard to the diagonal of the unit square (i.e. $\sqrt{2}$), and this is the example that Aristotle repeatedly invokes in his numerous discussions of the incommensurable (e.g. *Prior Analytics* 41a, 46b; *Posterior Analytics* 89a; *Topics* 163a; *Physics* 221b-222a; *Metaphysics* 983a, 1047b; *Nicomachean Ethics* 1112a; *Eudemian Ethics* 1226a; *Rhetoric* 1392a). Although $\sqrt{2}$ was the first quantity which was *proved* to be incommensurable to the arithmetic unit, mathematicians since Georg Cantor (1845–1918) have known that there is an uncountable infinity of such incommensurable quantities – an infinity which Cantor also proved to be larger than the countable infinity of the familiar counting numbers. Cf. Eugenia Cheng, *Beyond Infinity: An Expedition to the Outer Limits of the Mathematical Universe* (London: Profile Books, 2017), 130–46.

5   'Money, then, acting as a measure, makes goods commensurate and equates them ... Now in truth it is impossible that things differing so much should become commensurate, but with reference to demand [in the marketplace] they may become so sufficiently' (*Nicomachean Ethics* 1133b14-19). This and subsequent English translations of Aristotle are from Aristotle and Jonathan Barnes, *The Complete Works of Aristotle: The Revised Oxford Translation*, Bollingen series; 71:2 (Princeton, NJ: Princeton University Press, 1984).

6   'This is why it has the name "money" (νόμισμα) – because it exists not by nature but by law (νόμος) and it is in our power to change it and make it useless' (*Nicomachean Ethics* 1133a30-35). Contrast this with what Aristotle has to say about the mathematical truth of the incommensurability of the diagonal: 'To say, however, that you are at once standing and sitting, or that the diagonal is commensurable, is to say what is not only false but also impossible' (*On the Heavens* 281b30-35).

7   Plutarch, *The Lives of the Noble Grecians and Romanes Compared Together by That Graue Learned Philosopher and Historiographer, Plutarke of Chaeronea; Translated Out of Greeke into French by Iames Amyot ...; and Out of French into Englishe, by Thomas North*, ed. Thomas Sir North, Early English Books, 1475–640 / 1712:12

(Imprinted at London: By Thomas Vautroullier and Iohn VVight, 1579, 1579). Sig. PPPP. iiii. 1003.

8   Cf. James Hirsh, 'Rome and Egypt in Antony and Cleopatra and in Criticism of the Play', in *Antony and Cleopatra: New Critical Essays*, ed. Sara Munson Deats (New York: Routledge, 2005), 117.

9   Marc Shell, *Money, Language, and Thought: Literary and Philosophical Economies from the Medieval to the Modern Era* (Berkeley: Berkeley: University of California Press, 1982).

10 Hugh Grady, 'Timon of Athens: The Dialectic of Usury, Nihilism, and Art', in *A Companion to Shakespeare's Works: The Tragedies*, ed. Richard Dutton and Jean E. Howard (Oxford: Blackwell, 2005), 435.

11 'The Remedy for Vsury may be plenty of Money. For then, men will have no such cause to take Money at interest, as when Money is scant. For as it is the scarcitie of Money that maketh the high rates of interest: so the plentie of Money will make the rates Low, better than any Statute for that purpose'. Edward Misselden, *Free Trade. Or, the Meanes to Make Trade Florish Wherein the Causes of the Decay of Trade in This Kingdome, Are Discouered: And the Remedies Also to Remooue the Same, Are Represented*, Early English Books, 1475–1640 / 895:11 (London: Printed by Iohn Legatt, for Simon Waterson, dwelling in Paules Church-yard at the Signe of the Crowne, 1622, 1622).

12 Here, I am following the reading of the Second Edition of the *Norton Shakespeare*. The Third Edition has 'feared' where the Second has 'dearead'.

13 William Tyndale, *That Fayth the Mother of All Good Workes Iustifieth Us before We Ca[N] Bringe Forth Anye Good Worke*, Early English Books, 1475–1640 / 156:11 ([Printed at Malborowe [i.e. Antwerp] in the londe of hesse: y Hans luft [i.e. J. Hoochstraten], the. viii. day of May. Anno M.D.xxviii] [1528], 1528). Sig. f. v. Fol. xl.

14 I. Elizabeth, *Elizabeth I: Translations, 1592–1598*, ed. Janel M. Mueller and Joshua Scodel (Chicago: Chicago: University of Chicago Press, 2009), 144.

15 Boethius, *The Boke of Comfort Called in Laten Boetius De Consolatione Philosophie. Translated in to Englesse Tonge*, ed. John Walton, Early English Books, 1475–1640 / 604:02 ([Enprented in the exempt monastery of Tauestok in Denshyre: By me Dan Thomas Rychard monke of the sayd monaster, to the iu[n]stant desyre if ryght worshypful esquyer Mayster Robert Langdon, Anno d[omini] M D xxv. [1525]], 1535). Sig. E. iii.

16 'Money and language are both systems of signs: one produces meaning, the other value. As Goux puts it in *The Coiners of Language* (1994): "The parallel between language and money, literature and political economy, is not a mere juxtaposition, but is made possible and operative by processes at work simultaneously in both economies". This would become the basic, definitive and perhaps the only assumption shared by all new economic critics'. David Hawkes, *Shakespeare and Economic Theory* (London: Bloomsbury Arden Shakespeare, 2015), 70.

17 Don Tapscott, *Blockchain Revolution: How the Technology behind Bitcoin Is Changing Money, Business, and the World*, ed. Alex Tapscott (New York: Portfolio / Penguin, 2016), 31.

18 Cf. Philip Mirowski and Esther-Mirjam Sent, *Science Bought and Sold: Essays in the Economics of Science* (Chicago: University of Chicago Press, 2002), 284.

19 Northrop Fry, 'Antony and Cleopatra', in *Antony and Cleopatra*, ed. Neil Heims, Bloom's Shakespeare through the Ages (New York: Bloom's Literary Criticism, 2008), 214.

20 *De Officiis* 1.50: 'Homó, qui erranti cómiter monstrát viam, / Quasi lúmen de suo lúmine accendát, facit. / Nihiló minus ipsi lúcet, cum illi accénderit'. In the *Canterbury Tales*, Chaucer had adapted the very same lines as follows: 'He is to[o] greet a nygard that wolde werne [i.e., refuse] / A man to lighte a candle at his lanterne; / He shal have never the lasse light, pardee!' Geoffrey Chaucer, *The Riverside Chaucer*, ed. Larry Dean Benson and F. N. Robinson, 3rd edition (Boston: Houghton Mifflin, 1987). III. 333–5.

21 Marcus Tullius Cicero, *Marcus Tullius Ciceroes Thre Bokes of Duties to Marcus His Sonne, Turned Out of Latine into English, by Nicholas Grimalde. Cum Priuilegio Ad Imprimendum Solum*, ed. Nicholas Grimald, Early English Books, 1475–1640 / 315:09 ([Imprinted at London: In Fletestrete within Temple barre, at the signe of the hand & starre, by Richard Tottel], Anno domini. 1556, 1556). Sig. C. iiii. Fol. 21–22.

22 Pierre Bourdieu, *Language and Symbolic Power*, ed. John B. Thompson (Cambridge, MA: Harvard University Press, 1991), 43.

23 Cf. Thomas Whitfield Baldwin, *William Shakespere's Small Latine & Lesse Greeke*, vol. 2 (Urbana: Urbana: University of Illinois press, 1944), 590.

24 Thomas Sir Elyot, *The Boke Named the Gouernour Deuised by [Sir?] Thomas Elyot Knight*, Early English Books, 1475–1640 / 35:01; Early English Books, 1475–1640 / 1751:20 (Londini: In edibus Tho. Bertheleti, M.D. xxxi [1531], 1531). Sig. A. v. fol. 6; Sig. A. iii. fol. 3.

25   Harold C. Goddard, 'Antony and Cleopatra', in *Antony and Cleopatra*,
       ed. Neil Heims (New York: Bloom's Literary Criticism, 2008), 165.

26   'In Britain (more fully *imperial pint*), it is a measure equivalent to
       34.68 cubic inches (approx. 0.568 litre); in the United States (more
       fully *U.S. pint*), a measure equivalent to 28.87 cubic inches (approx.
       0.473 litre) for liquid measure, 33.60 cubic inches (approx. 0.551
       litre) for dry measure.' Oxford English Dictionary, '*pint, n*' (Oxford
       University Press). https://www.oed.com/view/Entry/144326?redirecte
       dFrom=pint.

27   Already in Shakespeare's lifetime, there was at least one
       book published in London which aimed to remedy these
       misunderstandings and inconveniences by providing '*Certaine Tables
       of the Agreement of Measures, and Waightes, of Diuers Places
       in Europe*'. Humfrey Baker, *The Well Springe of Sciences Which
       Teacheth the Perfect Worke and Practise of Arithmeticke, Bothe
       in Whole Numbres and Fractions, Set Forthe by Humfrey Baker,
       Londoner, 1562. And Nowe Once Agayne Perused Augmented
       and Amended in All the Three Partes, by the Sayde Aucthour,
       Whereunto Hee Hathe Also Added Certaine Tables of the Agreement
       of Measures, and Waightes, of Diuers Places in Europe, the One
       with the Other, as by the Table Folowing It May Appeare. 1574*,
       Early English Books, 14751640 / 307:06 ([Imprinted at London: By
       Thomas Purfoote, dwelling in Paules Church yarde at the signe of
       the Lucres, 1574], 1574).

28   John Donne, *An Anatomy of the Vvorld Wherein, by Occasion of
       the Vntimely Death of Mistris Elizabeth Drury the Frailty and the
       Decay of This Whole World Is Represented*, Early English Books,
       1475–640 / 881:20 (London: Printed [by William Stansby] for
       Samuel Macham. and are to be solde at his shop in Paules Church-
       yard, at the signe of the Bul-head, An. Dom. 1611). Sig. B. 3.

29   'For those men who have taken in hand to consider nothing else
       but the comparison of magnitudes, numbers, times, and motions,
       and their proportions one to another, have thereby been the authors
       of all those excellences, wherein we differ from such savage people
       as are now the inhabitants of divers places in America' (*Elements
       of Law*, Pt. 1, ch. 13, § 3). Thomas Hobbes, *Three-Text Edition
       of Thomas Hobbes's Political Theory: The Elements of Law, De
       Cive, and Leviathan*, ed. Deborah Baumgold and Thomas Hobbes
       (Cambridge: Cambridge University Press, 2017), 125.

30   '[I]f it be propounded that *two and three make five* ... to know
       this truth is nothing else, but to acknowledge that it is made
       by ourselves [...] *Truth* is the same with a *true proposition* ...
       And to *know truth* is the same thing as to *remember* that it was
       made by ourselves by the very usurpation of the words.' Thomas

Hobbes, *Man and Citizen: De Homine and De Cive* (Indianapolis: Indianapolis: Hackett Pub. Co., 1991), 373–4. For two important twentieth-century appraisals of Hobbes's constructivism, see Hannah Arendt, *Between Past and Future: Six Exercises in Political Thought* (New York: Viking Press, 1961). Leo Strauss, *Natural Right and History* (Chicago: University of Chicago Press, 1953). For a more recent treatment, see Victoria Ann Kahn, *The Future of Illusion: Political Theology and Early Modern Texts* (Chicago and London: The University of Chicago Press, 2014), 3.

31   Felix Martin, *Money: The Unauthorised Biography*, First American edition (New York: Alfred A. Knopf, 2014), 79.

32   Edward Wilson-Lee, 'Shakespeare by Numbers: Mathematical Crisis in Troilus and Cressida', *Shakespeare Quarterly* 64, no. 4 (2013). Adhaar Noor Desai, 'Number-Lines: Diagramming Irrationality in "the Phoenix and Turtle"', *Configurations* 23, no. 3 (2015).

33   There is, of course, a perfectly sober technical sense in which numbers such as $\sqrt{2}$ and π are 'irrational': none of them can be represented as the *ratio* of two finite integers. However, according to the Pythagoreans, anything which was irrational in this technical sense was also 'irrational' in the more substantial and lurid sense of turning a cosmos into a chaos. Cf. Richard D. McKirahan, *Philosophy before Socrates: An Introduction with Texts and Commentary* (Indianapolis: Hackett Publishing Company, 1994), 98.

34   Quoted in William Shakespeare and Horace Howard Furness, *A New Variorum Edition of Shakespeare: The Tragedie of Anthonie and Cleopatra* (Philadelphia: J. B. Lippincott Company, 1907), 344. The third edition of the *Norton Shakespeare* has 'an Antony' where the second edition has 'an autumn'.

35   Cf. Philippe Lacoue-Labarthe and Christopher Fynsk, *Typography: Mimesis, Philosophy, Politics* (Cambridge, MA: Harvard University Press, 1989), 255–6.

36   William Flesch, *Generosity and the Limits of Authority: Shakespeare, Herbert, Milton* (Ithaca: Cornell University Press, 1992).

37   Ida Kubiszewski, Joshua Farley and Robert Costanza, 'The Production and Allocation of Information as a Good That Is Enhanced with Increased Use', *Ecological Economics* 69, no. 6 (2010): 1346–7.

38   Lawrence Lessig, *Free Culture: How Big Media Uses Technology and the Law to Lock Down Culture and Control Creativity* (New York: Penguin Press, 2004). Yochai Benkler, *The Wealth of Networks: How Social Production Transforms Markets and Freedom* (New Haven: Yale University Press, 2006); *The Penguin and the Leviathan: The Triumph of Cooperation over Self-Interest* (2011).

39   Stephen Jay Greenblatt, *Shakespearean Negotiations: The Circulation of Social Energy in Renaissance England* (Berkeley: University of California Press, 1988).

40   'In perhaps one of the most startling papers on the economics of innovation published in the past few years, Josh Lerner looked at changes in intellectual property law in sixty countries over a period of 150 years. He studied close to three hundred policy changes, and found that, both in developing countries and in economically advanced countries that already have patent law, patenting both at home and abroad by domestic firms of the country that made the policy change, a proxy for their investment in research and development, decreases slightly when patent law is strengthened! The implication is that when a country – either one that already has a significant patent system, or a developing nation – increases its patent protection, it slightly decreases the level of investment in innovation by local firms. Going on intuitions alone, without understanding the background theory, this seems implausible – why would inventors or companies innovate less when they get more protection? Once you understand the interaction of nonrivalry and the "on the shoulders of giants" effect, the findings are entirely consistent with theory. Increasing patent protection, both in developing nations that are net importers of existing technology and science, and in developed nations that already have a degree of patent protection, and therefore some nontrivial protection for inventors, increases the costs that current innovators have to pay on existing knowledge more than it increases their ability to appropriate the value of their own contributions.' Benkler, *The Wealth of Networks*, 39.

8

Woman, warrior or witch? Fetishizing Margaret of Anjou on the early modern stage

Rebecca Steinberger

British theatre responded to the #MeToo Movement in various and innovative ways. Among them was a cultural renaissance of Shakespeare's femme fatale, Margaret of Anjou. Margaret appears in four of Shakespeare's history plays: *Henry VI, Parts I, II* and *III* and *Richard III*, but she has never been as fashionable as she is in our era. In 2018, Jeanie O'Hare's *Queen Margaret* was published and performed as a pivotal *her*story for the twenty-first century. By extracting Shakespeare's lines about the controversial regent and substituting her own, O'Hare makes Margaret into the subject of her own drama. In Elizabethan England, women could only wield power through an inherited title, money, magic, beauty and, of course, an advantageous marriage. Recent productions of the tetralogy and *Richard III* have dwelled on Margaret's metamorphosis from one kind of spectacle (beauteous French princess with huge dowry) to another (strategical warrior in the War of the Roses) to yet another (curse-wielding witch seeking revenge on those who have wronged her). What is it about Margaret that makes her such an attractively versatile commodity on the twenty-first-century stage?

Terry Eagleton acutely observes that 'Shakespeare is the quintessential commodity, at once ever-new and consolingly recognizable, always different and eternally the same, a magnificent feat of self-identity persisting through the most bizarre diversions and variations'.[1] One recent such topical variation is the focus of contemporary productions on Shakespeare's female characters, which in turn reflects a widespread desire to shift the general perspective of the plays to address the concerns of the twenty-first century. The dramatic figure of Margaret of Anjou has been straining against boundaries of power, space and gender from her stage debut in sixteenth-century London. She clearly enthralled Shakespeare, who gave her more lines than King Lear. He depicted her in roles ranging from the 'she-wolf of France' in *Henry VI, Part III*[2] to the 'foul, wrinkled witch' of *Richard III*.[3] Despite the fascination she can evoke in poets, however, Margaret is generally marginalized in English royal genealogy. As Nancy Bradley Warren explains, '[r]ather than being named or portrayed in the family tree, she is "translated into emblems," particularly into a bouquet of marguerites positioned in the centre of the bottom margin'.[4] Margaret of Anjou's space has quite literally been on the margins of historical and socio-political discourse.

Marginalization was, of course, an inherent quality of early modern theatre. The location of the playhouses in the 'liberties' south of the Thames reflected their exclusion from respectable social space. Like those who frequented the adjacent bear gardens, cockpits and stew-houses, the theatrical community (like the booksellers who set up shop in close proximity) was symbolically and literally alienated from the city and its government. Anti-theatrical attacks were relentless, condemning playwrights for marketing vice, with insouciant disregard of the theatre's considerable contribution to the burgeoning wealth and culture of the metropolis.[5] Puritanical factions attacked playwrights for contributing to drinking, dicing, prostitution – in fact the whole pantheon of illicit behaviour. Stephen Gosson's *The School of Abuse* (1579) compares the stage to the idolatrous sacrifices of the heathen:

He that thinks wanton plays a meet recreation for the mind of man is as far from the truth as the foolish Gentiles, which believe that their gods delight in toys; and we which carry our money to players to feed their pride may well be compared to the bath keeper's ass, which bringeth him wood to make his fire, and contenteth himself with the smell of the smoke.[6]

To such propagandists a powerful, beautiful, foreign and authoritative woman must have seemed the veritable embodiment of wantonness. These qualities were frowned on, for instance, by John Knox, whose influence remained strong in Calvinist London. His *First Blast of the Trumpet against the Monstrous Regiment of Women* (1558) pronounces: 'To promote a woman to bear rule, superiority, dominion or empire above any realm, nation or city is repugnant to nature, contumely to God, a thing most contrarious to his revealed will and approved ordinance, and finally it is the subversion of good order, of all equity and justice.'[7] On such grounds, Margaret's exercise of power could be construed as unnatural, opposed to God's will, ripe for invidious comparisons with witches, and likely to result in England's utter destruction.

Shakespeare's portrayal of Margaret in the first tetralogy is much more subtle than in *Richard III*. It moves through several distinct stages. On her initial entrance, it seems that Margaret's vice is limited to her role as vehicle of sexual and financial temptation. As the tetralogy progresses, however, her character shifts from wanton temptress to Amazonian warrior.[8] Over the course of this evolution, the tools of her trade change from the figurative magic of sexual 'glamour', through the economic power of finance, to the literal magic that Elizabethans believed to be prevalent all around them. By the time of her final appearance in Shakespeare's *oeuvre*, the aged Margaret has been relegated to the status of a witch – and in Renaissance England there was no more dangerous status to possess.

The price of peace

All this naturally raises the question of exactly how Margaret was able to achieve such power and influence at a time when women's opportunities for independent advancement were so limited? In her introduction to *The Last Medieval Queens*, J. L. Laynesmith explains:

> Ideas and assumptions about women in general were often contradictory in medieval society. Notions of women as weak,

passive, nurturing, and conciliatory contrasted with fear of them as temptresses with a potential for creating chaos and tongues that could do the devil's work. These fears and expectations were enhanced by the public position occupied by the woman who was queen and they shaped all attempts to establish what her role meant.[9]

This paints a bleak picture for women who did not fit into typical social roles. As Carole Levin and Patricia A. Sullivan note, 'Examining the rhetoric used by powerful women, by both men and women about such women, and the literary and dramatic weaving together of the themes represented by their lives can tell us a great deal about gender and power in the Renaissance, and also about how these themes echo in our culture today.'[10] An examination of Shakespeare's Margaret, an allegedly manipulative Machiavel who assumes the incapacitated king's office, can lay bare the ideological contradictions that necessarily arose when a woman came to occupy a position of authority in medieval culture.[11] With her husband unable to perform his kingly duties, Margaret seized a rare opportunity in an effort to protect her own assets and especially her son and heir.

Margaret of Anjou's arrival on English soil was deliberately staged as a spectacle. It followed months of anticipation. Helen Castor notes that '[f]or six months after the glittering celebrations that followed [her betrothal], Margaret remained with her mother in Anjou, honoured as a queen'[12] in a kind of rehearsal or prologue to her entrance into London.[13] As in later life, Margaret was not above spreading rumours that her enemies were using magic against her. According to Edward Hall's *The Vnion of the Two Noble and Illustre Fameilies of Lancastre Yorke* (1548), one of her later attempted invasions was thwarted by bad weather, although '[h]er frendes ... said, that she was kept awaie, and her iorney empeched by Sorcerers and Necromanciers'.[14] Margaret's position as a material asset to England is articulated prior to her first appearance in *I Henry VI*. She does not arrive until act 5, by which time the audience has been thoroughly prepared to perceive powerful women as skilled manipulators of rhetorical persuasion. The Duke of Alencon has warned that 'these women are shrewd tempters with their tongues',[15] while Talbot has described Joan la Pucelle as 'the devil's dam' and a 'witch'.[16] The performative power of Margaret's 'tongue' is particularly emphasized. Richard himself goes so far as to blame her words for making him commit murder: 'I was provokéd by her sland'rous tongue.'[17] Throughout the play Shakespeare elucidates the idea that Margaret's speech is more than merely persuasive; she seems to bewitch other characters into doing her will. As Cristina León Alfar observes: 'Margaret's power comes entirely from her words.... Margaret's actions are her words.'[18]

We are thus predisposed to suspicion when Gloucester informs the king that 'a great man of authority ... [p]roffers his only daughter to your Grace/ In marriage, with a large and sumptuous dowry'.[19] Whether the prospect of peace or of money primarily drives the transaction between Margaret and King Henry, her commodification is highlighted here. The picture Shakespeare paints of the financial anxieties circulating around the French princess is accurately drawn from history, and money concerns loomed over the historical Margaret even before she set sail for England. The English king was consumed with money worries: as one sixteenth-century chronicle succinctly puts it, he 'owed more than he was worth'.[20] Helen Mauer and B. M. Cron explain that 'Henry's marriage to Margaret was predicated upon the negotiation of a truce between England and France, in the hope that a temporary truce' might result in a resurgence of tranquillity and a consequent restoration of prosperity to both realms.[21]

Yet Margaret's 'gender denied her any recognized, concrete role in the negotiations that were supposed to lead to peace'.[22] At the time of her marriage Margaret was fifteen years old, so presumably her age also prevented her from playing an authoritative role in the talks. She was not even especially rich: Keith Dockray claims that although she was 'good-looking and vivacious ... and endowed with titles, her father possessed virtually no land beyond Anjou and little money'.[23] Yet Margaret's perseverance would soon pay off, as the ailing king's inability to rule propelled her into prominence. According to Laynesmith, 'Only those queens who publicly assumed a position independent from their kings ... received serious treatment in general histories, but this was as individual players on the political stage, not in the context of the office.'[24] Margaret's dramatic departure from this rule is the source of her central significance in Shakespeare's portrayal of England's national narrative.

When Margaret makes her initial entrance on Suffolk's arm, Shakespeare's stage directions indicate that he '*Gazes on her*'.[25] Before the audience even hears the princess speak, she is already objectified. She first asserts her identity ('Margaret my name') and asks about Suffolk ('whosoe'er thou art'),[26] even raising the question a second time: 'if thy name be so'.[27] Rapt at her sexual glamor, Suffolk notes: 'She's beautiful; and therefore to be wooed: She is a woman: therefore to be won.'[28] Margaret is reified, so that she can be used as a pawn in the peace negotiations, echoing the role played by Henry V's French princess Katherine (later to become Margaret's mother-in-law).[29] However, as Laynesmith reminds us:

> In stark contrast to Katherine of Valois, who was enthusiastically welcomed as a symbol of union between France and England following Henry V's victory over France, Margaret of Anjou arrived as part of a short-term compromise, sealing a twenty-two month truce between an increasingly powerful French monarch, Charles VII, and an English king too poor to pay his military commanders in France.[30]

The idea of Margaret as a reified spectacle recurs in act 5, when Henry is 'astonish'd' by Suffolk's 'wondrous rare description of Margaret',[31] and Suffolk quickly adds, 'She is content I be at your command.'[32] Although Henry is already engaged to be married, Suffolk assures him that '[a] poor earl's daughter is unequal odds'[33] and that her father's 'alliance will confirm our peace'.[34] Margaret's exploitation will be financial as well as political, as Exeter makes clear: 'his wealth will warrant a liberal dower'.[35] Money matters are further stressed by Suffolk:

> Henry is able to enrich his queen,
> And not to seek a queen to make him rich:
> So worthless peasants bargain for their wives,
> As market men for oxen, sheep, or horse.
> Marriage is a matter of more worth
> Than to be dealt in by attorneyship.[36]

A typical medieval marriage is based mainly on financial interests and, in spite of Suffolk's disgust, Henry behaves no differently from any other 'market man'. Henry rewards Suffolk's loyalty by levying a tax: 'For your expenses and sufficient charge, / Among the people gather up a tenth.'[37] As part of her coronation's pageantry, Margaret receives a welcome to London from the figure of 'Plente' who addresses her as the 'causer of welth, joie, and abundance'.[38]

The sexual appeal of the young Margaret impresses the king in *II Henry VI*, as he contemplates her 'beauteous face'.[39] Yet he also acknowledges the force of her words: 'Her sight did ravish, but her grace in speech, / Her words yclad with wisdom's majesty.'[40] An important factor in selecting a queen was virginity, and Laynesmith notes that '[t]he young virgin Margaret of Anjou fitted neatly in this tradition upon her arrival'.[41] At this stage, then, it seems that Henry has made the perfect match with the French princess, who possesses beauty, valuable linguistic skill and wisdom. Yet other courtiers hold a different opinion. Gloucester declares 'fatal this marriage',[42] and York complains:

> I never read but England's kings have had
> Large sums of gold and dowries with their wives,
> And our King Henry gives away his own,
> To march with her that brings no vantages.[43]

The financial implications of the transaction comfortably outweigh Margaret's beauty, words and wisdom in the view of the cynical courtiers. Yet as Helen Mauer points out in *The Letters of Margaret of Anjou*, the queen was hardly poor. On the contrary, her 'dower of duchy of Lancaster lands worth £2,000 made her a great magnate with extensive estates to manage. Some of her letters show her as a businesswoman, responsible for transactions as a landholder, as mistress of a large household or as someone who occasionally engaged in overseas trade'.[44] While this may seem like a lot of responsibility for a very young woman, her comfort in assuming roles of power appears remarkably consistent in Shakespeare and historical reality alike.

Queen of might and magic

Margaret's twentieth-century image mainly recalls her hag-like persona in *Richard III*. But a closer look at the texts forces us to ask how a historical figure of such beauty and power might degenerate into a witch. Although Margaret represents a significant

shift in the portrayal of women on the early modern stage, her aging
dictates that she must eventually relinquish femininity in favour
of 'male' character traits.[45] After Margaret's husband and son are
murdered, her reactions recall those of Richard III. This version
of Margaret serves as a precursor to Lady Macbeth, a character
written approximately fifteen years later. In 2 Henry VI we see
'two or three' murderers running off stage after the assassination
of Humphrey, Duke of Gloucester – an eerie foreshadowing of the
two or three murderers of Banquo in Macbeth. Upon learning of
his loyal friend's death, the King adopts a gender role-reversal that
anticipates Lady Macbeth's appeal to the 'spirits that tend on human
thoughts' to 'unsex me here' (1.5.38-39). The stage directions in 2
Henry VI reveal 'King sounds', which means that Henry literally
swoons. Margaret is quick to call for help and exclaims, 'Henry,
ope thine eyes!'[46] Not only does the King faint, fulfilling a feminine
stereotype, but his wife archly comments on his 'liquid tears or
heart-offending groans'.[47] Here is another connection to Lady
Macbeth, who alleges her husband's lack of manhood to goad him
into action. Margaret demands to be looked at, in an attempt to
distract her husband from his grief over Gloucester, and to hold
Suffolk accountable for his death:

Be woe for me, more wretched than he is.
What, dost thou turn away and hide thy face?
I am no loathsome leper, look on me.[48]

Margaret fits the stereotype of the wily, wanton woman here, as she
unabashedly asks for the male gaze to consume her. Her aggression
does not end there; she reminds the king of her hardships as she
voyaged to reach 'England's blessed shore,'[49] before appealing to the
power of both money and magic:

I took a costly jewel from my neck,
A heart it was, bound in with diamonds,
And through it towards thy land. The sea receiv'd it,
And so I wish'd thy body might my heart.
And even with this I lost fair England's view,
And bid my eyes be packing with my heart,
And call'd them blind and dusky spectacles,
For losing ken of Albion's coast.

How often have I tempted Suffolk's tongue
(The agent of thy foul inconstancy)
To sit and [witch] me, as Ascanius did
When he to madding Dido would unfold
His father's acts commenc'd in burning Troy!
Am I not witch'd like her? or thou not false like him?[50]

Margaret recalls her position as a spectacle on arrival on English
soil, connecting it to her subsequent status as 'witch'd'. Margaret is
often seen as a precursor of Lady Macbeth, but Eleanor, Duchess of
Gloucester, also exhibits damning similarities to Scotland's 'fiend-
like queen'.[51] Eleanor also asks to be 'unsex'd' and ridicules her
husband as unmasculine for chiding her ambition:

Were I a man, a duke, and next of blood,
I would remove these tedious stumbling blocks,
And smooth my way upon their headless necks;
And being a woman, I will not be slack
To play my part in Fortune's pageant.[52]

Money and magic collide as Eleanor enlists the aid of a conjurer
and witch in exchange for gold.[53] While both the Duchess and the
Queen desire power and status, Margaret cautions Suffolk on the
ways of Eleanor: 'More like an empress than Duke Humphrey's wife.
/ Strangers in court do take her for the Queen. / She bears a duke's
revenues on her back, / And in her heart she scorns our poverty.'[54]
While Margaret is extremely perceptive of Eleanor's will to power,
it is Buckingham who accuses her of having 'practic'd dangerously
against your state, / Dealing with witches and with conjurers'.[55]
As her banishment is pronounced, the Duchess comments: 'Look
how they gaze! / See how giddy multitude do point / And nod their
heads, and throw their eyes on thee!'[56] This recalls the spectacle
described by Kavita Mudan Finn:

In November 1411, the citizens of London were treated to the
fascinating spectacle of Eleanor Cobham, duchess of Gloucester,
wife to the Lord Protector and the most powerful woman in the
country, forced to do penance on their very streets after being
convicted of witchcraft and treason. It was a remarkable turn of
events, a story told and retold over the next century and a half,

spawning elaborate conspiracy theories, and inspiring writers as disparate as John Foxe, George Ferrers, Michael Drayton, and William Shakespeare.[57]

In a recapitulation of the earlier gaze, when Suffolk looked on Margaret for the first time, the audience appears charmed by their vision of the condemned. As with Lady Macbeth's final scenes, the Duchess of Gloucester appears with burning tapers in her hand, crying 'dark shall be my light, and night my day'[58] before retiring to prison. Rather than summoning spirits, however, Margaret commands an army for the House of Lancaster during the War of the Roses. The stereotype of the dangerous woman in power as bloodthirsty, untrustworthy, capricious and seductive was simply unavoidable, and Shakespeare merely holds the mirror up to what he assumed was nature. This is evident throughout his portrayals of seductive Cleopatra, pious Joan of Arc, traitorous Mary Queen of Scots and profligate Elizabeth I, in addition to bewitching Margaret of Anjou. In order to achieve a powerful voice, such women must be 'unsexed', transformed into she-wolves or, worse, into witches.

Warrior woman takes centre stage

In *III Henry VI*, Margaret has taken over monarchical responsibilities from her mentally ill husband. Historically, as Helen E. Maurer explains, 'Henry suffered a complete mental collapse that left him catatonic for roughly a year and a half. The king's illness and its aftermath brought Margaret to the political forefront.'[59] With tensions growing between Yorkists and Lancastrians, she confidently does what is necessary for her family and her crown. York warns: 'The Queen this day here holds her parliament, / But little thinks we shall be of her council.'[60] Yet the Queen continues to dominate the situation, cleverly reversing her husband's error in judgement:

> Had I been there, which am a silly woman,
> The soldiers should have toss'd me on their pikes
> Before I would have granted to that act.
> But thou prefer'st thy life before thine honor;
> And seeing thou doest, I here divorce myself

> Both from thy table, Henry, and thy bed,
> Until that act of parliament be repeal'd
> Whereby my son is disinherited.[61]

Not only does the Queen demand that her husband stay out of the battle, she actually forms an army herself. Margaret's shift from reified commodity to warrior woman is thus complete. Despite the messenger's warning to the Duke of York that the Queen has 'twenty thousand men',[62] Richard dismisses her based solely on her gender: 'A woman's general: what should we fear?'[63] Soon though, he must retract his sentiments and confess: 'The army of the Queen hath got the field.'[64] Whether or not Shakespeare had access to the historical Margaret's speeches, he accurately mirrors her aggressive language. In an address to the Citizens of London in 1461, Margaret proclaimed: 'I have often broken their battle line. I have mowed down ranks far more stubborn than theirs are now. You who once followed a peasant girl [Joan of Arc] now follow a queen.... I will either conquer or be conquered with you.'[65] The implication of 'mowing' anticipates the violent tone of *Henry V*'s warning to the French.[66] In *Shakespeare and Women*, Phyllis Rackin notes:

> All three parts of *Henry VI* ... feature women in what are now considered 'untraditional' roles – as generals leading victorious armies on the battlefield and as political actors who exercise significant power in the conduct of state affairs. Unlike Shakespeare's better-known history plays, these plays feature active, energetic female characters. Their roles may be unsympathetic, but they are real players in the theatre of history.[67]

It is York who most vehemently criticizes and even attacks the untraditional tendencies of the queen. His underestimation of female capability leads him to deploy gendered rhetoric as a means of characterizing Margaret as unnatural, though whether subhuman or superhuman seems in doubt:

> She-wolf of France, but worse than wolves of France,
> Whose tongue more poisons than the adder's tooth!
> How ill-beseeming is it in thy sex
> To triumph like an Amazonian trull
> Upon their woes whom fortune captivates![68]

Strong women warriors are referred to as she-wolves, adders and Amazons, whereas men victorious in battle are spoken of in fierce but admirable terms like 'Richard the Lionheart'. Despite copious comments about Margaret's beauty over the course of three plays, York brusquely dismisses her allure here: ''Tis beauty that doth oft make women proud,/ But God he knows thy share thereof is small.'[69] As he concludes this tirade, Margaret kills him out of sheer fury. Her warlike attributes are now prized above her femininity: she is recognized as possessing a 'tiger's heart wrapp'd in a woman's hide';[70] as 'stern, obdurate, flinty, rough, remorseless',[71] and above all as 'ruthless'.[72] As her actions are increasingly described in masculine terms, her husband becomes physically weaker. She advises him that his 'soft courage makes your followers faint',[73] and when battle strategy is discussed he is simply dismissed: 'I would your Highness would depart the field, / The Queen hath best success when you are absent.'[74] The alleged heir apparent, Edward, comments on this power shift: 'You that are king, though he do wear the crown, / Have caus'd him, by new acts of parliament, / To blot out me, and put his own son in.'[75] This scene reveals that a woman has taken control of the battlefield, and also of national politics, at the same time as attending to her unstable husband and ensuring her princely son's future. In response, several characters echo the kind of attacks on Margaret's gender and military strategy made in 1462:

> Also scripture saithe, woo be to that region
> Where ys a kyng unwise or innocent;
> Moreovyr it ys right a gret abusion,
> A woman of a land to be a regent,
> Qwene Margrete I mene, that ever hathe ment
> To goverene alle Engeland with might and poure,
> And to destroye the right lyne was here entente
> … Sche and here wykked affinité certayne
> Entende uttyrly to destroye theys regioun.[76]

The idea that Margaret always had a secret plan to destroy England verges on the paranoid, and this poem speaks clearly to the anxieties incited by a woman's power. The addition of Margaret's 'wykked affinite' casts her in an especially sinister light. An early modern audience would have been aware of Elizabeth I's legendary address to the troops at Tilbury: 'I know I have the body of a weak

and feeble woman, but I have the heart and stomach of a king.'
As Carole Levin observes, '[t]he issue of womanliness and peace
and kingship and war continued to be one Elizabeth explored in
the rhetoric at the end of her reign'.[77] Shakespeare draws a distinct
parallel between his 'Captain Margaret ... ready to put armour
on'[78] and the reigning monarch.[79] To solidify this bond, Margaret
is compared to an 'Amazon'.[80] While there are sundry unofficial
'accounts of Elizabeth arrayed like a warrior, fearlessly addressing
troops ... Amazons were almost always portrayed positively on
stage, possibly because they potentially alluded to the queen'.[81]
This kinship between the two queens might have led Shakespeare's
audience to view Margaret's armour-donning, war-waging character
traits with as much reverence as suspicion.

While the tetralogy shows Margaret's transformation from a
young, beautiful princess into a powerful, aggressive warrior, she
ultimately appears as a witch in *Richard III*. As with Lady Macbeth,
her traffic with the supernatural grants her an unusual degree of
agency. When the audience first sees her in the third scene, the stage
directions indicate: '*Enter old Margaret [behind]*.' The directions
dwell on her age rather than the physical charms on which the three
previous plays fixated, and the fact that she is positioned 'behind'
is telling. When she eventually reveals herself, she is referred to as
a '[f]oul, wrinkled witch' and a 'hateful, with'red hag'.[82] As S. Carr
Mason explains:

> On Margaret's first appearance, before Richard nominates her
> 'witch', Shakespeare calls on a mixed reaction from the theatre
> audience; there is an interplay of superstition and scepticism in
> the responses of the courtiers of I.3, the on-stage audience for
> Margaret's performance, which again helps both to differentiate
> their roles and to challenge multiple levels of response from the
> audience in the theatre.[83]

In her vow to Elizabeth that '[t]he day will come that thou shalt wish
for me / To help thee curse this poisonous bunch-backed toad',[84]
Margaret positions herself as a prophetess to the Queen of England.
As Geoffrey Bullough notes, 'her memories and curses enforce the
moral lessons of the tetralogy, especially later when one by one her
prophesies come true'.[85] Hastings acknowledges the efficacy of her
curses at the moment of his death: 'O Margaret, Margaret, now

thy heavy curse / Is lighted on poor Hastings' wretched head.'[86] Buckingham is yet more explicit: 'Now Margaret's curse is fallen upon my head. / "When he," quoth she, "shall split thy heart with sorrow, Remember Margaret was a prophetess."'[87] Even Queen Elizabeth acknowledges and covets Margaret's power of verbal efficacy: 'O thou well skilled in curses, stay awhile, / And teach me how to curse mine enemies!'[88] She understands that Margaret's words possess an agency that her own cannot match unaided: 'My words are dull. O, quicken them with thine.'[89]

As S. Carr Mason points out, however, Margaret herself takes some convincing that her magic is actually potent: '[h]aving been called a witch, Margaret at first remains dignified, only reminding the courtiers of the injustice of her situation. It is Richard who persists in a game of superstition, introducing the idea that curses are efficacious, by claiming that his father's curse has been fulfilled in the fate which has befallen Margaret'.[90] This might be considered a devaluation of her character, but it is also possible that her understanding of magical efficacy has evolved. It is important to remember that Margaret is not reduced to an aged witch until she experiences the murders of her husband and son. Her malignity is not motiveless: she sets her sights on vengeance and vows to take Richard down for his deeds. She may not be entirely unhappy with her status as a witch.

We do not see Margaret again until 4.4, when she once again is described as 'old' in the stage directions. The prophecy she made in the first act, that Queen Elizabeth would call for her, is now fulfilled, and Elizabeth even admires her former rival in her time of woe. The women bond over their urge to revenge the deaths of their husbands and sons. Equally bereft of the men in her life, Margaret comes to the aid of her fellow women, providing the agency that they lack. Instead of fashioning of Margaret as a typical witch, in fact, Shakespeare portrays her as a prophetess. As she boldly proclaims, the King will pay for his bloody deeds, and the debt of vengeance will be paid in full.

The final curtain

After Richard's death, Margaret retreats into exile in France. In her home country, the woman once celebrated as a beautiful queen, an independent ruler, a military strategist, and even as a warrior ends her days in obscurity. 'No woman is the protagonist in a Shakespearean history play,' observes Phyllis Rackin, but 'Shakespeare does give them a voice – a voice that challenges the logocentric, masculine historical record'.[91] Small in number as they may be, the female characters of Shakespeare's early history plays leave a lasting imprint on his work. Although *Henry VI, parts I, II, and III* are infrequently staged, such figures as Joan of Arc, Margaret and Lady Anne and Elizabeth from *Richard III* are at least familiar. It is nevertheless intriguing that, as Rackin points out, 'Margaret is ... the only character of either sex who appears in all four plays of the first tetralogy.'[92] Her character changes and develops dramatically across the plays, in notable contrast to her royal husband and the other, relatively static male characters. Margaret's image is in a constant state of flux. This may be because, as Rackin reminds us, depicted as 'blank pages awaiting the inscription of patriarchal texts, silenced by the discourse of patriarchal authority, the women could never tell their own stories'.[93] Yet Shakespeare *does* tell the story of Margaret, and this is now beginning to be reflected in contemporary theatre. Apparently this is what Jeanie O'Hare had in mind in her adapted *Queen Margaret*. Her 'Introduction' points out that '[Margaret] ruled England for over twenty years, but hardly a soul has heard of her. She is too important a role to be left unperformed, or, perhaps even worse, left in tatters yet again in another boys-own edit of the War of the Roses'.[94] O'Hare's rationale returns us to the question raised at the beginning of this chapter: why is interest in Margaret of Anjou resurgent now? Could it be that the present historical moment offers a glimpse into female agency of a kind that was invisible in the early modern epoch? If so, this provides an unrepeatable opportunity for contemporary theatre to show how the fabric of gender that informed early modern life remains threaded through discourse today. It is even possible that the resulting spectacle may, like Margaret of Anjou herself, 'prove a raging fire' to burn and purge the idols of patriarchal objectification.

Notes

1   Terry Eagleton, 'Afterword', in *The Shakespeare Myth*, ed. Graham Holderness (Manchester: Manchester University Press, 1998), 206.

2   William Shakespeare, *The Third Part of Henry the Sixth*, 1.4.

3   William Shakespeare, *Richard III*, 1.3.

4   Nancy Bradley Warren, 'French Women and English Men; Joan
      of Arc, Margaret of Anjou, and Christine de Pizan in England,
      1445–1540', *Exemplaria* 16, no. 2 (2004): 411.

5   See Henry Crosse, *Vertues Common-Wealth: Or the Highway to
      Honour* (London, 1603).

6   Stephen Gosson, 'The School of Abuse (1579)', in *Shakespeare's
      Theater: A Sourcebook*, ed. Tanya Pollard (Malden, MA: Blackwell,
      2004), 6, 19–33.

7   John Knox, *The First Blast of the Trumpet against the Monstrous
      Regiment of Women* (Geneva, 1558): fol. 16r.

8   The Elizabethans were intrigued by Amazons, and Shakespeare's
      A Midsummer Night's Dream addresses this trope through the figure
      of Hippolyta. Theseus alludes to this gendered power struggle when
      he asserts, 'Hippolyta, I wooed thee with my sword, / And won thy
      love doing thee injuries' (1.1.16–17).

9   J. L Laynesmith, *The Last Medieval Queens: English Queenship
      1445–1503* (Oxford: Oxford University Press, 2004), 2.

10   Carole Levin and Patricia A. Sullivan, *Politics, Women's Voices,
      and the Renaissance* (Albany: State University of New York Press,
      1995), 8.

11   As Sarah Burdett notes in '"Weeping Mothers Shall Applaud":
      Sarah Yates as Margaret of Anjou on the London Stage, 1797,'
      Margaret enjoyed exposure as a strong maternal figure at the end
      of the eighteenth century, as seen in George Coleman's *The Battle
      of Hexham* (1789); Edward Jerninghan's 'Margaret of Anjou:
      An Historical Interlude' (1777), and Richard Valpy's *The Roses:
      Or King Henry VI* (1795) (420).

12   Helen Castor, *She-Wolves: The Women Who Ruled England before
      Elizabeth* (New York: Harper Perennial, 2011), 333.

13   Transported to Westminster Abbey on a litter for her coronation,
      Margaret was 'dressed in white damask powdered with gold and
      a pearl-encrusted circlet resting on her loosened hair' (Castor,
      She-Wolves, 336).

14   Edward Hall, *The Vnion of the Two Noble and Illustre Famelies of
      Lancastre Yorke* (London: Richard Grafton, 1548).

15   Shakespeare, *I Henry IV*, 1.2.123.

16   Ibid., 1.5.

17   Ibid., 1.2.95.

18   Cristina León Alfar, 'Speaking Truth to Power as Feminist Ethics in
      Richard III', *Social Research: An International Quarterly* 86, no. 3
      (2019): 789–819.

19   Shakespeare, *I Henry VI*, V. I, 18-20.

20   An English Chronicle of the Reigns of Richard II, Henry IV, Henry
      V, and Henry VI, written before the year 1471, cit. Patricia-Ann
      Lee, 'Reflections of Power: Margaret of Anjou and the Dark Side of
      Queenship', *Renaissance Quarterly* 39, no. 2 (1986): 183–217, 188.
21   Helen Maurer and B. M. Cron, eds. *The Letters of Margaret of
      Anjou* (Woodbridge: Boydell Press, 2019), 114.
22   Ibid., 173.
23   Keith Dockray, *Henry VI, Margaret of Anjou and the War of
      the Roses: A Source Book* (Phoenix Mill, UK: Sutton Publishing,
      2000), 11.
24   Laynesmith, *The Last Medieval Queens*, 4.
25   Shakespeare, *I Henry VI*, V. iii. 46.
26   Ibid., 50–1.
27   Ibid., 72.
28   Ibid., 78–9.
29   After defeating the French at Agincourt, Henry V tells the French
      king and queen, 'leave our cousin Katherine here with us: She is our
      capital demand' (V.ii.95-6).
30   Laynesmith, *The Last Medieval Queens*, 42–3.
31   Shakespeare, *I Henry VI*, V. v, 1-2.
32   Ibid., 19.
33   Ibid., 34.
34   Ibid., 42.
35   Ibid., 46.
36   Ibid., 51–6.
37   Ibid., 92–3.
38   Laynesmith, *The Last Medieval Queens*, 84.
39   Shakespeare, *II Henry VI*, I.i.21.
40   Ibid., I.i.32-3.
41   Laynesmith, *The Last Medieval Queens*, 62; Importantly,
      Laynesmith notes that Margaret 'was the last of the traditional
      French royal virgins of the Middle Ages, but while queens had
      previously been chosen to protect English claims to continental
      territories, her marriage was accompanied by negotiations to
      surrender yet more of England's already dwindling French
      possessions' (70-1).
42   Shakespeare, *II Henry VI*, 1.1.99.
43   Ibid., 1.1. 128-131.
44   Helen E. Maurer, *Margaret of Anjou: Queenship and Power in Late
      Medieval England* (Woodbridge, Suffolk: Boydell Press, 2003), 57.
45   Judith Butler argues that '[t]he identification of women with
      "sex" … is a conflation of the category of women with the ostensibly
      sexualized features of their bodies and, hence, a refusal to grant

freedom and autonomy to women as it is purportedly enjoyed by
men'. Judith Butler, *Gender Trouble: Feminism and the Subversion of
Identity* (New York and London: Routledge, 1990), 27.
46 Shakespeare, *II Henry VI*, 3. 2. 34-5.
47 Ibid., 60.
48 Ibid., 72–5.
49 Ibid., 90.
50 Ibid., 106–19.
51 See Garry Wills, *Witches and Jesuits: Shakespeare's* Macbeth, p. 55.
52 Shakespeare, *II Henry VI*, I. ii, 83–87.
53 Eleanor was accused of witchcraft and banished from court in 1441,
     four years before Margaret arrived (*Riverside* 635).
54 Shakespeare, *II Henry VI*, I. ii, 78–81.
55 Ibid., II. i. 167-8.
56 Ibid., II. Iv. 20-2.
57 Kavita Mudan Finn, 'Tragedy, Transgression, and Women's Voices:
     The Cases of Eleanor Cobham and Margaret of Anou', *Viator* 2
     (2016): 281.
58 Shakespeare, *II Henry VI*, II. Iv. 40.
59 Maurer, *Margaret of Anjou*, 1.
60 William Shakespeare, '*The Third Part of Henry the Sixth*', in
     Riverside Shakespeare, ed. Gwynne Blakemore Evans (Boston:
     Houghton Mifflin, 1974), 671–707, I.i.35-6.
61 Shakespeare, *The Third Part* ..., I.i.243-50.
62 Ibid., I. ii. 51.
63 Ibid., 68.
64 Ibid., I. iv. 1.
65 English *Chronicle of the Reigns of Richard II, Henry Iv, Henry V
     and Henry VI*, ed. J. S. Davies (London: Camden Society, 1856);
     Quoted from Dockray, 16.
66 See *Henry V*, III.iii.10-14: 'The gates of mercy shall be all shut up, /
     And the flesh'd soldier, rough and hard of heart, / To liberty of
     bloody hand, shall range, / With conscience wide as hell, mowing
     like grass/ Your fresh fair virgins and your flow'ring infants.'
67 Phyllis Rackin, *Shakespeare and Women* (Oxford: Oxford University
     Press, 2005), 50.
68 Shakespeare, *III Henry VI*, I. iv. 110-15.
69 Ibid., 128–9.
70 Ibid., 137.
71 Ibid., 142.
72 Ibid., 156.
73 Ibid., II. Ii. 57.
74 Ibid., 73–4.

75 Ibid., 90–2.
76 T. Wright, ed., *Political Poems and Songs Relating to English History*, vol. 2, 1861), 268–9.
77 Carole Levin, '*The Heart and Stomach of a King*': Elizabeth I *and the Politics of Sex and Power* (Philadelphia: University of Pennsylvania Press, 1994), 145.
78 Shakespeare, *III Henry VI*, IV. i. 105.
79 See Thomas Cecil's print, *Truth Presents the Queen with a Lance*, c. 1622, where Elizabeth is depicted in armour and on horseback. British Museum. See Julia M. Walker, p. 253.
80 Shakespeare, *III Henry VI*, IV. i. 106; On the verso of the title page in *De claris mulieribus* (On Famous Women) (1497) is a detailed woodcut of Panthesilea (also Penthesilea), an Amazon Queen. She wears armour and a helmet and carries a spear and shield. See https://www.bl.uk/collection-items/engraving-of-amazon-warrior-queen-in-on-famous-women-1497.
81 Mary Villeponteaux, '"Not as women wonted be": Spenser's Amazon Queen', in *Dissing Elizabeth: Negative Representations of Gloriana*, ed. Julia Walker (Durham and London: Duke University Press, 1998), 213.
82 Shakespeare, *Richard III*, I.iii.162; ibid., 214; in *Discoverie of Witchcraft* (1584), Reginald Scot describes witches as 'women which be commonly old, lame, bleare-eied, pale, fowle, and full of wrinkles' (qtd. in Annabel Patterson, *Reading Holinshed's Chronicles*, p. 227).
83 Shirley Carr Mason, '"Foul Wrinkled Witch": Superstition, Scepticism, and Margaret of Anjou in Shakespeare's *Richard III*', *Cahiers Èlisabéthians: A Journal of English Renaissance Studies* 52, no. 1 (1997): 27.
84 Shakespeare, *Richard III*, I. iii. 244-5.
85 Geoffrey Bullough, *Narrative and Dramatic Sources of Shakespeare. Henry VI, Richard III, Richard II* (London: Routledge and Kegan Paul, 1960), 241.
86 Shakespeare, *Richard III*, III. Iv. 97-8.
87 Ibid., V, i. 25–7.
88 Ibid., IV, iv. 110–11.
89 Ibid., 118.
90 Mason, 'Foul Wrinkled Witch', 29.
91 Rackin, *Shakespeare and Women*, 147–8.
92 Ibid., 157.
93 Ibid., 147.
94 Jeanie O'Hare, *Queen Margaret* (London: Nick Hern Books, 2018), 6.

Works cited

Bullough, Geoffrey, *Narrative and Dramatic Sources of Shakespeare. Henry VI, Richard III, Richard II* (London: Routledge and Kegan Paul, 1960).

Burdett, Sarah, '"Weeping Mothers Shall Applaud": Sarah Yates as Margaret of Anjou on the London Stage, 1797'. *Comparative Drama* 49, no. 4 (Winter 2015): 419–44.

Butler, Judith, *Gender Trouble: Feminism and the Subversion of Identity* (New York and London: Routledge, 1990).

Castor, Helen, *She-Wolves: The women Who Ruled England before Elizabeth*. (New York: Harper Perennial, 2011).

Crosse, Henry, *Vertues Common-Wealth: Or the Highway to Honour* (London, 1603).

Dockray, Keith, *Henry VI, Margaret of Anjou and the War of the Roses: A Source Book* (Phoenix Mill, UK: Sutton Publishing, 2000).

Eagleton, Terry, 'Afterword', in *The Shakespeare Myth*, ed. Graham Holderness (Manchester: Manchester University Press, 1998).

Finn, Kavita Mudan, 'Tragedy, Transgression, and Women's Voices: The Cases of Eleanor Cobham and Margaret of Anjou'. *Viator* 2 (2016): 277–304.

Gosson, Stephen, '*The School of Abuse* (1579)', in *Shakespeare's Theater: A Sourcebook*, ed. Tanya Pollard (Malden, MA: Blackwell, 2004), 19–33.

Knox, John, *The First Blast of the Trumpet against the Monstrous Regiment of Women* (Geneva, 1558), fol. 16r.

Laynesmith, J. L., *The Last Medieval Queens: English Queenship 1445–1503* (Oxford: Oxford University Press, 2004).

Levin, Carole, '*The Heart and Stomach of a King': Elizabeth I and the Politics of Sex and Power* (Philadelphia: University of Pennsylvania Press, 1994).

Levin, Carole and Patricia A. Sullivan, *Politics, Women's Voices, and the Renaissance* (Albany: State University of New York Press, 1995).

Maurer, Helen E., *Margaret of Anjou: Queenship and Power in Late Medieval England* (Woodbridge, Suffolk: Boydell Press, 2003).

Maurer, Helen and B. M. Cron, eds., *The Letters of Margaret of Anjou* (Woodbridge: Boydell Press, 2019).

Mason, Shirley Carr, '"Foul Wrinkled Witch": Superstition, Scepticism, and Margaret of Anjou in Shakespeare's *Richard III*'. *Cahiers Èlisabéthians: A Journal of English Renaissance Studies* 52, no. 1 (1997): 25–37.

O'Hare, Jeanie, *Queen Margaret* (London: Nick Hern Books, 2018).

Patterson, Annabel, *Reading Holinshed's Chronicles* (Chicago and London: University of Chicago Press, 1994).

Philippus Foresti, Jacobus, *On Famous Women*, 1497, https://www.bl.uk/collection-items/engraving-of-amazon-warrior-queen-in-on-famous-women-1497

Rackin, Phyllis, *Stages of History: Shakespeare's English Chronicles* (Ithaca: Cornell University Press, 1990).

Rackin, Phyllis, *Shakespeare and Women* (Oxford: Oxford University Press, 2005).

Shakespeare, William, 'The First Part of Henry the Sixth', in *Riverside Shakespeare*, ed. Gwynne Blakemore Evans (Boston: Houghton Mifflin, 1974), 596–629.

Shakespeare, William, 'The Life of Henry the Fifth', in *Riverside Shakespeare*, ed. Gwynne Blakemore Evans (Boston: Houghton Mifflin, 1974), 930–75.

Shakespeare, William, 'Macbeth', in *Riverside Shakespeare*. ed. Gwynne Blakemore Evans (Boston: Houghton Mifflin, 1974), 1307–42.

Shakespeare, William, 'A Midsummer Night's Dream', in *Riverside Shakespeare*, ed. Gwynne Blakemore Evans (Boston: Houghton Mifflin, 1974), 217–49.

Shakespeare, William, 'Richard III', in *Riverside Shakespeare*, ed. Gwynne Blakemore Evans (Boston: Houghton Mifflin, 1974), 708–64.

Shakespeare, William, 'The Second Part of Henry the Sixth', in *Riverside Shakespeare*, ed. Gwynne Blakemore Evans (Boston: Houghton Mifflin, 1974), 630–70.

Shakespeare, William, 'The Third Part of Henry the Sixth', in *Riverside Shakespeare*, ed. Gwynne Blakemore Evans (Boston: Houghton Mifflin, 1974), 671–707.

Villeponteaux, Mary, '"Not as Women Wonted Be": Spenser's Amazon Queen', in *Dissing Elizabeth: Negative Representations of Gloriana*, ed. Julia Walker (Durham and London: Duke University Press, 1998), 209–25.

Walker, Julia., 'Bones of Contention: Posthumous Images of Elizabeth and Stuart Politics', in *Dissing Elizabeth: Negative Representations of Gloriana*, ed. Julia Walker (Durham and London: Duke University Press, 1998), 252–76.

Warren, Nancy Bradley, 'French Women and English Men; Joan of arc, Margaret of Anjou, and Christine de Pizan in England, 1445–1540'. *Exemplaria* 16, no. 2 (2004): 405–36.

Wills, Garry, *Witches and Jesuits: Shakespeare's* Macbeth (Oxford: Oxford University Press, 1995).

9

'The stone is mine': Theatre, witchcraft and ventriloquism in *The Winter's Tale*

Ja Young Jeon

> But of all, the burst
> And the ear-deaf'ning voice o'th'oracle,
> Kin to Jove's thunder, so surprised my sense
> That I was nothing.
>
> – *The Winter's Tale*, 3.1.8-11

In *The Winter's Tale* (1611) the envoys Cleomenes and Dion reminisce about the Delphic oracle, recalling the temple that surpasses 'the common praise' (3.1.3). Dion's reaction to the 'ceremonious, solemn, and unearthly' (3.1.7) ritual performed there centres on the visual spectacle, but Cleomenes's response is primarily about the ritual's sound: he evokes 'Jove's thunder', which deadens the hearing with its 'ear-deaf'ning voice'. Cleomenes's hyperbole highlights the oracle's extraordinary presence, which outdoes the

For comments and suggestions, I thank Tanya Pollard, Mario DiGangi, Will Fisher and David Hawkes, the seminar leader of 'Money and Magic on the Renaissance Stage' at the 2020 annual conference of Shakespeare Association of America.

cognitive ability of the mortal mind. He 'was nothing' in the face of the oracle's sonic power, and the oracle's divine voice exists in the realm of the supernatural not the secular. In this magical ritual of sound, the voice seems to work autonomously, as a result of forces beyond human control.

Although the allusion is to the male god's magic, the presence of women hovers behind this recollection. Cleomenes never refers directly to the priestesses who serve Apollo, yet his diction is telling. By centring our attention on the delivered sound itself – 'the ear-deaf'ning voice o'th' oracle' – rather than on the content of Apollo's message, Shakespeare directs our attention towards the women who mediate between the god and his audience. In Delphic practice, the thunderous voice does not come directly from Apollo himself but is mediated through his female vessels, the Pythia, who are inspired to channel the god's words. This fascination with the oracle suggests that ventriloquism meant something different in the early modern period than what it does now. In the period's literary imagination, ventriloquism was about one human channelling a voice that comes from elsewhere, as opposed to a human making their voice appear to come from an inanimate object or another human.

Shakespeare's depiction of the oracle alludes to early modern assumptions about ventriloquism inherited from the ancient Greek world. The ability to 'throw' the voice bestows a dangerous autonomy on the verbal statement, and ventriloquism involves a disconcerting disjunction between speech and the speaking subject, foregrounding the bodies of women who deliver the voice rather than the voice's origin. It is not simply that Cleomenes's observation about the oracle evokes a ventriloquism predicated on the bodies of women. It also invokes the well-known mythology of the ventriloquizing Pythia, a cultural belief that shaped English fascination with the Delphic oracle, as well as with demonic possession more broadly.

All Shakespeare's tragicomedies dramatize the apparent deaths and real recoveries of wives or daughters, and *The Winter's Tale* connects this resurrection of the seemingly dead to the supernatural speech of female ventriloquism. Since the Delphic Pythia play only a marginal role in the reports made by Dion and Cleomenes, however, critics have paid little attention to the play's engagement with female ventriloquism (literally 'belly-speech'). Scholars have identified the ritualistic significance of the oracle with Apollo's curative role, and

they have noted its parallels with the Eucharist.[1] Feminist critics
have proposed a link between the 'sealed up' (3.1.19) oracle and
Hermione's chaste pregnancy.[2] Jill Delsigne notes the oracle's
power to prompt excessive 'sensual experience', but although she
describes the ceremony's 'visual details' she stops short of focusing
on the Pythia.[3]

This chapter will concentrate on the Pythia in order to illuminate
the relationships between three morally dubious deployments of
performative representation: ventriloquism, necromancy and
theatricality. In the period's popular imagination, ventriloquism
might have been understood as involving a form of autonomously
powerful verbal performance. Just as linguistic signs operate in the
absence of a speaking subject, the process of ventriloquizing an
outside force such as Apollo's voice could be likened to magical or
occult effects in its ability to produce sound without the apparent
speaker. Audiences get to hear the voice of Apollo, but the god is
nowhere to be seen. In a play preoccupied by reflections on the
powers of magic, ventriloquism's presence in *The Winter's Tale*
responds to early modern ideas about occult effects of abstract
signs –including spells, money and theatrical representation.[4] The
magical effects of words included the curative power of spells,
whose sound and formulaic patterns were believed to effect physical
changes in the human body.[5] Similarly, theatrical representation
palpably affected the psyches of audiences and actors alike, as
the anti-theatrical pamphleteers loudly noted. Ventriloquism thus
offered a convenient, much-needed way of examining the ethical
status of efficacious representation in general.[6]

But according to early modern thought, ventriloquism was not
only broadly an autonomous speech-act but more specifically a
supernatural consequence associated with the female body. To
effect ventriloquism, bodies of the Pythia serve as vessels, prone to
the male god's spiritual takeover. Reflecting the openness typically
associated with the female body, ventriloquism set in motion
the binary frame of women placed in a passive status and men
actively giving voices to them. While ventriloquism operated as
an occult sign that is independent from the speaker, early moderns
also accepted that it was the female *bodies* that spoke from the
mouth of the male god, as Cleomenes and Dion do in the passage
I opened the chapter with. In what follows, I investigate how
Shakespeare responds to the fascination with the Pythia's ability to

produce the oracle and show the special place of women's bodies in ventriloquization contributing to the dubious witchcraft belief. Shakespeare wrote the play when the meanings of ventriloquism both inherited its supernatural contexts from classical thought and began to absorb its new associations with stage magic. *The Winter's Tale*, I argue, not only holds to the ancient premise that the Pythia possessed powers to move audiences' minds but especially seizes on the performative effects of ventriloquism that through magic and theatre, actors and playwrights alter both minds and bodies.

Belly-talking women

The word 'ventriloquist' was a recent import into English. It first appears in Reginald Scot's *The Discoverie of Witchcraft* (1584). The Latin *ventriloquist* literally translated the Greek *engastrimythos*, so both Greek and Latin identify the belly (*gaster* and *venter*) as the source of speech (*mythos* in Greek and *loqui* in Latin). Today, of course, we are familiar with professionals who can make their voice appear to issue from a dummy, and we do not usually associate a ventriloquist's skill with the belly. Yet the myth of 'belly-talking' proliferated in early modern England, and it shaped the period's cultural imagination of demonic possession as well as of ventriloquism.[7] The Greek model also suggested ventriloquism's gendered implications, since it was specifically female bellies that channelled the oracle.

Since they were vessels of the male god's divine power, chastity was crucial to the Delphic priestesses. Plutarch reports approvingly of their purity: 'the said Pythias keepth her bodie pure and cleane from the company of man'.[8] Yet the image of impregnation strongly resonated in the ritual. After the supernatural fume was emitted through a fissure of the earth, it entered the wombs of the Pythia, who sat on a tripod, intoxicating them and generating the divine voice.[9] This imaginary impregnation involved highly sexualized imagery, in which the virgin's body was possessed by the male god. The procreative power of ventriloquism was conceived as equivalent to pregnancy.[10]

Medieval attitudes departed from such pagan beliefs, as Christianity aimed to purge the demonic nature of the female body.[11]

The religious remodelling of ventriloquism saw the belly and the womb as inappropriate sources of human speech. As early as the third century CE, Origen announced that the Pythia's body could not be considered 'pure and cleane'. He questioned the sanctity of pagan prophecy, if the god's voice had to be channelled through the impure parts of the female body. The womb or the belly, he affirms, 'would be wrong for a self-controlled and sensible man to look upon, or ... even to touch'.[12]

Accordingly, the medieval model tried to separate ventriloquism from the belly, instead prioritizing mouth-speech 'as a standard for sacred vocal performance'.[13] Moreover, the controlling power over ventriloquism was now clearly assigned to the monotheist God. In this new, 'cleaner' version of ventriloquism, the voice of God was channelled through the mouth, and the importance of the belly correspondingly diminished. However, the late sixteenth-century-resurgence of witchcraft revived interest in the belly as the source of speech. Scot's *Discoverie* remarks: 'The Pythonists spake hollowe; as in the bottom of their bellis, whereby they are aptly in Latin called Ventriloqui.'[14] In Scot's account of the possession case of Elizabeth Barton, 'a wench, practising hir diabolicall witchcraft, and ventriloquie', the term 'ventriloquie' refers to the apparently supernatural speech of the typical witch.[15]

Scot's use of the word 'Pythonists' to describe 'ventriloqui' opens a set of echoes of the Pythia tradition. After Apollo slew the serpent Python, the temple of the Delphic oracle was established at the site of the monster's destruction, and the Pythia were named in honour of the god's triumph. Words referring to these female figures – 'Python', 'pythia' and 'pythonist', along with derivatives like 'phitonissa' – were used to designate belly-talkers throughout the medieval period. The Vulgate calls the Witch of Endor, the most famous example of a ventriloquizing witch in the Western tradition, 'mulier habens Pythonem' – a woman having a python.[16] Roger Bacon similarly locates the origin of ventriloquism in the charged figures of 'Pythonissae'.[17]

Scot's evocation of the Greek Pythia retrieves the pagan tradition, despite the Church's efforts to discredit the female belly and despite his scorn for superstition. Scot invites a comparison between the Delphic Pythia and the possessed witches, suggesting that their supernatural takeover of another's voice is nothing more than a trick. He first gives a list of the scriptural examples of 'Pythonists' like the Witch of Endor and goes on to introduce the Delphic oracle by the same title of 'Pytho' ('why Apollo was called Pytho whereof those witches were called Pythonists').[18] As observed, the word 'Pythonists' evoked the Greek origins of the Pythia and their special ability to produce speech from the bellies. Scot not only equates the Pythia with the Witch of Endor, whose ability to channel a dead male prophet offered a demonic model for female belly-speech as a version of necromancy. He especially identifies the sources of their supernatural speeches as the bellies. For him, as for his contemporaries, the witch figures' bellies point to its overwhelmingly feminine values. The female body's openness was a physiological commonplace, and the interest in belly-speech reveals profound cultural anxieties about women's bodies being susceptible to outside influences.[19]

Francis Beaumont and John Fletcher's tragicomedy *The Prophetess* (1622) repeats Scot's conflation of the Pythia with demonic necromancy. The title character Delphia is both a demonic witch and a holy priestess. In keeping with her name, she performs an oracular speech involving ventriloquism: 'I, presently inspired with holy fire, / And my prophetick spirit is burning in me, / Gave answer from the gods, and this it was: / Imperator eris Romae, cum Aprum grandem interfeceris' (1.2.31-34). The allusion to 'holy fire', combined with the 'prophetick spirit' that burns in her body, suggests the oracle's ancient Greek roots. Just as the Pythia receive the fume soaring through the earth's crack, Delphia receives the burning spirit in her body. Delphia's art is simultaneously holy and damnable: hailed as a druid for her sorcery, she also serves Hecate, exercises control over subordinate demons, conjures a she-devil and is despised as a 'damnable lewd woman' (2.3). The early modern conception of belly-talkers merged the virgin prophetess with the literary witch, pushing belly-speech further away from the sacred and towards the diabolical.

Later anti-witchcraft tracts presented 'ventriloqui' in an increasingly diabolical light. In a 1635 treatise, '*Ventriloqui*' are listed among the 'delinquents' who commit supernatural acts assisted by the devil, along with other demonic agents such as '*Pythonissae*', '*Magi*' and '*Negromancers*'.[20] The anonymous writer suggests that in England 'Witches' are 'one familiar terme with us'. Witches have great knowledge in supernatural science and become vessels for the devil; as a result they are both *Pythonissae* and

Ventriloqui, 'speaking with hollow voyces, as if they were possessed
with Devills'.[21] Edmund Porter's *Christophagia* (1680) links
witches to Satan, whose 'evil spirit used to speak from the belly of
Pythonists'.[22] For the author, Satan's cursed habit of crawling on his
belly suggests his natural recourse to the witch's belly as his most
convenient instrument.

The belly features prominently in these accounts of ventriloquism,
but another sense of the term emerges as Baconian science begins to
displace occult tradition.[23] Thomas Blount's entry for 'ventriloquist'
in his *Glossographia* (1656) gives a rational as well as a traditional
definition: 'One that has an evil spirit speaking in his belly, or one
that by use and practice can speake as it were out of his belly, not
moving his lips.'[24] Ventriloquism was becoming a kind of speech
that merely *looked* like 'belly-talking'. As Jan Purnis notes, this
definition suggests 'that the original etymological connection
between ventriloquism and the belly has been lost'.[25]

Thomas Hobbes attributed ventriloquism to the movement
of the air and the wind, in keeping with Baconian assumptions.
He mocks 'those [common audiences] that neither suspect the
artifice, nor observe the endeavour which they [the false users of
ventriloquism] use in speaking': the illusion of belly-speech results
from a low, inward sound artificially produced by the speaker so
that the listener mistakes it for a supernatural voice coming from a
distance.[26] This new definition reflected the dual role now attributed
to ventriloquists. The Pythia and the witches were ventriloquists
who mediated the voices of others. Once it became a technical skill,
on the other hand, those who could control their own vocal register
and lip movements were the ventriloquists. In the former instance,
ventriloquists were being manipulated; in the latter, they were doing
the manipulating.

Shakespeare's depiction of ventriloquism prefigures this
epistemological shift. Although the Delphic oracle offers a model
for legitimate belly-speech, Shakespeare mingles the Pythia into the
period's fascination with witchcraft and demonic possession. This
complicates the nature of Hermione's resurrection. It also offers
new theatrical possibilities for Paulina's climactic reanimation of
the statue, and her speaking in the dead queen's voice. Figured as
a witch, a ventriloquist and implicitly even a playwright, Paulina
simultaneously challenges and embodies the quasi-magical effects
of the theatre itself.

The actor's ventriloquism

Confirmed dead by Paulina, Hermione recedes from the stage into the
'wide gap' of time. Yet she never stops influencing either her husband
or her servant. The repentant Leontes, who has 'performed / A saint-
like sorrow' (5.1.2), and the forceful Paulina, who 'hast the memory
of Hermione' (5.1.50), act in unison for their 'recreation' of the dead
queen. Rejecting Dion's suggestion that he remarry, Leontes agrees
with Paulina that '[t]here is none worthy' (5.1.34). Pledging to cherish
his 'Queen's full eyes' and 'lips' (5.1.53-54), he imagines that his
treacherous remarriage would prompt his wife to return from death:

> One worse,
> And better used, would make her sainted spirit
> Again possess her corpse, and on this stage
> (Where we offenders now) appear, soul-vexed,
> And begin, 'Why to me'?

> (5.1.56-60)

This is not the first time Leontes expresses a kind of necromantic
wish to revive Hermione. Just after Paulina announces the queen's
death in 3.2, he vows to 'visit / The chapel where they [Hermione
and Mamillius] lie, and tears shed there / Shall be my recreation'
(3.2.235-37). On one level, 'recreation' denotes 'pastime', but it
also means 'creating anew', suggesting Leontes's spiritual rebirth
as well as the figurative restoration of his dead wife and son. Yet
the invocation also includes more dubious implications, as Leontes
imagines that the spirit of Hermione might 'possess her corpse'.

Leontes's fantasy of seeing his wife 'on this stage' is subsequently
echoed by Paulina, who offers a hypothetical setting for the queen
appearing as a ghost. As Hermione's spirit appears to him, Leontes
accepts that the 'soul-vexed' queen has 'just cause' to lament his
new marriage and 'incense [him] / To murder her [he] married'.
Paulina firmly responds:

> Were I the ghost that walked, I'd bid you mark
> Her eye and tell me for what dull part in't
> You chose her; then I'd shriek, that even your ears
> Should rift to hear me, and the words that followed
> Should be 'Remember mine'.

> (5.1.62-67)

In the span of six lines, Paulina uses seven first-person singular pronouns including 'I', 'me' and 'mine'. Yet the ambiguous syntax of this passage does not clearly indicate to whom these pronouns refer. Leontes and the audience both confuse Paulina with Hermione. Paulina's use of the pronoun 'I' channels Hermione's spirit as if she has already come back from the dead. Her impersonation intensifies when she employs the subjunctive mood in line 63: 'Were I the ghost that walked.' She reminds Leontes of Hermione's superior qualities as if she were the queen herself. Leontes's reaction adds further ambiguity: 'Stars, stars, / And all eyes else dead coals! Fear thou no wife; / I'll have no wife, Paulina' (5.1.67-9). The semicolon in the Folio text (1623) seems to separate his first use of 'thou' from the following address to Paulina, which suggests that 'thou' designates not Paulina but Hermione. As Lynn Enterline puts it, Paulina's address to the queen's spirit involves a 'movement between address, imitation, and identification'.[27]

Paulina lends her tongue to make the 'sainted spirit' speak, effectively conflating her voice with Hermione's. Her vocal identification with the queen recalls a specific, albeit unusual means of reviving the dead. In his in-depth study of ventriloquism's history, Steven Connor defines the act of ventriloquism as 'speaking with the voice of another, or the voice of another speaking through oneself'.[28] Paulina's assumption of the queen's voice could be a form of ventriloquism because she invites audiences, including Leontes, to see and react to her as if she were the very queen who has returned from death: she is 'speaking with the voice of' Hermione. When Leontes's preceding speech refers to necromancy, Paulina's more nuanced version draws together the act of channelling another's voice and the act of reviving that person. Her assumed utterance of the queen, 'Remember mine', is especially telling. The line recalls Old Hamlet's ghost urging his bewildered son to 'Remember me' (1.5.90), and early modern spectators would have been likely to associate Paulina with the biblical Witch of Endor, who summoned the voice of the dead prophet Samuel. Once again, Shakespeare links necromancy with ventriloquism.

Of course, the performance that revives Hermione primarily evokes the Delphic oracle rather than demonic necromancy. Paulina's ventriloquy helps reaffirm the queen's innocence, stressing Hermione's virtue and rebuking Leontes's persecution of her. The male auditors' reactions suggest similar emotional consequences. Leontes's ears 'rift to hear' the shrieking ghost, recalling the deafness of his emissaries. Just as Cleomenes expresses his inability to comprehend the soundscape of the oracle, Leontes is alarmed on hearing the spirit's command to 'remember me'. His pricked ear echoes Cleomenes's hearing stimulated by 'the ear-deaf'ning voice o'th'oracle' and implicitly pairs the ventriloquized voice of Hermione with the oracular voice of the Pythia. The play thus synthesizes Paulina's voice with the Pythia's, bestowing oracular authority on her words.

Paulina's ventriloquism is nevertheless distinguished from the Pythia's speech in crucial respects. The oracle is never directly presented on stage – unlike Paulina's imitation of the dead queen, which is performed immediately and physically. The oracle subjects female bodies to forces beyond their control. In contrast, Paulina exercises a decisive power over herself. Like the actor's theatrical power to move and animate spectators, Paulina's speech is performative. The Latin origin of the word 'act' – *agere, actus* – entails changes in actions and emotions that theatrical enactment can impose on audience and actor alike.[29] On hearing it, Leontes is not only inflamed with passion, but more crucially spurred to action – his vow never to remarry introduces another performative speech-act in response to Paulina's ventriloquial performance. Ventriloquism's connection to acting reflects a change in the public's understanding of the practice. Just as the general conception of 'magic' shifted towards the technical stagecraft designed to highlight the magician's dexterity, so 'ventriloquism' came to suggest the technical craft of throwing one's voice.[30] Departing from traditional notions of divine or demonic possession, Paulina's impersonation secularizes ventriloquism as a thespian stage skill.

The idea of ventriloquism as a technical craft resonates with the actor's habitual adoption of a fictional identity. Theatrical representation demands that actors carry out a convincing vocal performance to impersonate characters.[31] Just as Paulina summons, imitates and identifies with Hermione through her vocal performance, the actor manipulates his voice to create a character and makes the audience complicit with the illusion. The significance of vocal management in the production of dramatic identity is reflected in the importance of voice in early modern theatre. Brett Gamboa argues that the King's Men typically cast between nine and twelve actors to stage 'plots that involve 50 or more roles'.[32] Such casting required audiences to accept that a single actor might play a

Lord and the goddess Venus in the same play.[33] Versatility was a key
consideration in casting. Simon Palfrey and Tiffany Stern describe
a range of theatrical devices that helped actors rotate their roles:
rapid costume changes, fake beards, a special system of entering and
exiting the stage, and the wearing of masks or vizards.[34] The ability
to alter vocal register, like an ancient Greek actor ventriloquizing
behind his mask, would have been a vitally important skill.[35]

We have seen how *The Winter's Tale* alludes to a model of
'belly-speech' drawn from the Pythia and witches. Yet the play also
represents a shift towards the later model of ventriloquism that
highlights the actor's skill. The performative power of Paulina's
necromantic and theatrical ventriloquism evinces the association
between acting and sorcery. As Evelyn Tribble has shown,
Renaissance anti-theatrical writers attacked the acting body's
affective power over the spectator, which they often compared to
the power of a conjurer. Through trained bodily movements and
kinetic intelligence, the actor transfers his emotion to the audience
through an apparently spiritual exchange. As a version of sorcery
that bewitches, enthrals and animates the senses and spirits, then,
acting was understood to bring about 'quasi-magical' effects.[36]

Tribble does not mention speech among the actor's magical
powers, yet it is partly through words that the actor exerts his
influence, just as a conjurer transforms objective reality through
spells and charms. Eric Byville defines the transformative power of
the tragic witches such as Marlowe's Doctor Faustus through the
supernatural force of linguistic magic. Drawing on J. L. Austin's
speech act theory, Byville suggests that the witch's magical charms
have 'the ability to dictate, rather than describe, external reality'.[37]
Andrew Sofer suggests that in Shakespeare's time theatrical
performativity was likened to a form of magic in words' ability
to alter the audience's perception of reality.[38] In this occult model,
words uttered on stage might engender physical alterations
independently of the speaker, just as magical spells achieve their
effects by the performative power of the incantatory word.

According to the period's physiological assumptions, the tongue
epitomized not only the word's power to alter reality but also
women's proneness to witchcraft acts. As Carla Mazzio notes, the
organ was believed to have an especially important role in effecting
material changes: 'the tongue, unlike the ears, hands, and feet,
was able to move beyond the immediate material circumstances,

to *literally* influence lives from a distance'.[39] When the tongue constituted a model of autonomously powerful language, it was women, as opposed to men, who were overwhelmingly associated with this dangerous body part. The female tongue metonymically represented the feminized 'vices of credulity, curiosity, impressionability, tendency – like Eve – to fall, and implacability'.[40] Women were by nature more likely to become witches than men.[41]

Apparently, Paulina's association with the tongue highlights feminine verbal excess. Among thirteen uses of the word 'tongue', six are either spoken by or in reference to Paulina. Leontes calls her 'a callat / Of boundless tongue, who late hath beat her husband / And now baits me!' (2.3.90-92). Paulina's 'boundless tongue' elucidates her sharp words, and she is well aware of their power. She commands: 'Tell her [Hermione], Emilia, / I'll use that tongue I have' (2.2.50-51) and threatens to 'let my tongue blister' (2.2.32). The word 'boundless' looks beyond gendered volubility. Paulina's tongue is boundless both in the sense that she chides men excessively and in that her tongue can change the world from a distance. With a nod to Paulina's extended role-playing as a magic user later in the play, Leontes's description of her tongue as 'boundless' illustrates the representational power which women's speech could bring about.

Ventriloquism makes it obvious that words are 'bodily effects, built of voice, mouth, breath, and tongue', and the play's emphasis on Paulina's tongue indicates the magical powers of her verbal performance, as well as her ventriloquism's intimate connection to her body.[42] Hermione's resurrection through Paulina's is a double enchantment – a theatrical illusion, but also an embodied consequence of language's efficacious force. In *The Winter's Tale*, occult transformations through words are mediated by ventriloquism, which emanates from the depths of the female body.

The playwright's ventriloquism

The play's venture into necromancy through ventriloquism culminates in Paulina's reanimation of the statue in 5.3. This scene teems with allusions to pagan idolatry. The guests convened in Paulina's chapel, where she has kept the statue for sixteen years,

are awestruck by its 'dead likeness' (5.3.15). 'Performed by the rare
Italian master Giulio Romano' (5.2.82-3) the statue 'coldly stands'
(5.3.36), though it also seems to rebuke Leontes, to move, to breathe
and to turn its gaze upon the guests. Paulina eventually declares
that she will 'make the statue move indeed' (5.3.88), and the scene
hints at a disturbing idolatry, the effect of which 'would naturally
be more intense in the Protestant context of English drama, where
all the fantasies of the ancients might be considered idols, and none
more so than statues that are adored'.[43]

Idolatry is bound up with the play's pervasive necromantic wish.
Perdita kneels before her mother's statue to 'implore her blessing'
(5.3.44), despite acknowledging that her behaviour could be seen as
'superstitious' (5.3.43). Leontes echoes his daughter's attitude when
he desires to hear the statue scold him, thus again reminding the
audience of necromantic overtone. If, as some critics suggest, The
Winter's Tale was staged by the King's Men at the Blackfriars, a
new addition to the company's two live-in playhouses, the indoor
theatre's using of candlelight might have strengthened the uncanny
feelings of the moving statue.[44] The actor playing Paulina would
have opened the curtain of the discovery space to unveil the statue.
As the inner space was lit by candles, the stage effects produced by
lighting, darkness and shadow could beguile the onlookers' visual
senses, making the cold stone appear to move and breathe.[45] They
'think anon it lives' (5.3.70).

The desire for and the effect of the moving statue in turn evoke
Christ's power of ventriloquism. Pagans saw arbitrary natural
events as mediating the messages of deity and would have found
the idea of a statue speaking for divinity quite plausible. In an early
Anglo-Saxon hagiographic text, some Jews pray to and admire the
statue because they believe that Christ's voice emanates from it.[46]
Christianity attacked the practice as an explicit sign of paganism,
and, as such, the text recounts how Christ himself throws a divine
revelation into the pagan effigy and converts the pagans. Christ not
only turns the pagan belief in ventriloquism into a real event but
also effectively translates the talking idol into the lawful vehicle for
his divine speech.[47] Unlike the medieval Church official's wholesale
rejection of ventriloquism, an older account shows Christ's 'power
to command it [an idol] to walk and talk' becoming the origin of
the pagan statue's speech. Christ, in other words, makes use of
idolatry to demonstrate 'an unbeatable ventriloquism'.[48]

This evocation of reclaiming ventriloquism situates Paulina's reanimation of the statue in a context of paganism ruled by Christ's power. Improving on her project of bringing Hermione's ghost onto the stage, she miraculously revivifies the Queen:

'Tis time. Descend. Be stone no more. Approach.
Strike all that look upon with marvel. Come,
I'll fill your grave up. Stir, nay, come away.
Bequeath to death your numbness, for from him
Dear life redeems you.

(5.3.98-102)

Here Paulina builds on the language of necromancy used by Leontes in the preceding scene. Where he longed for the spirit of his wife to possess the corpse, Paulina literalizes his necromantic desire by way of restoring the statue to life: 'If you can behold it, / I'll make the statue move indeed, descend / And take you by the hand' (5.3.87-89). The spirit of Hermione re-enters her body, and the 'cold' stone turns into a warm, living figure. Leontes celebrates the transformation, again endorsing the scene's implicit idolatry.

Paulina identifies her invocation as 'unlawful business' (5.3.95) and fears the accusation that she is 'assisted / By wicked powers' (5.3.90-91). Embodying the rhetorical power, midwifery and emasculation associated with witchcraft, Paulina receives the disparaging titles of 'mankind witch' (2.3.67), 'crone' (2.3.76) and 'hag' (2.3.107). Yet the power of enchantment that promises 'more amazement' (5.3.85) casts Paulina as a more active and authoritative figure than the marginalized old woman usually evoked by such terms.[49] One might even argue that Paulina's embrace of the witch's role challenges the pejorative associations of magic. Just as Christ alters unsettling necromancy and unorthodox divinity inherent to the pagan mode of ventriloquism, Paulina revises demonic possession widely associated with witchcraft in the period and conjures ventriloquism's theatrical possibilities that Shakespeare also seems to associate with Christ. In carving out a powerful yet authoritative witch character who is also the play's most verbally vigorous woman, Shakespeare interweaves Paulina's magical reanimation with Christ's revision of ventriloquism.

The witch's ventriloquism was typically understood as a passive submission to the devil's power, in keeping with the gendered hierarchy between male sorcerers and female witches. Men were exclusively granted the ability to command spirits, while female witches were regarded as submissive supplicants to Satan.[50] Yet Paulina's resurrection of the statue brings into question the passivity of the belly-talking witch.[51] Although she worries that her action may be called 'unlawful', her version of ventriloquism is not about receiving a voice or being manipulated. It is about becoming the one doing the manipulating in order to make the stone move and talk. Her words have the capacity to alter objective reality. Paulina transforms the ventriloquist from a passive vessel of supernatural powers beyond her control to an active practitioner of efficacious representation. Her reconfigured role puts her in a position less typically female than the traditional witch and, as Lucy Munro has observed regarding the witch's challenge to the hegemony of male magicians, it strengthens her powers of illusion and miracle.[52]

Paulina's affirmative portrayal of the witch not only enables her to restore voice to the statue; it also establishes her as a representative of the playwright. Anti-theatrical writers claimed that theatrical illusions had a dangerously infectious impact on audiences as well as on actors. Dramatic illusions were just as contagious as magical effects. This fear of deceptive spectacles suggests that the figurative language of drama, like the incantations of ritual magic, is able to manipulate the senses, prompting the audience to credit cunning illusions.[53] In this model of theatrical fraudulence, the illusion-creating language of the stage identifies playwrights with witchcraft.[54] The chain of equation identifies the playwright with the witch, and the witch with the ventriloquist. Shakespeare presents Paulina as a creating theatrical illusion through ventriloquism. In developing ventriloquism as a figure for the performative power of the poet-playwright, Shakespeare depicts a dramatist who deploys ventriloquism as performative language.

Paulina gives the statue directions about when to speak and how to move, and the statue, or the boy actor playing Hermione pretending to be the statue, passively accepts such theatrical cues. Within this hierarchy of performance, Hermione's dependence on Paulina's orders represents the playwright's control over the actor. The playwright-ventriloquist provides words and designs movements that the actor faithfully performs on stage. Although the actor's voice is not manipulated by remote vocal control as in a puppet show, the playwright nonetheless ventriloquizes the actor, dictating and controlling his speech.[55] The playwright, in short, makes the actor talk.

The trope of ventriloquism thus reflects the dramatist's effort to adapt acting to writing. The actor's 'ministerial' role was to mediate the author's language from page to stage.[56] Richard Flecknoe's wistful reflection in 1664 on the 'the ideal authors' with 'their subservient actors' idealizes the preceding era's hierarchy.[57] Due to the playwright's greater knowledge of theatrical labour and literary language, Thomas Middleton suggests that actors should 'submit always to the writer's wit'.[58] Bound by the privileged knowledge of the playwright, actors are denigrated by the authors of *Return from Parnassus II* as 'leaden spouts / That nought down vent but what they do receive'.[59] This passage shows that at least some playwrights perceived actors as purely passive vehicles and expected them to add 'grace to the poet's labours' rather than alter them.[60] In the epilogue to *The Roaring Girl* (1611), Moll Cutpurse similarly pleads pardon for faults committed by 'either the writers' wit / Or negligence of the actors' (Epilogue, 31-32). The accusation against actors is echoed by Ben Jonson in the title page to the 1631 Octavo of *The New Inn*. Because the play was 'most negligently play'd, by some the Kings Servants', Jonson claims that 'it was never acted'. As Robert Weinmann observes, Jonson's rebuke is a conspicuous example of privileging playwriting over acting.[61] Writers like Jonson maximized their influence by demanding that actors accurately deliver their words.

In this text-based understanding of representation, theatrical representation never exists independently of the text, whose privileged authority averts any improvisations, additions or alterations, underscoring the ultimately scripted nature of theatrical performance.[62] Paulina's ventriloquism reveals the pre-existence of a 'script' – words that do not directly emanate from the actor. In turn, the text reflects the pre-existence of design, indicating the ultimate power of authorial intent to frame and animate the actor's performance. Just as a ventriloquist induces his dummy to speak with his voice, so the playwright puts his words into the mouths of actors, and Paulina throws her speech into the statue. The performative verbal signs haunt the stage through ventriloquism, which is therefore vindicated as 'an art / Lawful as eating' (5.3.110-1).

Notes

1   David M. Bergeron, 'The Apollo Mission in *The Winter's Tale*', in
    The Winter's Tale: Critical Essays, ed. Maurice Hunt (New York:
    Garland Publishing, 1995), 361–79; and Jill Delsigne, 'Hermetic
    Miracles in *The Winter's Tale*', in *Magical Transformations on the
    Early Modern English Stage*, ed. Lisa Hopkins and Helen Ostovich
    (Burlington, BT: Ashgate Publishing Group, 2014), 91–108.
2   Lowell Gallagher, '"This seal'd-up Oracle": Ambivalent Nostalgia
    in *The Winter's Tale*', *Exemplaria* 7 (1995): 465–98; and Tanya
    Pollard, *Greek Tragic Women on Shakespearean Stages* (Oxford:
    Oxford University Press, 2017), 171–204.
3   Delsigne, Hermetic Miracles in *The Winter's Tale,* 96.
4   See Brian Vickers, 'Analogy versus Identity: The Rejection of Occult
    Symbolism, 1580–1680', in *Occult Scientific Mentalities in the
    Renaissance*, ed. Brian Vickers (Cambridge: Cambridge University
    Press, 1984), 95–164.
5   For the curative power of magical spells, see Tanya Pollard,
    'Spelling the Body', in *Environment and Embodiment in Early
    Modern England*, ed. Mary Floyd-Wilson and Garrett A. Sullivan
    (Basingstoke: Palgrave Macmillan, 2007), 171–86.
6   See David Hawkes, *Idols of the Marketplace* (New York: Palgrave,
    2001) and Andrew Sofer, 'How to Do Things with Demons:
    Conjuring Performatives in Doctor Faustus', *Theatre Journal* 61,
    no. 1 (2009): 1–21, for the performativity of spells and symbolic
    utterances. For the early modern period's understanding of
    performance in terms of material transformation, see Mary Thomas
    Crane, 'What Was Performance?' *Criticism* 43, no. 2 (2001): 169–87.
7   Other terms used in Renaissance England for those who channel
    another's voice include 'ob, python or pythonist, engastrimyth, and
    gastriloquist'. See Leigh Eric Schmidt, 'From Demon Possession
    to Magic Show: Ventriloquism, Religion, and the Enlightenment',
    Church History 67, no. 2 (1998): 278, n.7.
8   Pollard cites the quotation from Plutarch's 'Of The Oracles That
    Have Ceased To Give Answere'. The original passage appears on
    page 1350. See Pollard, *Greek Tragic Women*, 190.
9   See Giulia Sissa, *Greek Virginity*, trans. Arthur Goldhammer
    (Cambridge, MA: Harvard University Press, 1990); and Hugh
    Bowden, *Classical Athens and the Delphic Oracle: Divination and
    Democracy* (Cambridge: Cambridge University Press, 2005).
10 For the evocation of pregnancy in the oracle, see Pollard, *Greek
    Tragic Women*, 190–2.

11   See Mary Hayes, *Divine Ventriloquism in Medieval English Literature: Power, Anxiety, Subversion* (New York: Palgrave Macmillan, 2011).

12   Origen. *Contra Celsum*, 397, cit. Hayes, *Divine Ventriloquism in Medieval English Literature*, 3.

13   Hayes, *Divine Ventriloquism in Medieval English Literature*, 4. The medieval idea of the hierarchy between the upper and lower body parts is useful in understanding the demonization of belly-speech. In this conception, the parts above the belly held the loftier functions of reason and cognition; the parts beneath were associated with polluted functions like excretion. Belly-speech reverses this hierarchy by turning the belly, interchangeably figured as the womb or the genitals, into a verbalizing organ.

14   Reginald Scot, *The Discoverie of Witchcraft* (Carbondale: Southern Illinois University Press, 1964), 120.

15   Ibid.

16   1 Samuel 28:7: 'dixitque Saul servis suis quaerite mihi mulierem habentem pythonem et vadam ad eam et sciscitabor per illam et dixerunt servi eius ad eum est mulier habens pythonem in Aendor'. The King James Bible translates: 'Then said Saul unto his servants, Seek me a woman that hath a familiar spirit, that I may go to her, and enquire of her. And his servants said to him, Behold, there is a woman that hath a familiar spirit at Endor.' Here 'python' is translated as 'a familiar spirit'. See also Hayes, *Divine Ventriloquism in Medieval English Literature*, 3–4; 114–15.

17   '& Pythonissae vocum varietaté in ventre, & gutture fringentes, & ore, formant voces humanas á longè vel propè prout volunt, ac si spiritus cum homine loqueretur; (The Pythonesses, twittering (?) with a variety of voices in their stomach, throat, and mouth, make human voices from a long way off or close by, as they will, as if a spirit were conversing with a man)'. In *De Secretis Operibus Artis et Naturae, et de Nullitate Magiae*, Cit. Philip Butterworth, *Magic on the Early English Stage* (Cambridge: Cambridge University Press, 2005), 109. The English translation is Butterworth's.

18   Scot, *The Discoverie of Witchcraft*, 127.

19   For the female body's particular leaky and porous nature, see Gail Kern Pastor, *The Body Embarrassed: Drama and the Disciplines of Shame in Early Modern England* (Ithaca: Cornell University Press, 1993). For *The Winter's Tale*'s anxieties about the belly's openness, see Chapter 5 of David Hillman, *Shakespeare's Entrails: Belief, Scepticism and the Interior of the Body* (New York: Palgrave Macmillan, 2006).

20   *Witchcrafts, Strange and Wonderfull* (London: M.F. for Thomas Lambert, 1635).

21 Ibid.
22 Edmund Porter, *Christophagia: The Mystery of Eating the Flesh and Drinking the Blood of Christ* (London: Tho. Newcomb for Tho. Collins, 1680).
23 See John S. Mebane, *Renaissance Magic and the Return of the Golden Age: The Occult Tradition and Marlowe, Jonson, and Shakespeare* (Lincoln: University of Nebraska Press, 1989).
24 Cit. Schmidt, 'From Demon Possession to Magic Show', 281.
25 Jan Purnis, 'The Belly-Mind Relationships in Early Modern Culture: Digestion, Ventriloquism, and the Second Brain', in *Embodied Cognition and Shakespeare's Theatre: The Early Modern Body-Mind*, ed. Laurie Johnson, John Sutton and Evelyn Tribble (New York: Routledge, 2014), 241.
26 Thomas Hobbes, *Elements of Philosophy the First Section, concerning Body* (London: R. & W. Leybourn for Andrew Crooke, 1656), 369–70.
27 Lynn Enterline, *The Rhetoric of the Body from Ovid to Shakespeare* (Cambridge: Cambridge University Press, 2000), 166.
28 Steven Connor, *Dumbstruck: A Cultural History of Ventriloquism* (New York: Oxford University Press, 2000), 49.
29 See Pollard, 'Acing Like Greeks', in *Thomas Heywood and the Classical Tradition*, ed. Tania Demetriou and Janice Valls-Russell (Manchester: Manchester University Press, 2021), 232–3.
30 See Donald Hedrick, 'Distracting Othello: Tragedy and the Rise of Magic', *PMLA* 129, no. 4 (2014): 649–71.
31 Andrew Gurr suggests that in the sixteenth century 'acting' primarily referred to oratory skill rather than to stage performance. See Gurr, *The Shakespearean Stage 1574–1642* (Cambridge: Cambridge University Press, 1970). For the actor's primary skill as an orator, see Robert Weinmann, *Author's Pen and Actor's Voice*, ed. Helen Higbee and William West (Cambridge: Cambridge University Press, 2000).
32 Brett Gamboa, *Shakespeare's Double Plays: Dramatic Economy on the Early Modern Stage* (Cambridge and New York: Cambridge University Press, 2018), 70.
33 This example is from Thomas Preston's 1569 play *Cambyses*. The playtext's title page provides a full casting plan, in which one actor is cast in around five roles, of varying gender and class. See Gamboa, *Shakespeare's Double Plays: Dramatic Economy on the Early Modern Stage*, 73.
34 Simon Palfrey and Tiffany Stern, *Shakespeare in Parts* (Oxford: Oxford University Press, 2007), 50–6.
35 See C. B. Davis, 'Distant Ventriloquism: Vocal Mimesis, Agency and Identity in Ancient Greek Performance', *Theatre Journal* 55, no. 1 (2003): 45–65.

36 Evelyn Tribble, *Early Modern Actors and Shakespeare's Theatre: Thinking with the Body* (London and New York: Bloomsbury Arden Shakespeare, 2017), 24.
37 Eric Byville, 'How to Do Witchcraft Tragedy with Speech Acts', *Comparative Drama* 45, no. 2 (2011): 3.
38 Sofer, 'How to Do Things with Demons', 9.
39 Carla Mazzio, 'Sins of the Tongue', in *Body in Parts: Fantasies of Corporeality in Early Modern Europe*, ed. David Hillman and Carla Mazzio (New York: Routledge, 1997), 57.
40 Jonathan Gil Harris, '"To Stop Her Mouth with Truths Authority": The Poisonous Tongue of the Witch and the Word of God', in *Foreign Bodies and the Body Politic: Discourses of Social Pathology in Early Modern England* (Cambridge: Cambridge University Press, 1998), 118.
41 In his 1616 *Treatise of Witchcraft*, for example, Alexander Roberts attributes the higher number of the female witches than their male counterparts to women's possession of 'slippery tongue', which is 'full of words'. See Frances E. Dolan, *Dangerous Familiars: Representations of Domestic Crime in England, 1550–1700* (Ithaca and London: Cornell University Press, 1994), 198. The original quotation is taken from Alexander Roberts, *Treatise of Witchcraft*, sig, G2.
42 Pollard, 'Spelling the Body', 180. This reflects Agrippa's view: Ficino and Agrippa were two important thinkers whose ideas on the words' bodily nature influenced the early modern English understanding of language and its physical effects.
43 Leonard Barkan, '"Living Sculptures": Ovid, Michelangelo, and the Winter's Tale', *ELH* 48, no. 4 (1981): 659. See also Julia Reinhard Lupton, *Afterlives of the Saints: Hagiography, Typology, and Renaissance Literature* (Stanford: Stanford University Press, 1996); and Michael O'Connell's *The Idolatrous Eye: Iconoclasm and Theater in Early Modern England* (Oxford: Oxford University Press, 2000). For Post-Reformation England's revision of the lifelike quality found in idols, see Jennifer Waldron, 'Of Stones and Stony Hearts: Desdemona, Hermione, and Post-Reformation Theater', in *The Indistinct Human in Renaissance Literature*, ed. Jean E. Feerick and Vin Nardizzi (New York: Palgrave Macmillan, 2012), 205–27.
44 The first recorded performance of *The Winter's Tale* took place at the Globe in 1611, a production Simon Forman attended and wrote about in his diary. Gurr proposes that the play was likely performed both at the Globe and the Blackfriars, adding a question mark after the indoor playhouse ('Globe / Blackfriars?') in his select list of Renaissance plays and their playhouses. Gurr, *The Shakespearean Stage 1574–1642*, 298.

45 On the lighting effect of the indoor theatre, see Martin White, '"When Torchlight made an Artificial Noon": Light and Darkness in the Indoor Jacobean Theatre', in *Moving Shakespeare Indoors: Performance and Repertoire in the Jacobean Playhouse*, ed. Andrew Gurr and Farah Karim-Cooper (Cambridge: Cambridge University Press, 2014), 115–36 and Sarah Dustagheer, '"So Glistred in the Torchy Fryers": Effects of Candlelight Indoors', in *Shakespeare's Two Playhouses: Repertory and Theatre Space at the Globe and the Blackfriars, 1599–1613* (Cambridge: Cambridge University Press, 2017), 123–38.

46 Hayes introduces this episode from Boeing's translation of *The Acts of Andrew*, 38–9. See Hayes, *Divine Ventriloquism in Medieval English Literature*, 53–79, especially 67.

47 Ibid., 67–70.

48 Ibid., 67, 68.

49 See Heidi Breuer, *Crafting the Witch: Gendering Magic in Medieval and Early Modern England* (New York: Routledge, 2009), and Diane Purkiss, *The Witch in History: Early Modern and Twentieth-Century Representations* (New York: Routledge, 1996).

50 Gareth Roberts, '"An Art Lawful As Eating"?: Magic in *The Tempest* and *The Winter's Tale*', in *Shakespeare's Late Plays: New Readings*, ed. Jennifer Richards and James Knowles (Edinburgh: Edinburgh University Press, 2010), 128–9.

51 Kirilka Stavreva similarly suggests that '*The Winter's Tale* is unique in Jacobean drama for its endorsement of women's "potent" witch-speak as politically revitalizing art' (118).

52 See Lucy Munro, *Shakespeare in the Theatre: The King's Men* (London: Bloomsbury, 2020). Investigating the power relations between a male leading actor and a boy actor apprenticed to him, Munro suggests that *The Winter's Tale* shifts the focus from the leading actor to the boy actor playing Paulina (124).

53 Kirstie Gulick Rosenfield, 'Nursing Nothing: Witchcraft and Female Sexuality in *The Winter's Tale*', *Mosaic: A Journal for the Interdisciplinary Study of Literature* 35, no. 1 (2002): 95–112.

54 See Stephen Greenblatt, 'Shakespeare Bewitched', in *New Historical Literary Study: Essays on Reproducing Texts, Representing History*, ed. Jeffrey N. Cox and Larry J. Reynolds (Princeton, NJ: Princeton University Press, 1993), 127; and Roberts.

55 Scott Cutler Shershow suggests that puppet theatre provides a useful metaphor to imagine the author's mastery, in which actors are merely 'puppet-like slaves of a sovereign poet' (192).

56 Douglas Bruster and Robert Weinmann, *Shakespeare and the Power of Performance: Stage and Page in the Elizabethan Theatre* (Cambridge and New York: Cambridge University Press, 2008), 7.

57   Cit. Tiffany Stern, *Rehearsal from Shakespeare to Sheridan* (Oxford: Oxford University Press, 2000), 86. The original passage appears in Richard Flecknoe's *Love's Kingdom ... with a short Treatise of the English Stage* (1664), G6b.
58   Cit. Stern, 85. The line is taken from *No Wit, No Help Like a Woman's* (1657), 78.
59   *The Return from Parnassus (Part II), or The Scourge Of Simony*, 4.3.1887-8. Cit. in Scott Cutler Shershow, '"The Mouth of "hem All": Ben Jonson, Authorship, and the Performing Object', *Theatre Journal* 46, no. 2 (1994): 192.
60   Thomas Overbury, 'An Excellent Actor', in *Character Writings of the Seventeenth Century*, ed. L. L. D Henry Morley (1891), http://gutenberg.org/files/10699/10699-h/10699-h.htm.
61   Weinmann, *Author's Pen and Actor's Voice*, 132.
62   See Preiss, *Clowning and Authorship in Early Modern Theatre* (Cambridge: Cambridge University Press, 2014). Preiss comments on the early modern 'theater's legibility as pre-produced, as something purely recitative and rehearsed. Today, we expect performers to mask such "scriptedness," because we are all too aware of it; Elizabethans needed it revealed, because to them it was a new idea' (10).

Works cited

Barkan, Leonard, '"Living Sculptures": Ovid, Michelangelo, and the *Winter's Tale*', *ELH* 48, no. 4 (1981): 639–67.
Beaumont, Francis and John Fletcher, 'The Prophetess', in *The Works of Francis Beaumont and John Fletcher*, vol. 5, ed. A. R. Waller (New York: Octagon Books, 1969), 320–89.
Bergeron, David M. 'The Apollo Mission in *The Winter's Tale*', in *The Winter's Tale: Critical Essays*, ed. Maurice Hunt (New York: Garland Publishing, 1995), 361–79.
Bowden, Hugh, *Classical Athens and the Delphic Oracle: Divination and Democracy* (Cambridge: Cambridge University Press, 2005).
Breuer, Heidi, *Crafting the Witch: Gendering Magic in Medieval and Early Modern England* (New York: Routledge, 2009).
Bruster, Douglas and Robert Weinmann, *Shakespeare and the Power of Performance: Stage and Page in the Elizabethan Theatre* (Cambridge; New York: Cambridge University Press, 2008).
Butterworth, Philip, *Magic on the Early English Stage* (Cambridge: Cambridge University Press, 2005).
Byville, Eric, 'How to Do Witchcraft Tragedy with Speech Acts', *Comparative Drama* 45, no. 2 (2011): 1–33.

Connor, Steven, *Dumbstruck: A Cultural History of Ventriloquism* (New York: Oxford University Press, 2000).

Crane, Mary Thomas, 'What Was Performance?' *Criticism* 43, no. 2 (2001): 169–87.

Davis, C. B., 'Distant Ventriloquism: Vocal Mimesis, Agency and Identity in Ancient Greek Performance', *Theatre Journal* 55, no. 1 (2003): 45–65.

Delsigne, Jill, 'Hermetic Miracles in *The Winter's Tale*', in *Magical Transformations on the Early Modern English Stage*, ed. Lisa Hopkins and Helen Ostovich (Burlington, BT: Ashgate Publishing Group, 2014), 91–108.

Dolan, Frances E., *Dangerous Familiars: Representations of Domestic Crime in England, 1550–1700* (Ithaca and London: Cornell University Press, 1994).

Dustagheer, Sarah, '"So Glistred in the Torchy Fryers": Effects of Candlelight Indoors', in *Shakespeare's Two Playhouses: Repertory and Theatre Space at the Globe and the Blackfriars, 1599–1613* (Cambridge: Cambridge University Press, 2017), 123–38.

Enterline, Lynn, *The Rhetoric of the Body from Ovid to Shakespeare* (Cambridge: Cambridge University Press, 2000).

Gallagher, Lowell, '"This seal'd-up Oracle": Ambivalent Nostalgia in *The Winter's Tale*', *Exemplaria* 7, no. 2 (1995): 465–98.

Gamboa, Brett, *Shakespeare's Double Plays: Dramatic Economy on the Early Modern Stage* (Cambridge and New York: Cambridge University Press, 2018).

Greenblatt, Stephen, 'Shakespeare Bewitched', in *New Historical Literary Study: Essays on Reproducing Texts, Representing History*, ed. Jeffrey N. Cox and Larry J. Reynolds (Princeton, NJ: Princeton University Press, 1993), 108–35.

Gurr, Andrew, *The Shakespearean Stage 1574–1642* (Cambridge: Cambridge University Press, 1970).

Harris, Jonathan Gil, *Foreign Bodies and the Body Politic: Discourses of Social Pathology in Early Modern England* (Cambridge: Cambridge University Press, 1998).

Hayes, Mary, *Divine Ventriloquism in Medieval English Literature: Power, Anxiety, Subversion* (New York: Palgrave Macmillan, 2011).

Hawkes, David, *Idols of the Marketplace: Idolatry and Commodity Fetishism in English Literature, 1580–1680* (New York: Palgrave, 2001).

Hedrick, Donald, 'Distracting Othello: Tragedy and the Rise of Magic', *PMLA* 129, no. 4 (2014): 649–71.

Hillman, David, *Shakespeare's Entrails: Belief, Scepticism and the Interior of the Body* (New York: Palgrave Macmillan, 2006).

Hobbes, Thomas, *Elements of Philosophy the First Section, Concerning Body* (London: R. & W. Leybourn for Andrew Crooke, 1656). EEBO, http://ezproxy.gc.cuny.edu/login?url=https://www-proquest-com.ezproxy.gc.cuny.edu/books/elements-philosophy-first-section-concerning-body/docview/2240980833/se-2?accountid=7287.

Lupton, Julia Reinhard, *Afterlives of the Saints: Hagiography, Typology, and Renaissance Literature* (Stanford: Stanford University Press, 1996).

Mazzio, Carla, 'Sins of the Tongue', in *Body in Parts: Fantasies of Corporeality in Early Modern Europe*, ed. David Hillman and Carla Mazzio (New York: Routledge, 1997).

Mebane, John S., *Renaissance Magic and the Return of the Golden Age: The Occult Tradition and Marlowe, Jonson, and Shakespeare* (Lincoln: University of Nebraska Press, 1989).

Munro, Lucy, *Shakespeare in the Theatre: The King's Men* (London: Bloomsbury, 2020).

Overbury, Thomas, 'An Excellent Actor', in *Character Writings of the Seventeenth Century*, ed. L. L. D Henry Morley (1891). Project Gutenberg, http://gutenberg.org/files/10699/10699-h/10699-h.htm.

O'Connell, Michael, *The Idolatrous Eyes: Iconoclasm and Theater in Early Modern England* (Oxford: Oxford University Press, 2000).

O'Gorman, Myles and Bonnie Lander Johnson, 'Shakespeare's Statuary Women and the Indoor Theatre's Discovery Space', *Early Theater* 24, no. 1 (2021): 89–112.

Origen, *Contra Celsum*, trans. Henry Chadwick (Cambridge and New York: Cambridge University Press, 1980).

Palfrey, Simon and Tiffany Stern, *Shakespeare in Parts* (Oxford: Oxford University Press, 2007).

Pastor, Gail Kern, *The Body Embarrassed: Drama and the Disciplines of Shame in Early Modern England* (Ithaca: Cornell University Press, 1993).

Plutarch, 'Of the Oracles That Have Ceased to Give Answere', in *Moralia*, trans. Philemon Holland (London: 1603), 1320–50. *Early English Books Online Text Creation Partnership*, http://name.umdl.umich.edu/A09800.0001.001.

Pollard, Tanya, 'Spelling the Body', in *Environment and Embodiment in Early Modern England*, ed. Mary Floyd-Wilson and Garrett A. Sullivan (Basingstoke: Palgrave Macmillan, 2007), 171–86.

Pollard, Tanya, *Greek Tragic Women on Shakespearean Stages* (Oxford: Oxford University Press, 2017).

Pollard, Tanya, 'Acting like Greeks', in *Thomas Heywood and The Classical Tradition*, ed. Tania Demetriou and Janice Valls-Russell (Manchester: Manchester University Press, 2021), 229–43.

Porter, Edmund, *Christophagia: The Mystery of Eating the Flesh and Drinking the Blood of Christ and the Modus or Manner thereof Discovered* (London: Tho. Newcomb for Tho. Collins, 1680). EEBO, http://ezproxy.gc.cuny.edu/login?url=https://www-proquest-com. ezproxy.gc.cuny.edu/books/christophagia-mystery-eating-flesh-drinking-blood/docview/2240878573/se-2?accountid=7287.

Preiss, Richard, *Clowning and Authorship in Early Modern Theatre* (Cambridge: Cambridge University Press, 2014).

Purkiss, Diana, *The Witch in History: Early Modern and Twentieth-century Representations* (New York: Routledge, 1996).

Purnis, Jan, 'The Belly-Mind Relationships in Early Modern Culture: Digestion, Ventriloquism, and the Second Brain', in *Embodied Cognition and Shakespeare's Theatre: The Early Modern Body-Mind*, ed. Laurie Johnson, John Sutton and Evelyn Tribble (New York: Routledge, 2014), 235–52.

'The Return from Parnassus (Part II), or The Scourge of Simony', in *The Pilgrimage to Parnassus, with The Two Parts of The Return from Parnassus*, ed. W. D. Macray (Oxford: Oxford University Press, 1886), 76–154.

Roberts, Alexander, *A Treatise of Witchcraft* (London: N. O. for Samuel Man, 1616).

Roberts, Gareth, '"An Art Lawful As Eating"?: Magic in *The Tempest* and *The Winter's Tale*', in *Shakespeare's Late Plays: New Readings*, ed. Jennifer Richards and James Knowles (Edinburgh: Edinburgh University Press, 2010), 126–42.

Rosenfield, Kirstie Gulick, 'Nursing Nothing: Witchcraft and Female Sexuality in *The Winter's Tale*', *Mosaic: A Journal for the Interdisciplinary Study of Literature* 35, no. 1 (2002): 95–112.

Schmidt, Leigh Eric, 'From Demon Possession to Magic Show: Ventriloquism, Religion, and the Enlightenment', *Church History* 67, no. 2 (1998): 274–304.

Scot, Reginald, *The Discoverie of Witchcraft* (Carbondale: Southern Illinois University Press, 1964).

Shershow, Scott Cutler, 'The Mouth of "hem All": Ben Jonson, Authorship, and the Performing Object', *Theatre Journal* 46, no. 2 (1994): 187–212.

Shakespeare, William, *Hamlet*, ed. Philip Edwards (Cambridge: Cambridge University Press, 2003).

Shakespeare, William, *The Winter's Tale*, ed. Susan Snyder and Deborah T. Curren-Aquino (Cambridge: Cambridge University Press, 2007).

Sissa, Giulia, *Greek Virginity*, trans. Arthur Goldhammer (Cambridge, MA: Harvard University Press, 1990).

Sofer, Andrew, 'How to Do Things with Demons: Conjuring Performatives in *Doctor Faustus*', *Theatre Journal* 61, no. 1 (2009): 1–21.

Sokol, B. J., *Art and Illusion in The Winter's Tale* (Manchester and New York: Manchester University Press, 1994).

Stavreva, Kirilka, 'Courtly Witch-Speak on the Jacobean Stage', in *Words Like Daggers: Violent Female Speech in Early Modern England* (Lincoln: University of Nebraska Press, 2015), 103–27.

Stern, Tiffany, *Rehearsal from Shakespeare to Sheridan* (Oxford: Oxford University Press, 2000).

Tribble, Evelyn, *Early Modern Actors and Shakespeare's Theatre: Thinking with the Body* (London and New York: Bloomsbury Arden Shakespeare, 2017).

Vickers, Brian, 'Analogy versus Identity: The Rejection of Occult Symbolism, 1580–1680', in *Occult Scientific Mentalities in the Renaissance*, ed. Brian Vickers (Cambridge: Cambridge University Press, 1984), 95–164.

Waldron, Jennifer, 'Of Stones and Stony Hearts: Desdemona, Hermione, and Post-Reformation Theater', in *The Indistinct Human in Renaissance Literature*, ed. Jean E. Feerick and Vin Nardizzi (New York: Palgrave Macmillan, 2012), 205–27.

Weinmann, Robert, *Author's Pen and Actor's Voice: Playing and Writing in Shakespeare's Theatre*, ed. Helen Higbee and William West (Cambridge: Cambridge University Press, 2000).

White, Martin, '"When Torchlight Made an Artificial Noon": Light and Darkness in the Indoor Jacobean Theatre', in *Moving Shakespeare Indoors: Performance and Repertoire in the Jacobean Playhouse*, ed. Andrew Gurr and Farah Karim-Cooper (Cambridge: Cambridge University Press, 2014), 115–36.

INDEX

Printed in the USA
CPSIA information can be obtained
at www.ICGtesting.com
LVHW020312201023
761647LV00005B/21

9 781350 247048